Promises and Pitfalls of Special Education

for parents and professionals

– LYNN ATTWOOD –

www.fast-print.net/store.php

PROMISES AND PITFALLS OF SPECIAL EDUCATION
FOR PARENTS AND PROFESSIONALS

Copyright © Lynn Attwood 2013

All rights reserved

No part of this book may be reproduced in any form by photocopying
or any electronic or mechanical means, including information storage
or retrieval systems, without permission in writing from both the
copyright owner and the publisher of the book.

The right of Lynn Attwood to be identified as the author of this work has
been asserted by her in accordance with the Copyright, Designs and
Patents Act 1988 and any subsequent amendments thereto.

Real life case studies and separate quotations have been included
but names have been changed to protect identities.

A catalogue record for this book is available from the British Library

ISBN 978-178035-695-2

This book contains:
Parliamentary information licenced under the Open Parliament Licence v1.0.
Available online from:
www.parliament.uk/site-information/copyright/open-parliament-licence
and
Public sector information licensed under the Open Government Licence v2.0
Available online from:
www.nationalarchives.gov.uk/doc/open-government-licence/version/2/

An environmentally friendly book printed and bound in England by
www.printondemand-worldwide.com

This book is made entirely of chain-of-custody materials

Acknowledgements

I would like to thank Doctor Jane Tarr and Ms Karen Lewis (University of the West of England) for their timely advice and support during the process of writing this book and Mrs Joan Cooper for proof reading the manuscript. I would also like to thank friends and family for their patience and suggestions at various stages of writing.

And finally, to all the parents I have had the privilege of knowing and working alongside - this book is dedicated to you.

The Author

Lynn Attwood has experience in managing a Parent Partnership Service in the South West of England. As both a professional manager and educationalist, she had strategic and operational responsibility for providing a statutory service for parents of children with special educational needs and disabilities, providing information, advice and support when they had concerns about their children's education. This confidential service comprised both local authority staff and volunteers, who were trained to provide support and advice to parents. Through parents receiving support and relevant training, they became empowered when meeting with professionals and acquired a *'voice'* with respect to influencing local policies and procedures. And most importantly, it made a difference to the educational provision for their children.

Whilst managing this service, Lynn completed a research project which included parents, local authority educational professionals, a representative sample of schools in the area and colleagues from other Parent Partnership Services. This research examined some of the *'background'* issues that affect parent and professional communication and its impact upon families when communication and professional relationships break down, entitled:

An Evaluation of Communication between Educational Professionals and Parents and its impact on families and Working in Partnership with Parents (2007).

Lynn achieved an MA in Professional Learning (Professional Practice) and as a result of issues raised in her research, was awarded the prestigious Erika Lovelady Prize (2007) by the International Professional Development Association where the research abstract was disseminated to members at the annual conference held in Belfast.

Research findings were subsequently disseminated to headteachers, school senior management teams, special educational needs co-ordinators, chairs of governors, senior local authority managers and strategic teams within Children's Services, local authority conferences, regional Parent Partnership Service leads and national colleagues through the confidential Parent Partnership Service website. In addition, Lynn has tutored Special Educational Needs Co-ordinators registered on the National Award (MA level) for Special Educational Needs Co-ordinators, accredited by Bath Spa University.

Additional experiences that contribute to her expertise in this field include management roles within the NHS and being strategic training lead for a local authority in the South West of England during the pilot phase of the Single Assessment Process for Older People. Teaching experience has included colleges of Further Education, a Sixth Form College, a girls' grammar school; maintained secondary schools and universities. This diverse experience has resulted in support being provided to children, young people and adults spanning a range of learning difficulties and disabilities, including significant numbers of children and young people with a range of behavioural, social and emotional difficulties.

Lynn has continued to provide support to parents through writing and being an Occasional Associate Lecturer at the University of the South West of England, periodically teaching undergraduates completing BA (Hons) in Education in Professional Practice.

CONTENTS

		Page
Preface		1
Chapter 1	Setting the Scene	3
Chapter 2	Labelling, Guidance and Politics	14
Chapter 3	Special Provision for Children	32
Chapter 4	Support for Parents	62
Chapter 5	Legislation and Promises	73
Chapter 6	Communication with Parents	86
Chapter 7	The Impact of Parent and Professional Relationships	124
Chapter 8	Parents and Children's Experiences	156
Chapter 9	SEN Reform – will it deliver?	176
Chapter 10	Academies and School Discipline	193
Chapter 11	Where do we go from here?	200
Useful Contacts		204
Glossary		210
Bibliography		214

Promises and Pitfalls of Special Education

for parents and professionals

PREFACE

This book has been written against the background of the daily struggles experienced by parents of children with Special Educational Needs and disabilities who encounter not only difficulties with *'the system'* and its bureaucratic mechanisms, but also have to contend with the nuances involved in professional and parent relationships. Many parents are fortunate in that the practitioners supporting their children are committed to doing whatever is possible to improve their children's educational achievements and outcomes; they also fully embrace the concept of working in partnership with parents and acknowledge the value of parental knowledge in relation to their children. At the opposite end of the spectrum are practitioners who avoid working in partnership with parents, discount parental expertise and readily become defensive at the slightest hint of challenge. Others engage in tokenistic partnership with parents and willingly meet with them and commit to undertake specific actions which are subsequently unfulfilled, all of which add to the angst of parents who are already weary.

Who is this book for?

This book is for all parents who have struggled or are currently struggling *'to be heard'* in respect of having their children's difficulties identified, acknowledged and catered for with respect to their education. Equally, this book is for professionals – to help them gain a greater understanding of the parental perspective, with the possibility of informing their own professional practice and avoiding situations that work against the ethos of *'partnership'*.

The current approach to addressing children's additional needs is outlined as well as changes that were originally proposed in the Government's *Green Paper, Support and aspiration: A new approach to special educational needs and disability (DfE 2011).* These have now been incorporated into the *Children and Families Bill (2013)* and discussion will enable both parents and professionals to align current and future systems, thereby acquiring a greater understanding with respect to what the future might hold for them.

In an attempt to *'peel back layers'*, a multi-dimensional approach has been adopted to explore some of the underlying issues and concerns that relate to special education. Historical legislation and policy provide some insight into the evolving role of parents with respect to their children's education, travelling through that of *'partnership'*, *'consumer'*, *'choice'* and *'control'*. The implementation of educational provision, set against national legislation and policy is discussed and explores some of the reasons why there are sometimes failures in *'the system'*. Partnership and communication are explored from the perspective of the detrimental effects upon families when such relationships disintegrate. Case studies are included from which parents may align their own experiences, whilst, hopefully, drawing strength, hope and inspiration in how to satisfactorily resolve their own difficulties, whilst professionals will be alerted to practice and procedures that cause additional stress for families.

Parents will gain a greater understanding of what advice and practical support is available and will generally be better equipped to negotiate the *'minefield'* of Special Educational Needs (SEN) – the term adopted by government in legislation and guidance. It is hoped that parents will become empowered in their interactions with professionals in health, education and social care, in the knowledge of what they can influence and change and that which is not possible. From this position, they will have a better understanding of what is worth *'fighting'* for whilst saving time and emotional effort in other areas. Professionals will acquire knowledge of practices that cause parental grief and through this will be better placed to develop more productive relationships with parents.

Other Readership

Policy makers may acquire further insight into the dynamics of special education with the potential of informing future policy decisions.

Chapter 1
Setting the Scene

Introduction

As an educationalist, I have a particular interest in the area of Special Educational Needs and how children with learning difficulties and disabilities have those needs supported in school. In my experience, one of the best ways of helping children to be happy and achieve at school is to inform and empower their parents; to help them gain a better understanding of the system and to manage their expectations regarding the extent and type of provision available. This has never been more important than in the current economic climate as the Coalition Government pushes forward an educational reform which will affect all children with learning difficulties and disabilities. Parents with children already in the educational system will be affected as well as those with children just embarking on their educational journey. This book will briefly explain the existing system and inform parents of changes contained in the *Children and Families Bill (2013)* so they will gain some understanding of any impact upon their particular circumstances.

Explanation of Terms

Before going any further, some terms must be explained.

- *'Special Educational Needs' (SEN)* is the legal term applied to pre-school and school children who require different or additional support to help them learn. Broadly, it applies to children with a range of learning difficulties and/or disabilities which affect their ability to learn. Under Special Educational Needs reform the term also applies to young people in further education and training.
- *'Additional Needs'* refers to the type of extra support that some children need to help them learn. *'Additional Needs'* is a euphemism for the legal term of Special Educational Needs which is used in government legislation and documentation such as the *Special Educational Needs and Disability Act 2001,* the *Special Educational Needs Code of Practice (DfES 2001), Education Acts 1981,1996* and the *Children and Families Bill (2013).*

- *'Disabilities'* refers to both overt and *'hidden'* disabilities which are protected in law under the *Equality Act 2010* which has superseded the *Disability Discrimination Act 1995*.
- SENCO is an abbreviation for Special Educational Needs Coordinators who are either lead teachers or Early Years practitioners with responsibility for the assessment and planning of support for children with Special Educational Needs and disabilities. In schools, they usually lead a team of learning support assistants or higher level teaching assistants.
- *'Statement'* – the term used for a Statement of Special Educational Needs for children with learning difficulties and disabilities. Statements record children's difficulties and detail the support required to address them. Under SEN reform, Statements are being replaced by Education, Health and Care Plans (EHC Plans).
- *'Green Paper'* refers to the Coalition Government's proposals for SEN reform published in *Support and aspiration: A new approach to special educational needs and disability (2011)*.

Government Spending

As a result of the *Government's Comprehensive Spending Review (HM Treasury 2010)*, local authority budgets were significantly reduced, with further reductions being implemented under the latest *Spending Review (2013)*. This has resulted in public sector job losses and services being restructured in an endeavour to meet increasing demands, with fewer people and greatly limited financial resources to deliver them. I have worked in an environment where I have supported parents of children with Special Educational Needs, initially starting my role before the full impact of the economic crises became evident - at a time of reasonable *'excess'* where decisions made by professionals regarding the use of resources were less critical than they are now; sometimes with a degree of flexibility and negotiation being possible. In contrast, I have experienced first-hand some of the tensions in the workplace when there is a greater demand for services and support than can realistically be delivered by the human and financial resources available.

Government Priorities

Successive governments have introduced legislation and guidance that provide the basis of initiatives designed to improve the circumstances of vulnerable members of society, from addressing poverty, protecting the disabled from discrimination through the *Disability Discrimination Act 1995,* now superseded by the *Equality Act 2010* and addressing educational provision through a number of Acts, Guidance, White Papers and other policy documents, with the general intention of improving the educational attainment, life experiences and opportunities of children who would or could otherwise be disadvantaged. Sure Start Centres were established in 1999 as a means of providing support to families of pre-school children who were living in poverty. Centres were strategically positioned in areas of social deprivation to make them easily accessible to families considered most in need of support. Centre staff provided support and advice in an endeavour to reduce any negative influences from the home environment as a means of improving life chances and reducing social inequalities.

The *Children Act 2004* and its accompanying implementation guidance, *Every Child Matters: Change for Children (DfES 2004)* resulted in local authorities appointing *parenting commissioners* with strategic responsibility for devising Parenting Strategies (subsequently re-named Think Family Strategies) for each local authority; their responsibilities included commissioning a range of services for parents and families. At that time, the Labour Government adopted a *'deficit'* model of parenting and attributed poor behaviour by children as being due to their parents' lack of parenting skills; this resulted in many evidence-based parenting programmes being established. In 2004, Sure Start Centres generally became known as Children's Centres and many new ones were established around the country, with some being located in more affluent neighbourhoods. Services were extended to cater for families with adolescent children and those with Special Educational Needs and disabilities.

The Labour Government published *Aiming High for Disabled Children: better support for families (2007)* which established the over-arching principles of delivering services to disabled children, with the *Early Support* scheme providing co-ordinated services to disabled pre-school children or those with difficulties just emerging *(DfES 2007: 7).* The Coalition Government's *Green Paper (2011)* declared this family-centred approach remains a priority, with practitioners promoting children's development whilst ensuring the early identification of needs so that essential support is in place ready for when children start school (DfE 2011: 61-62).

Transition Arrangements

Seamless support between settings is an idealistic goal and is dependent upon the robustness of transition programmes between settings as well as the dedication of practitioners in ensuring transition takes place as smoothly as possible for all children. Early years settings, primary and secondary schools all have procedures and structures in place to help ease the transfer of children from one setting to another; relevant information is forwarded to the new setting prior to transfer taking place and children have an opportunity to attend the new school prior to becoming a pupil on the school role. Despite systems and protocols being in place, for some children with learning difficulties and disabilities, transition between school settings is often less successful as children progress through the educational system and for those about to leave compulsory education, sometimes transition arrangements are not implemented or take place too late to benefit the young person upon leaving school. This is despite the fact that children with Statements are supposed to participate in person-centred transition planning in combination with their year 9 Annual Review. The Coalition Government is addressing this anomaly under its educational reforms, but whether there will be improvements in the future, remains to be seen.

Reform under the Children and Families Bill

Publication of the *Children and Families Bill (2013)* makes it possible to inform parents of legislative changes to SEN provision that will affect them and their children. The revised *SEN Code of Practice* will contain implementation procedures for professionals, when published in 2014. Aspects of reform will be discussed so that parents have a clearer notion of what they can expect from the system. This will be set alongside aspects of *'human behaviour'* which sometimes distort systems and practices whilst influencing relationships between parents and professionals.

History and Best Intentions

A brief review of government legislation and policies will contextualise the current reforms for children with Special Educational Needs and will help illuminate the position of parents with respect to their children's education today. Furthermore, it will help establish whether systems introduced by previous governments are merely being *'reshuffled'* or re-packaged in the Coalition Government's quest *'to be seen to be doing something'* or whether the reforms include innovative policies and practice. Whilst there are benefits from SEN reform, there might also be some unintended consequences and these will be discussed.

Who are Parents?

Throughout this book, there are references to *'parents'*. The *Childcare Act 2006* defines a parent as any individual with parental responsibility or care of a young child. To elaborate further - the person with parental responsibility could be a an older brother or sister, a legal guardian, foster carer, adoptive parent or other adult (such as grandparents, aunts and uncles) with caring responsibilities for a child. Furthermore, an individual's professional role might involve having *'parental responsibility'* for children placed in local authority care. So the term *'parent'* includes carers as well. Readers will know if the role of *'parent'* applies to them or someone they are helping.

Children and Young People

In compliance with the *Children and Families Bill (2013)*, *'children'* applies to young children of pre-school and school age, including those passing through adolescence whilst *'young people'* applies to students entering further education or those entering employment or training.

An Outline of Content

This book has been approached from several perspectives – education law and guidance clarifies the position regarding support, the political arena is examined in relation to the role of parents and how some policies have evolved, parent and professional relationships are discussed in relation to communication skills and psychological theories help explain some of the causes of relationship breakdown. Throughout this book, there is anecdotal evidence and recourse to research and theoretical models. An overview of chapters is below:

Chapter 2: Labelling, Guidance and Politics. This chapter explains the legal framework and government guidance relating to the provision and protection of children with Special Educational Needs and disabilities. Examples of learning difficulties and disabilities are included so that parents can determine whether their children have learning difficulties or disabilities or both. Other aspects include professional sensitivity, labelling and the effects of disability on family life. The *'ladder of intervention'* is explained, enabling parents to understand both the current system and some of the changes being introduced under reform. Medical and social models of disability are explained as well as the economic and emotional effects of disability.

Chapter 3: Special Provision for Children. Despite the best endeavours of Government, it is questionable as to whether children with learning difficulties and disabilities receive *all* the necessary support needed to help them learn and become useful members of society; in fact, due to the current economic climate and the stronghold on government spending, the likelihood of this occurring becomes increasingly remote. Realistically, the *Special Educational Needs Code of Practice (2001)* makes a commitment to educational provision that enables children to make *'adequate'* progress *(DfES 2001:52)*. This potentially means that if children make progress as a result of extra support they do receive, other difficulties may not be addressed. Media hype and political rhetoric would have us believe that *all* children, with additional needs and disabilities, *always* receive the appropriate provision to address *all* of their particular difficulties, but the reality is somewhat different.

An outline of current Special Educational Needs provision serves to illuminate how some decisions are arrived at and reveals potential obstacles to achieving desired goals. Changes to SEN provision are included to help parents through the transition period (if already in the system) whilst informing parents just embarking upon this most important journey.

Chapter 4: Support for Parents. Information is provided for parents on the role of Parent Partnership Services, which were specifically created to provide information, advice and support to parents of children with Special Educational Needs and disabilities. As statutory services, with staff knowledgeable on legislation, education law and local policies and procedures, they can provide significant support to parents when they have cause to challenge their children's teachers or local authority Special Educational Needs team. An overview of other services is also included.

Chapter 5: Legislation and Promises. The language of *'working with parents'* will be examined with a review of the position of parents. There will be an attempt to determine the current relationship that parents have with professionals – such as whether they are *'involved'*, *'partners'* or *'consumers'*. In recent years, there has been significant emphasis on the notion of *'parent power'* and how parents may influence educational standards and be involved in decisions regarding their children. This can sometimes result in parents having false expectations regarding the extent to which they may influence their children's education.

The reality for many parents is that their children's needs are not always appropriately addressed, even following identification of specific difficulties, nor are parents' concerns necessarily given any weight when they share them with professionals. Choosing schools and moving between schools (within a school year) is not necessarily as straightforward as parents might hope. Schools vary in their admissions criteria, dependent upon the type of school, whilst other factors may further limit *'choice'*. An examination of the role of parents, underpinned by legislation and guidance, will help establish the real position of parents with respect to their involvement and will highlight those areas in which they might exert some influence.

Chapter 6: Communication with Parents. Professional and parent communication is fundamental to establishing effective relationships and impacts upon subsequent services provided and received. Good communication with parents and children is at the heart of all services provided for children, including educational provision, and if communication is not effective, then children may suffer lasting consequences. This chapter will discuss the goals of communication, *'bad news'*, *'critical communication'* and what parents and educational professionals consider is important when communicating with each other. Drawing upon theory, research and anecdotal evidence, the chapter will explain the reasons for communication between parents and professionals, common assumptions and motivators. There will be an overview of how professionals should communicate with parents, and an outline of some psychological theories to explain how and why communication may become distorted and how the effects of poor communication may be mediated. Meetings, language and active listening skills are also discussed.

Chapter 7: The Impact of Parent and Professional Relationships. The manner in which professionals exert their power in relation to parents may affect the extent to which it is possible for them to work together. Some educational professionals refuse to work with parents, using their position to reject requests for meetings, ensuring any contact is always at *'arm's length'*. Parents may find that their efforts in dealing with *'the system'* results in anger, disappointment, fear, turmoil, humiliation and broken relationships with those professionals upon whom they most depend for their children's welfare and progress. Few parents could imagine or anticipate the *battleground* they are about to enter when their children start attending school, while for some parents this starts even earlier. The impact that professional relationships can have upon parents and family life will be explained and how hostility with parents may result in a spiral of negativity, which can lead to school disaffection.

Chapter 8: Parents and Children's Experiences. This chapter will illustrate how effective communication and working in partnership with statutory services have the potential to enhance the emotional well-being of parents and their children. Conversely, examples of less than desirable professional communication will reveal the detrimental effects upon children and their parents, supported by research and anecdotal experience. Case studies demonstrate the tenacity and determination of parents to secure appropriate and consistent provision for their children and the impact that *'battles with the system'* have had on family life and their children's outcomes.

Chapter 9: SEN Reform – will it deliver? This chapter examines some additional aspects of SEN reform, originally proposed in the Coalition Government's Green Paper: *Support and Aspiration: A new approach to special educational needs and disability (DfE 2011)* and subsequently incorporated into the *Children and Families Bill (2013)*. Key elements will be discussed including eligibility criteria for school-based SEN support while some possible unintended consequences of reform will be illuminated.

Chapter 10: Academies and School Discipline. There has been much media controversy regarding the position of Academies in relation to the admission of children with Special Educational Needs. This chapter will attempt to explain some of the freedoms granted to Academies in relation to the requirement to comply with SEN legislation. The new system of redress following permanent exclusions will also be explained.

Chapter 11: Where do we go from here? This chapter reflects upon SEN provision, including aspects which are outside of reform. The additional demands being placed upon teachers are illuminated, leaving readers to consider whether SEN reform will enhance parent and professional relationships and whether provision for children will improve to the extent hoped for.

This overview will enable readers to proceed to those chapters most relevant to them. However, parents who are new to the special educational needs system will benefit from reading the book from the beginning.

Measuring Service Quality

Finally, it's pertinent to raise the issue of service quality and how this is evaluated. This book includes a combination of evidence (data), for example, analysis of government legislation and other documentation that provides *'hard'* evidence with respect to how parents are viewed and valued as well as quantifiable data with respect to the benefits of good communication, whilst *'soft'* evidence, acquired through case studies and interviews, reveal some of the struggles experienced by parents when attempting to get appropriate educational provision for their children. Both types of evidence have their place and together form a picture of the experiences of parents and their children.

Performance Data

Successive governments have been zealous in collecting performance data that is supposed to demonstrate the standard of service delivered; combined with this is the quest for *'continuous quality improvement'* that has demanded that services, including health, education and social care, must monitor their performance and continually seek ways to *'better their best'* standards. There are many and varied methods used to achieve and measure service improvement and these are just a few examples for illustration purposes:

- Increased staff training (more of it, higher standards, evidence of achievement through *'tick box'* methods, accreditation to demonstrate achievement).

- Practitioners must comply with Core Standards of professional practice to demonstrate their professional competence.
- Measurement of the *'customer journey'* where fewer contacts with the customer, to resolve their concerns, is considered indicative of a better service.
- Statistics that demonstrate case load number and time dedicated to working with clients.
- Measurements of success (or failure) – whether objectives were achieved.
- Whether outcomes have improved and what they were. (This can be difficult to quantify when a number of services have contributed to the overall outcome, but is often requested.)
- Qualitative evaluation of customer satisfaction through completion of survey questionnaires.

This is aside from quests to obtain *'Quality Marks'* such as the *Inclusion Quality Mark (Coles and Hancock 2002)* which many schools achieve as a means of demonstrating their inclusive practices and relationships with parents whilst other organisations might achieve the Government's *'Customer Service Excellence'* award which involves departments and teams demonstrating effective *'customer journeys'* and achievement of desired results.

No doubt, many working parents will be aware of which exacting standards they must demonstrate in order to *'prove'* they are good at their jobs and have *'made a difference'*. In my previous role, considerable time was spent producing anonymised statistical data for local authority and government departments as a means of demonstrating fluctuating demand upon the service and the effectiveness of the team. In this day and age, so much *'success'* is measured by the production of data which merely glosses over aspects of the system which are immeasurable. There is increased emphasis on customer reviews which evaluate the service provided. Such feedback is usually voluntary with the proportion of customers responding often being small in relation to the total number served. Positive or negative criticism may be influenced by the extent to which customers receive exactly the outcomes they desired. Where a service is acting as an intermediary using influence to bring about change, but having no control over the eventual outcome, the quality of the service delivered may be masked by the necessity to compromise on customer demands. Conversely, there may have been poor customer service, with the practitioner lacking appropriate skills in how they addressed and served the customer but where the customer ultimately received the outcome they wanted this may have resulted in positive feedback.

Excellent policies and procedures may exist, but implementation may fall short of the documented standard. A contributing factor to schools receiving a *'good'* rating by Ofsted is the quality of their documentary evidence, but this can mask parental dissatisfaction with respect to relationships with teachers and the education provided for individual children. Data alone will always mask the true nature of the service delivered and we need to get to the heart of what really goes on. It is hoped this book will, at least, provide some enlightenment.

Chapter 2
Labelling, Guidance and Politics

Introduction

This chapter will examine what is meant by Special Educational Needs and disabilities. Legal definitions and examples of learning difficulties and different types of disabilities will help illustrate which types of condition are categorised as SEN, disabilities or whether they meet both criteria. Some of the issues around labelling, professional sensitivity, working in partnership and professional practice will also be addressed.

In addition, there is a brief introduction to the current system of provision for children and young people with Special Educational Needs and disabilities, drawing upon the principles contained in the *Special Educational Needs Code of Practice (DfES 2001)*. Economic and social factors will be briefly examined in relation to their effects upon parental involvement, subsequent provision for children and impact upon family life.

Legal Definitions of Need

Definitions of Special Educational Needs and disabilities are provided in the *Children and Families Bill (2013)*, the *Special Educational Needs Code of Practice (DfES 2001), Education Acts 1981,1996*, the *Children Act 1989 and Equality Act 2010*. Government publications are accessible online (at least for a limited time) and may be downloaded whilst hard copies may be free or chargeable, depending upon the type of publication.

Special Educational Needs applies to children who have *'special educational provision made for them'* (DfES 2001: 6, DfE 2013: 17-18) when they experience:

"*significantly greater difficulty in learning than the majority of children of the same age*' or (have) a disability *'which prevents or hinders them from making use of educational facilities*"
    (DfES 2001: 6; DfE 2013: 17-18).

Children who attend pre-school settings may receive extra support in an attempt to prevent them from falling too far behind their peers. Disabilities include a myriad of conditions that include overt physical disabilities, *'hidden'* disabilities, long-term medical and mental health conditions. *The Equality Act 2010 (c15: 4)* defines disability as being:

"a physical or mental impairment which has a substantial and long-term adverse effect on a person's ability to undertake their normal day-to-day activities".

Conditions categorised as *'long-term'*, must usually have been present for a year or more, or are expected to continue for that time. Life-long conditions and those which are expected to re-occur are also included whilst individuals with new conditions may meet the criteria for being disabled when the disability is expected to last more than a year.

What type of Need?

The *Warnock Report (1978: 37)* introduced the term *'Special Educational Needs'* as a means of emphasising that such children are *'special'* and that they require additional educational support. The Report widened the scope of SEN provision by including children with behavioural, social and emotional difficulties as well as those with short-term needs. Being mindful of the stigma associated with earlier terms, new language was introduced to define specific needs, which continue to be used today. Even with this change in terminology, many people find the existing terms unacceptable, viewing them as derogatory, although categorisation of difficulties does have its place and helps to ensure children receive educational provision, appropriate to their needs. Since the *Warnock Report* was published, children with *'hidden'* disabilities have received support alongside those with overt physical disabilities. Under the *Special Educational Needs Information Act 2008*, the government collects statistical information on the number of children and young people with specific difficulties, ranging from pre-school age through to those who take 'A' levels. Learning difficulties and disabilities are officially categorised as follows:

1. *"Specific learning difficulty*
2. *Moderate learning difficulty*
3. *Severe learning difficulty*
4. *Profound and multiple learning difficulty*
5. *Behaviour, emotional and social difficulties*

6. Speech, language and communication needs
7. Hearing impairment
8. Visual impairment
9. Multi-sensory impairment
10. Physical disability
11. Autistic spectrum disorder
12. Other difficulty/disability."

(DfE, Special Educational Needs Information Act – An Analysis 2011: 73)

Categorisation by type of need contributes to government planning with respect to the allocation of funds to local authorities and schools. Data is broken down into sub-categories such as age, gender and ethnicity with current statistics indicating that more boys than girls are issued with Statements, both at primary and secondary school *(DfE 2011: 12)*.

Most Prominent Difficulties

The Government's SEN Statistical *Analysis (2013: 5)* indicates that for children with Statements, across all types of school - primary, secondary and special, the most prevalent conditions are behavioural, emotional and social difficulties (approximately 24%), moderate learning difficulties (approximately 23%), followed by autistic spectrum and speech, language and communication disorders (approximately 22% each). Figures were considerably lower for these categories at School Action Plus *(DfE 2013)* which might suggest that the majority of children with such needs have them managed through statutory provision. Furthermore, from my experience in supporting parents, many of them had children with these difficulties which could further suggest they are more likely to require support in their relationships with educational professionals due to concerns associated with the management of behaviour, school discipline or educational provision.

The Warnock Report (1978: 41) estimated that 20% of pupils would have Special Educational Needs at any time. This means that a considerable number of parents are likely to have regular contact with educational and health professionals and for some families, this will include social care services as well. Parents who are new to this territory may, mistakenly, believe that the law has provided for *all* their children's needs and that their difficulties simply have to be identified in order for *all* relevant support to be provided. In principle, this is exactly what should happen, but the reality, regrettably, is often quite different for a significant number of parents and their children. Let us now look at what the law has to say about special educational needs provision for children.

Law and the Code of Practice

The Special Educational Needs Code of Practice (DfES 2001) provides the framework and practical guidance on how educational professionals should discharge their duties in relation to the identification, assessment, provision, monitoring and review of progress for children with Special Educational Needs and disabilities. Guidance specifically relates to the statutory duties and responsibilities of school and local authority professionals and those services which provide support and guidance to parents, such as Parent Partnership Services, whether employed in the public or voluntary sectors. The first Code of Practice was published in 1994, following the *Education Act 1993*. Part IV of this Act was subsequently incorporated into the *Education Act 1996*. Both the *Education Act 1996* and the *Special Educational Needs and Disability Act 2001* underpin guidance contained in the current *SEN Code of Practice (2001)*. Other legislation and guidance has resulted in changes which affect working relationships with parents, provide greater legal protection for children with disabilities and affect the way in which local authority services are delivered; not forgetting, of course, that we now have Academies and Free Schools which operate outside of local authority control, all of which impact upon parents and SEN provision.

Professional Guidance

The *Children and Families Bill (2013)* is the legislative framework for reform of the SEN system. With publication of the Bill, Part IV of the *Education Act 1996* has now been repealed. The Bill has, largely, incorporated the original proposals published in the *Green Paper, Support and Aspiration: A new approach to special educational needs and disability (DfE 2011)*. Changes relating to procedures and professional practice will be contained in the revised *SEN Code of Practice*, expected sometime during 2014. Until then, existing guidance remains relevant to education professionals working in pre-school settings, primary and secondary schools, local authority staff and others who support parents (such as Parent Partnership Services) on all procedures relating to the identification, assessment, provision and monitoring of children with special educational needs.

Chapter 2 of the current guidance provides Parent Partnership Services with the foundational principles upon which they must operate and stipulates local authority responsibilities in relation to providing and supporting such services. Guidance advises services on how to work in partnership with parents and how to include the involvement of children and young people, at a level that is appropriate to their age and capacity to understand what is taking place in meetings. This is a useful document for all parents of children with special educational needs or disabilities, especially if they need to query the provision being made for their children *(DfES 2001)*.

Government Policy

Between the years 1997-2010, the Labour Government continued to develop the concept of *'working in partnership'* with parents when this was promoted in the schools' *White Paper: Higher Standards, Better Schools for All, More choice for parents and pupils (2005)* where strategies placed parents in the position of *'equal'* or *'lead'* partners, with the emphasis they could drive forward change *(DfES 2005)*. City Academies were introduced to improve the standards of under-performing schools and through the *Children Act 2004* and accompanying guidance, *Every Child Matters: Change for Children (2004)* the Labour Government reformed the delivery of children's services. Separate local authority departments for Education and Social Services were abolished, replaced by Children's Services Departments and Children's Trusts.

The Labour Government lost its right to govern at the 2010 General Election, which subsequently resulted in a Coalition Government being formed. Since then, radical decisions have been taken regarding public spending, which has resulted in significant reductions in resourcing throughout the public sector. The Academy programme has continued to forge ahead, whilst the schools' *White Paper: The Importance of Teaching (DfE 2010)* introduced the option for parents and other interested stakeholders to establish Free Schools which, like Academies, operate outside of local authority control. Many of the commitments made in the *White Paper* were subsequently replicated in the *Green Paper (2011)* which committed to raise teaching standards through improved teacher training, scholarship schemes, continuing professional development (CPD), headship qualifications and networks of Teaching Schools sharing knowledge and expertise *(DfE 2011)*. Local authority commissioning functions were strengthened (having their origins under the Labour Government's *Every Child Matters agenda (2004)* and continued in their role as *'champions for parents'*. As a consequence, local authority *school improvement partners were* abolished and there are now minimal opportunities for local authorities to have any direct influence on the majority of failing schools.

Professional Services

Families of children with additional needs and/or disabilities frequently have more contact with a range of professionals that include education, health services and possibly social care as well. These services are often inextricably interwoven into the lives of families of children with additional needs, and are frequently influential in the type and extent of support provided in the school environment as well as at home. For example, to increase independence and mobility, social care services are likely to be involved in making arrangements for disabled children to have wheelchairs. Local authority Disabled Children's teams, as part of their forward planning, monitor the needs of disabled children so that equipment is available as children grow and develop. On the other hand, paediatricians correspond with schools regarding diagnoses and how conditions affect specific children in order to help schools implement the most appropriate educational provision for them. Children with behavioural, social and emotional difficulties may be assessed by *specialist behaviour teachers* who devise individual behaviour management programmes; some children may also attend Child and Adolescent Mental Health Services (CAMHS) both to address their emotional needs and to receive advice on specific ways of managing their difficulties. This type of professional involvement necessitates a partnership relationship between parents and professionals, with parents being expected to work cooperatively with their children's school by consistently applying the same strategies in the home environment as those implemented at school in order to modify their children's behaviour. When all parties work cooperatively to bring about change, children's behaviour can sometimes be turned around, preventing permanent exclusions from school, whilst enabling them to achieve educationally, without disrupting the education of other pupils.

A myriad of physical impairments exists, including those relating to vision, hearing and speech that will usually require support from specialist services in the health, education and social care professions. Children who find learning more difficult than their peers may require additional support in the classroom through the implementation of *'additional'* or *'different'* teaching strategies, use of targeted learning programmes and teaching aids as a means of helping them learn more effectively. Depending upon the severity of children's learning difficulties, an educational psychologist may have performed an assessment in order to advise the school of appropriate strategies to use in the classroom. It is not unusual for children and young people to have both a learning difficulty and a disability (or multiple disabilities) and examples will be provided to explain this further.

Learning Difficulties

There are many types of difficulty that can be described as Special Educational Needs and some children present with overlapping conditions. Sometimes, it takes a while before difficulties experienced by particular children can be identified and addressed as the presenting picture may make it difficult to determine the exact nature of what is going on. During this time period, teachers should be observing, monitoring, assessing and recording achievements and difficulties in order to develop a profile. Case Studies in Chapter 8 illustrate the considerable amount of time it sometimes takes before children's difficulties are fully recognised and addressed.

The *'Ladder of Intervention'*

Children with learning difficulties should receive extra support, described in the *Special Educational Needs Code of Practice (DfES 2001: 52)* as being *'additional to'* or *'different from'* those methods adopted for their peers. The type of support will be determined by the class teacher, sometimes under the guidance of the school or pre-school SENCO (Special Educational Needs Co-ordinator). Additional advice will be obtained, when necessary, from support services such as Learning Support or Behaviour Support, which will most likely be provided by in-house teams or purchased from external providers, due to few local authorities now providing such services. Other factors that influence the type and amount of additional or different support provided for children include the age of the child, resources available in school and the difficulties being presented and how best to meet their needs.

Teaching assistants (or *higher level teaching assistants*) may provide one-to-one support or extra group work activities with the amount of support being dependent upon assessed need and the availability of such support in the school environment. From my experience, children are more likely to receive one-to-one support from teaching assistants at primary school than at secondary school where whole class support is more common. However, children should receive individual support when this is written into their Statements and this will most likely apply under the new Education, Health and Care Plans.

Currently, there is a graduated approach to intervention, which I refer to as the *'ladder of intervention'*. There are three levels to this *'ladder'* which comprise:

- School Action (and Early Years Action)
- School Action Plus (and Early Years Action Plus)
- Statements of Special Educational Needs

SEN Code of Practice (2001: 48)

For the majority of children, the process is not usually linear in that having been placed on School Action they do not necessarily progress to School Action Plus nor require a Statement of Special Educational Needs, although a small number of children might progress through each stage of provision. Some children with extremely complex needs will usually have had these identified before they attend school or even pre-school settings and Statements would have been issued at pre-school stage, in readiness for starting formal education. Occasionally, children who have had a Statement for several years may make sufficient progress so that a Statement is no longer justified, resulting in it being withdrawn, with further support being provided at a lower level. Pupils at School Action may only need low-level support for a limited period of time and once they make progress that is comparable to their peers or better than their former rate of progress, the extra support is usually withdrawn. If pupils require support again, at a later stage, then they can simply be placed back on School Action or School Action Plus; the level of intervention is determined by the complexity of their needs and whether external support, from professionals outside the school, is necessary. Changes to provision will be explained in Chapter 3.

Perspectives on Disability

Several models of disability exist, although the most commonly used, and publicly recognised are the Medical and Social Models of Disability. Children with both physical and *'hidden'* disabilities will invariably be assessed under the Medical Model of Disability. Educational professionals will have to consider the medical implications (such as impairments that restrict activity) as well as elements under the Social Model of Disability with regard to how they impede children's learning and participation in school life. An outline of these models will help the reader's understanding in relation to their children's experiences and with respect to the legal position.

The Medical Model: This is primarily a deficit model with its focus on the individual and what is *'wrong'* with them *(Terzi 2010: 64)*. Medicine is concerned with diagnosis, labelling, assessment, monitoring and programmes of treatment where individuals are defined by their illness or condition. Impairment is judged against the *'normal'* range to determine the extent of disability. Families in receipt of Disability Benefits will usually be aware of the Medical Model of Disability, due to parents having to provide information regarding the extent of their children's disability, including restrictions in daily living and the amount of supervision required such as part-time or 24 hour care.

The Social Model: This model regards the organisation of society as being a contributor to individual impairment and adopts the position that removal of barriers will enhance participation in everyday life. Terzi asserted this model was influential in schools becoming more inclusive *(ibid: 64)* and its principles underpinned the *Disability Discrimination Act 1995,* which determined that shops, restaurants, public buildings and businesses should become accessible to *all* people. Modifications to premises included widening doors, installing ramps and lifts and generally ensuring that disabled people could access and use all facilities at any venue or service they chose. In 2005, educational settings were expected to comply with the Act, with local authorities having a duty to ensure their school premises could accommodate disabled pupils and that, at least, some of their schools were fully accessible to pupils with mobility difficulties, enabling them to use facilities and move around school sites and buildings easily.

Children with learning difficulties may or may not have a diagnosis that explains the difficulties they experience. Interventions at school with respect to *'additional'* or *'different'* strategies to help them learn will primarily focus on how difficulties are presented and the best way of reducing their effects so that children can learn and achieve. We shall now look at some examples of learning difficulty.

Dyslexia

Dyslexia is categorised as a Specific Learning Difficulty. Children (and adults) with dyslexia find reading and spelling difficult. The Labour Government commissioned Sir Jim Rose to produce a review, *Identifying and Teaching Children and Young People with Dyslexia and Literacy Difficulties (DCSF 2009)* which explained that dyslexia is characterised by:

"difficulties in phonological awareness (the ability to identify and manipulate units of language), verbal memory and verbal processing speed."
(DCSF 2009: 10).

Children of any intellectual ability may have dyslexia, which can range from very mild to severe. Other difficulties which may co-exist with dyslexia include dyspraxia and dyscalculia *(DCSF 2009: 10).*

Speech and Language and Communication

Children may develop their speech, language and communication skills more slowly than their peers and their delayed development can impact upon their learning ability in all areas of the curriculum. *The Bercow Report: A Review of Services for Children and Young People (0-19) with Speech, Language and Communication Needs (DCSF 2008)* identified the primary difficulties as:

- *"Being unable to form sounds and words, use sentences and speak fluently.*
- *Being unable to communicate in social situations due to difficulties in understanding what has been spoken and responding appropriately."*
(DCSF 2008: 13)

Children do not necessarily experience all of these difficulties but may have difficulties in some areas only. Children with speech, language and communication difficulties may be excluded and ridiculed by their peer group due to others being unable to understand them. Some difficulties may be mild and require only short term intervention from a speech and language therapist. In contrast, others may be complex and long-term, sometimes combined with disabilities, such as those along the autistic spectrum. Such children may require support during critical periods of childhood and adolescent development. To help children learn, teachers or teaching assistants may need to re-phrase instructions so the meaning is understood and then check that children have understood and know what they are expected to do.

Disabilities

Advances in medicine have resulted in many children being born and surviving with a number of complex conditions that have, in the past, considerably affected their chances of survival. As with learning difficulties, there are innumerable types of physical disability, but broadly speaking, physical difficulties encompass those affecting sight, hearing and speech, mobility problems that may require the use of a wheelchair or walking aids, conditions that necessitate help with feeding and personal hygiene and a range of medical conditions including those that require the use of apparatus, for which staff have to be trained in their use. Often such children have severe learning difficulties as well.

Autistic Spectrum Disorders

These are generally regarded as life-long *'hidden'* disabilities due to individuals not having obvious physical impairments, but they do experience a range of difficulties that impact upon every area of their lives. The Labour Government's *Inclusion Development Programme (2009)* noted that difficulties include:

- "Being unable to behave in socially acceptable ways.
- Having difficulty in understanding what has been spoken, especially in relation to jokes and sarcasm.
- Being inflexible in thought – which means that children prefer regular routines and become anxious when they are unexpectedly changed".

Additional difficulties might include being unable to play imaginatively, make decisions and being over-sensitive to the environment by reacting to noise, smells and objects *(DCSF 2009: 10-12)*. Autistic spectrum disorders may co-exist with learning disabilities which further impact upon learning ability and being able to manage personal needs and live independently.

Asperger's Syndrome: Is another form of autistic spectrum disorder which affects how individuals make sense of their world, process information and relate to other people. As routines are important, schools should advise pupils of changes to their routine, in an effort to avoid emotional upset. Children can react badly when presented with a new (or substitute) teaching assistant when they have not had advance warning and no time in which to emotionally prepare themselves for change.

Attention Deficit Hyperactivity Disorder (ADHD)

Children with ADHD have difficulties with their attention span, completing tasks and are easily distracted. Hyperactivity is demonstrated by constant movement such as getting up and down from their seats, wandering around or fidgeting. Impulsivity and inappropriate behaviour can result in school disciplinary procedures being implemented. Attention deficit disorder (ADD) is similar to attention deficit hyperactivity disorder (ADHD) without the hyperactivity component.

Depression

Depression is a condition which affects mood; each individual's experience is unique and personal to them; feelings can vary from mild sadness to despair whilst others may feel *'flat'*, neither experiencing joy nor sadness. The severity and way in which depression affects an individual can change over time and someone's internal mood may not always be evident to others. External characteristics which may be more noticeable include changes in sleeping pattern (insomnia or over-sleeping), lethargy, lack of motivation and difficulty with concentration and changes to appetite (either over-eating or barely eating anything). Children who have formerly been high achievers at school may become disinterested and *'careless'* and withdraw from school activities. Some children and young people will disengage from their peers and become socially isolated whilst others may appear more sociable by putting on a *'front'* in an endeavour to conceal their inner turmoil.

Anxiety

Anxiety may co-exist with depression or may exist alone. There are a number of anxiety disorders that children may experience. Anxiety can be described as an irrational fear that causes individuals to act in a particular way. For example, school children may become *'school phobic'* and refuse to attend school; specialist support will be required to help manage the anxiety and, where possible, address the underlying cause. Children may have obsessive compulsive disorders (OCD) resulting in repetitive actions, such as constant hand washing or avoiding cracks on pavements - the focus of the obsession can be anything and strict routines may need to be followed each day when getting ready for school or performing certain tasks. If routines are interrupted, it may be necessary to re-start the whole sequence from the beginning. Experiences can be disabling and affect children's ability to attend school and learn.

Co-occurring Difficulties

Special Educational Needs and disabilities do not fit neatly into compartments, being delineated from each other with no overlap. Learning difficulties and disabilities may be viewed along a continuum of need (ranging from the mild to the severe) and the examples provided will have illustrated that several conditions may simultaneously exist within one individual.

Labelling

As already mentioned, the Medical Model of disability is concerned with diagnosis, labelling and treatment, so the majority of children who are assessed by medical professionals will sooner or later receive a diagnosis. Some parents become frustrated when their children's difficulties are not immediately given a diagnosis, especially with children along the autistic spectrum, where the full nature of their difficulties only becomes apparent when they enter adolescence. Prior to that point, most children will usually have experienced periodic assessment and monitoring by paediatricians, other consultants and/or educational psychologists, but the presentation of such disabilities, which often co-occur with other conditions, is that initially, it might be difficult to ascertain the primary condition and until it becomes clear, paediatricians may be hesitant in providing a definitive diagnosis, although they may have advised parents of their suspicions. Once a label has been given, it may satisfy months or years of uncertainty and provide parents with a sense of relief after wrestling with the cause of their children's difficulties, as illustrated Mrs B and Mrs H in Chapter 8.

A diagnosis may provide the gateway for parents being able to find out more information about their children's difficulties, perhaps through local support groups or internet forums where they can share experiences with other parents and learn from each other. Without a label, parents may flounder - not knowing where to turn for additional support in how to manage their children's difficulties. Although not strictly necessary for educational purposes, having a label may improve upon children's educational provision, as teaching staff become informed about how specific conditions present and learn of appropriate strategies to manage them, as illustrated by Mrs E's story in Chapter 8.

Some parents question the need for children to be categorised as having Special Educational Needs or specific disabilities and have particular concerns about stigma attached to such labels. Whilst labelling *can* have negative connotations and society can sometimes separate those with labels from the majority of the population, there can also be advantages to having a *'label'*. Whilst supporting parents, it became apparent there are distinct benefits in having a definitive diagnosis; not only were children with disabilities protected by disability legislation, but a diagnosis sometimes *'steered'* teachers to apply appropriate strategies to help overcome some of the difficulties being experienced. Furthermore, when parents know which type of organisation to approach for further support in learning about and managing their children's conditions, they become better informed and more skilled with respect to strategies to use at home, as the following statement, from my own research, corroborates.

"I'm in favour of early diagnosis and using labels, although they aren't popular these days. Labels give parents clarity. Once you have labelled a child, for example, having Asperger's, parents can then go to the ASD website and link up with parent groups and so forth."
Educational Psychologist
(Attwood 2007 Appendix E1: 5)

With additional knowledge, the parental position becomes stronger when they meet with local authority staff, teachers and attend multi-agency meetings, with a number of different professionals present. Instead of being daunted by such meetings, parents are generally more confident and able to hold their own – being experts on their own children as well as having a wider understanding about their children's difficulties and/or disabilities. This ultimately has a positive impact upon their children's education. Case Studies in Chapter 8 demonstrate a label does not necessarily make *everything* fall into place, but it *tends* to help. Labels help parents fight their corner when seeking further support for their child - far more than any vague discussion around *'difficulties'* of an imprecise nature ever will; a specific diagnosis always adds weight to any requests being made. Finally, children *'labelled'* with disabilities are afforded protection under the *Equality Act 2010* which means that schools must have regard to how they manage pupils with both physical and *'hidden'* disabilities which impact upon behaviour and emotions. Labels help educational professionals make sense of difficulties being presented by children although will not necessarily indicate the seriousness of the condition, nor the specific number of symptoms experienced from a whole range of possibilities. Labels do (or should) contribute to professional understanding of children's behaviour and learning in the classroom and should encourage examination of the characteristics being displayed by children, some of which may previously have been disregarded or attributed to other causes. Professionals may re-assess the presenting picture and react more positively towards children with a definitive diagnosis, rather than when the same children *'merely had a confusing set of undefined difficulties'* to deal with. To state it bluntly, it is harder for educational professionals to ignore a label, although there are occasions when this does occur.

Professional Sensitivity

Whilst labelling can be invaluable with respect to ensuring *reasonable adjustments* are implemented and that children receive extra provision, as required, this doesn't mean that it's appropriate to constantly remind parents that their children have Special Educational Needs or disabilities. Parents may find such terms offensive or be in denial of their children's differences. In particular, children's disabilities may be rejected when they do not match their parents own notions of disability. Sensitivity is therefore, required in how professionals reach out to parents, including the language they use, in both face-to-face and written communication. Parents who may be reluctant to accept their children have Special Educational Needs may find the term *'additional needs'* more palatable to their psyche. A professional helper will soon determine the most appropriate language to use when supporting specific parents and should make adjustments accordingly.

Family Life and Disability

Parents of children with Special Educational Needs and disabilities are often swamped by the complexity of their lives; some parents have health concerns or learning difficulties or disabilities of their own which may be of the same type as their children, adding to their struggles with daily living. Disability is frequently a cause of poverty; parents may be unable to work because of their own disabilities or health issues and must then survive on benefits. Some families have more than one sibling with additional needs which further complicates the practicalities of daily living.

Families living on low incomes are at increased risk of having children with disabilities due to poor diets and stressful living conditions, both of which increase the possibility of premature births or low birth weight babies which can contribute to disabilities. Services that work with and support families of children with Special Educational Needs and disabilities should adopt a holistic approach when supporting such families as their living circumstances may significantly impact upon the advice and support that is being offered. In my experience, some families are simply unable to pursue avenues, which professionals regard as being beneficial to them, due to being over-whelmed by their situation and being unable to take any further responsibilities on board. Whatever someone's professional role, they should have regard to the bigger picture, even when their involvement with a family only addresses one small element.

Research undertaken by *The Children's Society (2011)* acknowledged additional pressures on families such as costs associated with attending frequent medical appointments, purchase of specialist equipment and the need to replenish home furnishings due to damage caused by disability aids. In addition, the prohibitive costs of childcare can be an obstacle to parents being able to undertake paid employment *(The Children's Society 2011: 5, 14)*.

Families with disabled children may experience insurmountable stress and life may become untenable. Few are likely to be part of a social network and many may not approach professionals who could help them. Parents may separate under the strain, resulting in children living in single-parent households. Research commissioned by the *Department for Work and Pensions (2008: 26)* noted that parents are at their greatest risk of separation during the first two years of their children's lives, which may be attributed to the significant challenges and upheaval in lifestyle associated with having a disabled child. However, *Shapiro (2004)* asserted that risk factors can be reduced if parents can spend quality time with each other and have a network comprising friends, family and professionals who can support them (*Shapiro 2004 cited in Department for Work and Pensions report 2008*). Families should ensure they receive all benefits to which they are entitled and that they do not struggle alone, especially when there are professional services available to support and advise about a range of matters.

Educational Concerns

Additional stress occurs when parents have concerns about their children's education such as when needs have not been fully acknowledged and are, therefore, not being addressed or when teachers have raised concerns about children's behaviour or some other issues appertaining to their education. Some parents have no difficulty in meeting with *'authority figures'* to raise their concerns or address issues being raised by school or local authority professionals; others, for a variety of reasons, are unable to contemplate such meetings and shy away from attending their children's school whenever possible. Parent Partnership Services, in each local authority area, are available to provide information, advice and support to such parents, and can accompany parents to meetings and advocate on their behalf. Furthermore, services can work with parents and educational professionals to improve relationships between them as well as mediating on concerns raised by each party. Such involvement ultimately benefits children's education and can, in some small way, help reduce family stress.

Commentary

In my experience, children with behavioural, emotional and social difficulties or *'hidden'* disabilities, combined with speech, language and communication needs are more likely to be at risk of school exclusion due to their non-conforming and disruptive behaviour. Frequently, teachers attribute the characteristics and behaviours associated with *'hidden'* disabilities as being due to adolescent rebellion or indiscipline as a result of poor parenting and it's paramount that teaching staff become knowledgeable about such disabilities and how they affect behaviour; fortunately, the Coalition Government is currently attempting to address this through additional training for teachers.

Children with speech, language and communication needs may become highly frustrated because of their inability to communicate effectively with their peers and adults and this may be demonstrated through their behaviour; this can be in addition to any co-occurrence of other recognised conditions. Difficulties in the language and communication arena may result in a young person giving an inappropriate response due to their inability to correctly process and understand what has been said to them. For example, parents have sometimes reported that their children have been disciplined, due to their inability to understand questions directed to them; where they admitted to actions which they personally hadn't undertaken, but because they had *'admitted'* to *'crimes'* they were punished. The reality was that such children had failed to comprehend what they were being asked and didn't respond appropriately. Even when their peers corroborated the truth of the situation, this was usually disregarded because the *'crime'* had been admitted to.

In supporting parents of children with Special Educational Needs, there were few occasions when there was only one learning difficulty or disability being presented; often there would be a primary concern, such as dyslexia which would trigger the parent's contact with the service, but upon further questioning and working with the parent, it was not unusual for other issues to surface such as dyspraxia or emotional problems. As well as concerns associated with the child, case work with parents (and their children) would often reveal a myriad of additional factors affecting the family, and these would often compound the difficulties being experienced by the child and often hindered relationships between school and family. When supporting parents of children with Special Educational Needs, there are multiple factors that can impinge upon the family situation and affect children's learning. All of these factors should be considered when attempting to understand children's difficulties in order to provide the most effective support.

Chapter 3
Special Provision for Children

Dispelling Myths

In an ideal world, every child with additional needs (Special Educational Needs and/or disabilities) would receive *all* the help and support they needed in their school environment. Unfortunately, there are several myths concerning educational provision which sometimes lead parents to have false and unrealistic expectations. I will attempt to dispel these, whilst presenting a more realistic perspective on what may happen and what parents can expect for their children. We are on the brink of SEN Reform which is expected to become law in Spring 2014. Meanwhile, schools and local authorities are preparing to implement the changes whilst continuing with the existing system which still remains largely unchanged. Readers will now be guided through some common misconceptions about Special Educational Needs provision. The myths are set against the current system, but the essence of the points raised will still apply when SEN reform is implemented. Against each statement, there will be a *'true'* or *'false'* response with more detailed explanations following.

1. *All* children with learning difficulties and disabilities have their difficulties identified early. *False. Some do, but not all.*
2. *All* children with learning difficulties and disabilities receive appropriate additional support in accordance with the *Special Educational Needs Code of Practice (2001)*. *False. They should do, but it doesn't always happen.*
3. *All* children with learning difficulties and disabilities receive a Statement of Special Educational Needs. *False. Not all children with learning difficulties and/or disabilities need a Statement. Even some children who could be advantaged by having a Statement do not always get one.*
4. *All* children with Statements of Special Educational Needs have the provision that is written into the Statement, met at *all* times. *False. Legally, there should be no interruptions or disruption to the provision detailed in the statement, but unfortunately, there are situations in which the stated provision is not fulfilled, even though it should be.*

5. *All* children with disabilities have *reasonable adjustments* put in place, appropriate to their needs and disability. *False. It should happen if a child needs them, but there are many reasons why this might not occur.*

You will notice that in each case, *'all'* children were referred to. In theory, all legislated systems and procedures should ensure that no children with Special Educational Needs slip *'through the net'*, but the reality is often quite different. Detailed responses will now be provided to the above statements, keeping to the same number order.

Late Identification of Difficulties (1): Many children with overt disabilities have them identified from birth, during their pre-school years or whilst at primary school but for others it may take many years before the cause of their difficulties is recognised; this particularly applies to *'hidden'* disabilities which may become more pronounced during the course of children's development, but can also apply to more subtle learning difficulties. Regrettably, not all children with learning difficulties and/or disabilities have them identified, with additional support being put in place during their school years, despite having government guidance on assessment methods, identification, monitoring and provision required for children with Special Educational Needs and disabilities. For example, whilst employed at a sixth form college and colleges of further education, I encountered students with Specific Learning Difficulties and disabilities, in particular, dyslexia (which affects literacy skills) and dyscalculia (which is the mathematical equivalent) where their difficulties had only been identified and diagnosed in post-compulsory education settings. The young people informed me that during their school years, class teachers had attributed their difficulties as being due to laziness or low intelligence, which had subsequently had a damaging effect on their self-esteem. Following assessment, appropriate teaching strategies were applied and the students made significant academic progress. Furthermore, as a result of positive affirmation from teaching staff and their own recognition that they were finally able to achieve, their self-worth and self-esteem improved considerably. For whatever reasons, teachers had failed to recognise the nature of the student's difficulties and instead, had adopted judgemental attitudes towards them and their abilities, which meant they had no additional support or strategies put in place to help them overcome their obstacles to learning. Such situations will continue to occur. More recently, parents have reported that children with dyslexia have spent hours on homework tasks that were expected to take a maximum of an hour to complete. With a Specific Learning Difficulty affecting their ability to read and write, pupils spent a disproportionate amount of time completing their work, but through their own perseverance had managed to achieve results. Whilst teachers were aware of the diagnosis and because pupils were viewed as being able to manage, no additional support was provided to help them overcome some of their difficulties and relieve some of the stress experienced due to their need to *'over-work'*.

Lack of Support (2): As an educationalist and challenger of professional practice, I am able to view the educational system from *'both sides of the fence'*, recognising there are many reasons why children and young people may not receive the support they need whilst at school. Some common reasons are given below.

- Stereotypical attitudes regarding pupil behaviour may sometimes hinder recognition of what is really being presented.
- Sometimes bright children and young people are just good at *'working around'* their difficulties so the full extent of their conditions may be unrecognised by practitioners and therefore, not acknowledged as requiring additional support.
- Children and young people with learning difficulties sometimes *'mask'* their differences by preferring to be viewed as lazy or unmotivated rather than admitting to their difficulties with regards to learning; this may account (in part) for inaccurate teacher perceptions of the cause of pupils' difficulties.
- Practitioners may lack the skills and/or insight required to recognise difficulties that are presented.
- Too much time may be spent in *'waiting to see'* if a difficulty is temporary or of a longer-term nature, meaning that precious time is wasted before children receive additional support. This position is most likely to apply during primary school years, when parents might *'wait'* two years before having their concerns addressed due to teachers viewing their children's difficulties as being due to *'slow development'*, which in itself should have served as a trigger for investigation. Mrs E's story in Chapter 8 illustrates this point.

Whilst supporting parents of children with Special Educational Needs and disabilities, it was not uncommon to encounter such *'reasons'* to explain lack of educational support being provided. This is something that no amount of legislation can eradicate; factors that influence professional responses include experience, lack of respect for parental concerns and attitudes taken towards children all of which ultimately rest upon subjective judgement of the presenting situation.

Criteria for Obtaining Statements (3): Not all children with learning difficulties or disabilities receive a Statement of Special Educational Needs, nor do they all need one. Currently, children's difficulties are addressed through a graduated response, known as School Action or School Action Plus (or the Early Years equivalent). In my experience, changes to the economic and political climate have resulted in more vigorous criteria being applied against the statutory guidance before children obtain a Statement. Sometimes, Statements are only issued when an Appeal has been lodged with the First-tier Tribunal (SEND), following initial refusal by the local authority.

Complex cases may initially be refused a Statement because of lack of supportive documentary evidence that explains children's difficulties. Whilst health reports will have been sought during the Statutory Assessment process, they may not have sufficiently reflected the extent of children's learning difficulties and/or disabilities, or may simply have been out-of-date and not representative of the current position. When professional reports refer to *'suspected'* conditions, rather than provide a definitive diagnosis, there is a risk of non-medical practitioners concluding that difficulties are less severe than they actually are. Therefore, a firm diagnosis is always helpful, even though such labelling is often disliked by parents and their children.

Regrettably, parents' hopes are sometimes raised regarding the prospect of obtaining Statements for their children with some believing that Statements are automatically issued following requests for Statutory Assessment. The reality is that many parents have their hopes dashed. Sometimes parents may have had their expectations raised due to advice received from other parents or services that lack a full understanding of how the system works. They may know of children, with similar difficulties to their own children, who were issued with a Statement and assume that the condition itself is the basis for a Statement being issued. However, as a general rule, Statements are not issued according to specific types of learning difficulty and/or disability, but are issued according to children's needs and the complexity of difficulties being experienced and the extent to which they create barriers to learning.

Non-compliance of Statement (4): By law, children with Statements of Special Educational Needs *'must'* have their educational needs met, but the reality is *sometimes* different. The most usual reason for non-compliance is due to lack of resources to meet the needs and provision identified in the Statement. For example, if a teaching assistant leaves her post (most are female) or is absent from work due to ill health, it's a legal requirement, when written into a child's statement, that such support is maintained. Whilst technically, schools should find a substitute when teaching assistants are absent, this is sometimes easier said than done. When there is no capacity within the existing staff compliment, schools may need to recruit, even if only on a temporary basis but, of course, this takes time. One only has to consider the stages involved in recruiting new staff - advertising, shortlisting of applicants, interviewing and carrying out Disclosure and Barring Service (DBS) checks, etc. before a new recruit is finally able to commence work in their new post. When someone has left their job, a whole term may be spent, without support being provided while the recruitment process is underway.

Aside from the practicalities involved in recruitment, schools may even resist recruiting a new member of staff, if they are already paying a salary to someone on sick leave, as this would effectively mean they are paying twice over for the duties to be fulfilled. Such scenarios do not only apply to school provision. Statements of Special Educational Needs are *only* legally enforceable with respect to the educational provision written into them and this position will continue when Education, Health and Care Plans are introduced. Whilst local authorities have a duty to ensure that special educational provision is provided in accordance with EHC Plans *(DfE 2012: 22)* there will be no such guarantee regarding health and social care – merely a *'commitment'* to provide services.

However, under reform, health and social care services can be written into EHC Plans as educational provision, separate provision or a combination of both. If categorised as *educational* provision this *may* provide the leverage necessary to ensure such services are provided. Currently, parents may complain under the standard NHS or local authority complaints procedures for lack of (planned) health or social care provision, although the revised *SEN Code of Practice* may publish alternative arrangements.

Stretched resources do not necessarily result in *'all or nothing'* provision; sometimes, services are delivered less frequently than they are supposed to be, or responsibility may be delegated to teaching assistants or other staff to undertake therapy programmes with children. This permits specialists, such as speech and language therapists, to check upon children's progress by telephone or infrequent school visits, in order to maximise use of available resources. This means that children receive their therapy but its effectiveness is dependent upon the skills of the practitioner, the training they have received and the time they have available to deliver such programmes.

Non-delivery of statutory provision may also be due to the need for schools to purchase specialist teaching materials or equipment as well as any weaknesses in professional practice. These are being addressed by the Coalition Government's *Schools' Funding Reform (2013-14)* where the expectation is that schools will receive sufficient delegated funds to enable them to purchase necessary SEN resources *(DfE 2012)*, whilst the Government's *White Paper, 'The Importance of Teaching' (DfE 2010)* and the *Green Paper, Support and aspiration: A new approach to special educational needs and disability (DfE 2011: 59-60)* have both committed to enhanced continuing professional development (CPD) and improvements to teacher training in order that teachers have more expertise in managing and teaching children with Special Educational Needs.

Unfortunately, having a Statement of Special Educational Needs, or the new Education, Health and Care Plan, is no guarantee that everything will operate smoothly from the time of being issued. Best intentions are sometimes outweighed by other factors such as having the resources available to deliver programmes, finances, professional expertise and sometimes, simply having the *'heart'* to expend extra time and effort, when necessary. Chapter 8 describes parents' and children's experiences and demonstrates that, for some families, statutory provision is no guarantee that everything will happen as it should. Parents should be vigilant and work closely with teaching staff to ensure that their children's needs are being met at *all* times.

Reasonable Adjustments (5): Under the *Equality Act 2010*, schools are expected to make *reasonable adjustments* for children with disabilities. Their duty is *'anticipatory'* in that they should already have systems in place or be ready to implement them as soon as required. For some children, *reasonable adjustments* are not implemented or not applied consistently, especially in relation to children along the autistic spectrum. Some teachers are conscientious about the application of *reasonable adjustments* with respect to the appropriate application of discipline methods and communication strategies, whilst others disregard the disability and treat all undesirable behaviours as being due to other causes.

Parents have reported that primary school children have been denied the opportunity to attend school trips when overnight sleeping arrangements have been involved, with the excuse that there were insufficient staff available to supervise them, when there were concerns about their behaviour. Even though trips had been organised weeks in advance, parents would only be informed a few days before the excursion was due to take place. This obviously distressed the children concerned whilst *'catching'* parents unawares. Without being aware of the legal position, parents accepted the school's explanation, but subsequently sought advice on how to address similar occurrences in the future. On one occasion, an assertive parent, who was presented with this *fait accompli*, persuaded the school to allow her to accompany her son on an overnight trip in order to supervise him whilst he enjoyed the learning experience with his peers. The school agreed to this proposal, the child enjoyed the excursion, and relations between parent and school subsequently improved! I'm sure there must be other parents who have resolved matters in the same way. Having now addressed the myths at the beginning of this chapter, this will be followed by an outline of current support with information, as currently known, on future changes to provision.

Current Practice

The current practice in relation to educational provision for children with Special Educational Needs and disabilities will be outlined; this is not meant to address every situation that can occur, nor describe every stage of the Statutory Assessment Process, as detailed information is provided in the official guidance, the *Special Educational Needs Code of Practice (DfES 2001)*. Whilst reading this section, readers should be mindful that this system has a limited life-span, with SEN reform being implemented sometime during 2014 onwards. Nevertheless, this section is useful for parents whose children are already receiving SEN provision as it should help address some of their uncertainties about what will happen in the future. For parents who are new to the world of SEN, it will provide some general information about how the system operates as well as familiarising them with current terminology.

There are currently three tiers to SEN provision. These are known as School Action, School Action Plus and Statements of Special Educational Needs. For children in Early Years provision, the first two stages are known as Early Years Action and Early Years Action Plus. These terms will be explained more fully as we proceed. To avoid duplication, both pre-school and primary school provision will be collectively referred to, unless there is specific need to allude to one or other stage of education. The purpose is to explain the general principles, whilst advising readers about what might occur, based upon my own professional experience.

Identifying Needs

As children progress through the education system, travelling through pre-school provision to primary school and progressing through secondary, there are numerous opportunities for teaching staff (including pre-school practitioners) to identify any difficulties and obstacles to children's learning. Many difficulties are of a transient nature and children are quickly able to catch up with their peers, following a short period of intervention that addresses their area of need, such as reading skills or behaviour management. This type of support is provided within the setting's existing resources and when progress and development is comparable with their peers, support for individual children is discontinued. Children with temporary difficulties are *not* regarded as having Special Educational Needs under *The Special Educational Needs Code of Practice (DfES 2001: 46)*.

Pre-School and School Assessment

Teachers and Early Years practitioners continually observe, monitor, assess and record the progress of all children for whom they are responsible. Both formal (objective) and informal (subjective) methods of assessment are used for noting and recording children's achievements and difficulties. Whilst some learning difficulties are quickly and easily recognised, others are much more complex; it may take considerable time to identify and gain an understanding of the presenting picture before professionals are certain children have specific Special Educational Needs that require longer term support.

In accordance with the *SEN Code of Practice (ibid: 16-17)*, Early Years practitioners and child minders assess children to ensure they are developing in accordance with national standards. *Tickell's Early Years Foundation Stage Review (DfE 2011: 27)* resulted in revised assessment criteria for young children, with the primary focus being on three main areas:

- "personal, social and emotional development
- communication and language and
- physical development".

Children will be expected to demonstrate such skills through literacy, mathematics, expressive arts and design and their understanding of the world *(DfE 2011: 27)*.

Intervention may arise from parental concerns being raised with Early Years practitioners, the practitioner's own awareness of prevailing difficulties or by assessments undertaken by general practitioners, health visitors or social workers. Concerns identified by Early Years practitioners (or school teachers), should be reported to children's parents so they are aware of specific strategies being used to help their children's development and, where necessary, can co-operate with the setting. Currently, a graduated response is applied, known as Early Years Action and Early Years Action Plus for pre-school settings and School Action and School Action Plus for schools. Strategies used for children experiencing difficulties are either *'additional to'* or *'different from'* those used for their peers. The *SEN Code of Practice (2001)* categorises children with Special Educational Needs, when teaching interventions and use of appropriate resources have failed to help children make progress and they continue to perform below the level of their peers. This includes children who require individual support to help them overcome communication difficulties, children with persistent behavioural difficulties and those with sensory and physical impairments *(DfES 2001: 35)*.

Changes Under Reform: the *Children and Families Bill (2013)* states that Early Years Action and Early Years Action Plus (and the school equivalent) are ceasing to exist. Instead, there will be one school-based level (or Early Years equivalent) of Special Educational Needs and statutory provision under Education, Health and Care Plans only. Children with existing Statements will continue to have these honoured and are afforded the same protection and provision. At some stage, Statemented children may be required to undergo a full assessment to be transferred to Education, Health and Care Plans. The *Green Paper, Support and aspiration: A new approach to special educational needs and disability (2011)* states that in order for children to receive school-based SEN provision, their difficulties must be of a kind that *"exceed what is normally available in schools" (DfE 2011: 59).* Teachers will be expected to implement a range of strategies, use comparative data and possibly discuss issues with parents and support services before children are categorised as having Special Educational Needs and receive Additional SEN Support in school *(DfE 2013).* The implications for this approach are that some children already receiving Special Educational Needs provision might not meet the new criteria. Teachers will be expected to manage the most commonly encountered difficulties as an integral aspect to their teaching practice. It is realistic to assume, therefore, that teaching practice will have an increased emphasis on whole-class strategies, rather than individualised programmes.

Transition between Educational Settings

Once children have been identified as having certain difficulties at pre-school, information regarding the nature of their difficulties and how they have been managed should be passed onto the next educational setting to help ease children into the next phase of their education. The new setting will use the existing information regarding children's difficulties while they make their own assessment of needs. Usually, the new setting is a primary school, but it may be another pre-school setting. For some children, their difficulties only become apparent when they enter formal education so may first be discovered at primary school, either by teacher observation and assessment, or through parents raising concerns.

The *SEN Code of Practice (2001)* indicates the measures to be undertaken by schools and pre-school settings in order to ascertain whether children have Special Educational Needs. When children enter into the primary phase of education, schools routinely undertake baseline assessments within the first few weeks. The results are then used to help chart children's future progress and development. Assessment includes monitoring, observation and measurement against national objectives *(DfES 2001: 46).* As part of formal transition arrangements, primary schools pass on pupil information to secondary schools. In compliance with the *SEN Code of Practice (2001),* secondary schools use existing pupil information and further develop pupil profiles through observation and assessment to determine pupil strengths and weaknesses. Both pupils and their parents may work with teachers to establish future targets to be achieved *(DfES 2001: 60).*

Early Years Provision

Between the ages of 3-5 years, many children attend some form of Early Years provision, known as the Foundation Stage in Education. There are many types of provider for young children that include maintained nursery schools, independent schools, playgroups and approved childminders. Each local authority has a Family Information Service that is able to provide parents and practitioners with a full list of settings in their area; they can also inform parents about local Children's Centres and eligibility criteria with respect to accessing free Early Years provision for 2 and 3 year olds.

Identification of a Problem

Unless a child has already been diagnosed with a disability or learning difficulty soon after birth, it may only be when they attend an Early Years setting, that any difficulties first become apparent. Early Years practitioners must provide learning opportunities and record children's progress and achievements on their pupil record, noting progress from when they first joined the setting, as well as comparisons with their peers. Obviously, children are not the same as each other and develop at different rates with some progressing faster or slower than others. Delayed or non-existent progress may be generalised, covering all aspects of development, or may relate to one or more specific areas only. If development in key learning areas causes concern, strategies will be put in place to help children progress, in keeping with their peers. Early Years settings (and schools) will have a practitioner with responsibility for Special Educational Needs, known as the Special Educational Needs Co-ordinator, more usually referred to as the *SENCO.* Childminders will usually need to seek advice from their local network Co-ordinator who has SENCO responsibilities.

Special Educational Needs

As time progresses, it becomes easier to determine if a child has delayed development and whether the gap between their achievements and that of their peers is widening. Should this be the case, under the current system, they may then be considered as having Special Educational Needs that require longer term support to help them learn and achieve. As already stated, support is always *'additional to'* or *'different from'* that required for other children in the class. When children experience a number of difficulties in relation to their development, it should be noted that it is not usually possible to address all the difficulties at once. The type of support provided for children will be dependent upon their needs and the resources available within the setting (both material and human). When difficulties have become apparent, the Early Years practitioner (or school teacher) should discuss their concerns with the parent(s), prioritise which aspects should be targeted first, and then as progress is made, implement strategies for the other difficulties in turn. When children with behavioural, social and emotional difficulties are having their needs addressed through a management and support programme, it is common for *'motivators'* to be applied as an incentive to encourage appropriate behaviour. For younger children this may involve *'star'* charts (or similar approaches) whilst other incentives are generally adopted for older children. The *Warnock Report (1978)* stated it was necessary to implement multiple approaches for children with Special Educational Needs and strategies implemented include use of specialist equipment, facilities and resources, teaching strategies, modification of the curriculum and consideration of the physical and emotional environment *(Warnock 1978: 41)*. The Coalition Government is intending to improve the outcomes of children with Special Educational Needs which will necessitate a range of strategies being applied under reform *(DfE 2013)*.

In accordance with the *SEN Code of Practice (2001)* children with Special Educational Needs are currently issued with Individual Education Plans (commonly referred to as *IEPs*). This document details the difficulties being experienced, short-term targets to be achieved and teaching strategies and resources. Named individuals are usually identified who will implement specific aspects of the programme, whilst other details should include the frequency and time periods of interventions, methods of monitoring, recording achievement of targets and review dates *(DfES 2001: 70)*. Behavioural, social and emotional difficulties are usually addressed through use of Pupil Inclusion Plans (known as *PIPs*) which adopt a similar format.

In recent years, many schools have switched to using Provision Maps, which generally contain the same type of information as Individual

Education Plans, so although the documentation may be different, the general content should be the same. In my experience, educational professionals sometimes mistakenly believe that whole class Provision Maps are sufficient, but irrespective of whether these are used, individual target sheets should be completed for children with identified needs, in order to note their own individual difficulties, strategies used, monitoring of progress and review dates. The Government may review the system of recording, but the general principles will still apply – in particular there must be evidence of monitoring of achievement as without this it's impossible to know whether strategies are being effective. The purpose of intervention is to help children make progress *(DfES 2001: 52)* and once there is consistent evidence that targets have been achieved (through monitoring and recording), new targets can then address other areas of difficulty.

'P' Scales

Sometimes children with Special Educational Needs work on 'P' scales. This is a set of targets, specifically for children who are unable to manage work at National Curriculum Key Stages. Children work through stages 1-8 in national curriculum subjects, with a view to joining Key Stage 1 of the National Curriculum, although realistically, this is not an achievable target for all children. Teachers precisely record progress which is measured against national levels of attainment *(DfE 2010)*. Class teachers should inform parents if their children are working on 'P' scales and will be able to provide more detailed information about the system.

Specialist Support

The Warnock Report (1978: 47) endeavoured to provide for children with a whole range of difficulties, in assorted settings that could meet their educational, physical and emotional needs. Under the *Special Educational Needs Code of Practice (2001),* there are circumstances under which school support should be escalated. This applies to children who fail to make progress, have been unable to achieve previously agreed targets or the nature of their difficulties has changed as well as those who are unable to sustain relationships with others. Any of these reasons should trigger the SENCO in approaching external support services *(DfES 2001: 71)*. For example, children may be referred to educational psychologists, Learning Support or Behaviour Support

Services, or health professionals such as occupational therapists, paediatricians, physiotherapists, audiologists, psychiatrists or speech and language therapists. Of course, there are many other professional specialisms which may be called upon too. Referrals will be based on identified need, and are quite often, through a process of elimination. As soon as external professionals become involved, children on Early Years Action (or School Action) will be elevated to the next level of support, known as Early Years Action Plus or the school equivalent. As well as diagnosing potential conditions, both education and health specialists will provide advice and guidance for managing and improving children's difficulties in the educational setting.

Changes under Reform: From the description of school-based provision provided in the *Green Paper (2011: 58)*, this system has similarities to School Action Plus as external support services are likely to be involved to help children progress in school. The expectation under reform is that teachers might be required to implement a full range of strategies, meet with parents *and* discuss concerns with external professionals (as required) *before* a classification of Special Educational Needs applies *(DfE 2011: 58)*. SENCOs will need to be skilled in liaising with agencies and parents whilst having the ability to secure quality services within budget that appropriately addresses children's needs. Therefore, the extent to which children's difficulties are addressed may be largely dependent upon the skills and experience of SENCOs as well as support provided by senior management in commissioning quality support services.

Late Identification of Difficulties

The majority of disabilities and learning difficulties are identified during the early years or while children attend primary school, but some are not detected until secondary school age or beyond. Delays in identification may be due to having been missed during earlier years of schooling, parents' concerns may have been disregarded by educational professionals or conditions might have been relatively mild (and imprecise), during earlier childhood but became more pronounced during the adolescent years, which is not an uncommon occurrence for *'hidden'* disabilities. Having Special Educational Needs does not mean that children's learning difficulties or disabilities remain static over time. This is not to ignore the fact that *'life events'* may also be responsible for a later diagnosis, where accidents or illness cause a change in circumstances, with formerly healthy children becoming disabled, often with accompanying learning difficulties.

How Children Cope

In my experience, children with any type of difficulty often manage better whilst attending pre-school and primary school settings, due to their more nurturing environments and effective support systems in place. For instance, primary schools often have teaching assistants available in class to provide general support (even when not allocated to children on a formal basis). The environments also have fewer changes taking place and are less stressful for pupils. In contrast, secondary schools place greater demands upon children – the pace of learning is more intense, children must navigate their way around school sites to attend different lessons and are expected to take responsibility for their own organisation and management of time. Furthermore, secondary schools are usually much larger and have a wider age range of pupils, usually between the ages of 11-18, which to a newcomer may be quite daunting and intimidating, especially when they are vulnerable children with Special Educational Needs. Many children, with additional needs, will have received one-to-one support at primary school from a teaching assistant, even without the need for a Statement, and will be accustomed to having help in organising their day and receiving support during lessons. Such children will find it extremely challenging to discover there is no support for them when they attend secondary school, because of how schools allocate their resources. Even children with Statements, which provide for teaching assistant support, are sometimes let down by the system, and find they are expected to cope on their own. This often becomes a *'sink or swim'* scenario. Against this background, difficulties which may have been controlled or remained just beneath the surface at primary school, become exacerbated due to the pressures associated with secondary education, compounded by the surge of adolescent hormones.

Secondary schools adopt a graduated response to provision in the same way that earlier stages of education provide for needs – through Individual Education Plans (IEPs), or Provision Mapping at School Action or School Action Plus. Children are more likely to become involved in helping to set targets for areas of improvement at IEP meetings and parents should be invited to attend where possible, although it is acknowledged this is not always possible. Decisions are meant to be jointly taken between educational professionals, parents and children.

Some schools adopt the practice of presenting new Individual Education Plans to parents during parent consultations, with the request that parents sign their agreement, without having had the opportunity to be involved in the planning process. Professional opinion differs on the appropriateness of this approach, although there are reasons why this might not be considered good practice. For instance, parent consultations are extremely time limited and presenting a new IEP to parents at such events, gives them insufficient time to read and digest the contents and ask questions. Parents may become flustered and sign without really taking in the contents or knowing if they even agree with them. Presenting IEPs to parents in this way, prevents their engagement in the decision making process and keeps them at *'arms-length'*; furthermore, parent consultations are *'public events'* and the personal nature of IEPs and the reasons for having them should be discussed in more private settings. Assertive parents when presented with this scenario may prefer to request a separate meeting to discuss the contents.

Changes under Reform: Children who receive SEN support at school will continue to have their targets and progress documented *(DfE 2013).*

Involvement of Specialist Support Services

Support and advice from external professionals may be obtained in several ways. Unless provided in-house by schools, support services must be commissioned from external providers, or occasionally through local authorities, although this is largely being phased out. Systems are likely to vary from area to area and even between schools, so this can only be taken as a general guideline.

Educational Psychology, Learning Support and Behaviour Support Services will be contacted by the SENCO, who may only require telephone advice regarding strategies to use. After a number of strategies have been tried, with limited success, the SENCO may refer children to support services or health services for further assessment. Assessment may involve observation of children in the setting and use of assessment tools in order to determine the nature of the difficulties. The specialist service will then advise on a range of strategies in order to improve children's cognitive development, social skills or behaviour.

Each child will be assessed individually, although observations often take place within a classroom or playground context when children are interacting with their peers. Children are usually unaware that observations are taking place so that naturally occurring behaviour is observed. Direct contact with specialist services may follow once the results of observations are known, or there may be no further action.

Referrals to health services are usually diagnostic and may result in treatment programmes such as speech and language therapy or occupational and physiotherapy being implemented in educational settings. It is not uncommon for health professionals to go into educational settings to train teaching assistants or staff in other types of support role, to deliver programmes of therapy for individual children. Educational professionals are then responsible for reporting upon progress and ensuring that programmes of therapy are completed. Health professionals then periodically check upon progress, either by telephone or by visiting the setting, but may see children infrequently, following initial assessment.

Special Educational Needs Co-ordinators will always advise parents of the need to make such referrals and they shouldn't be surprised when action has been taken. In relation to health appointments, parents will usually accompany their children to hospitals, Children's Centres or whatever local provision has been made regarding access to such services. They will usually advocate on behalf of their children, explaining their difficulties and discussing with specialists the most appropriate course of action. When referrals are made to educational psychologists, it is not uncommon for children to be observed or assessed without their parents being present, although a meeting usually follows, once test results are known. With respect to Learning Support Services, parents may be required to collaborate with the school with respect to undertaking specific tasks with their children at home, in order to reinforce the strategies being used at the educational setting. In a similar way, when Behaviour Support Services are involved, parents and children may agree a *'contract'* committing their cooperation in following the programme at home, ensuring continuity of strategies between home and school.

Listening to Parents

It is important that parents and educational professionals at pre-school or school settings work together, especially when children have difficulties associated with Special Educational Needs and disabilities; it is vital that parents keep professionals informed of any additional concerns that may only be evident in the home environment, and that professionals take such concerns on board, as they may impact upon what is experienced in the school environment. It is easy for professionals to dismiss parents' concerns when they raise issues that are not evident in the educational setting, although such occurrences are a typical feature of children with *'hidden'* disabilities and are not necessarily due to a lack of parenting skills, which is sometimes asserted by professionals. The following excerpts from an interview with a parent illustrate this point.

"You cannot get them to see how a child like him can appear perfectly normal. Somebody can go into the classroom and look around and would not spot him as having Special Needs, but that does not mean he hasn't got an invisible need. Because they can't see it does not mean it isn't there, and to not support him is the worst thing you can do."
(Attwood 2007 Appendix C10: 77)

"The teachers have congratulated him at school because he is fine there and then at home, he explodes because of everything he has stockpiled from school. We were told we obviously needed help to control him at home. They won't see that what they do at school has a knock-on effect."
Parent of boy with Asperger's Syndrome.
(ibid Appendix C10: 77-78)

Requesting Assessment

Schools and parents may request that a local authority carry out a Statutory Assessment. An application does not necessarily mean that an assessment will take place, nor guarantee that a Statement will be issued if an assessment is completed. To support an application, parents should provide as much evidence as possible to validate the request by enclosing any reports and letters about their children's condition whether obtained from NHS consultants, therapists or independent assessments. Evidence from specialist organisations or websites may also be enclosed. Under the *Education and Inspections Act 2006* and the *Children and Families Bill (2013),* local authorities have a duty to consider parental requests and must respond by either informing parents of what action they intend to take, or advising them of the reason(s) for taking no further action.

Special Educational Needs Panels

Requests for Statutory Assessment are considered by local authority Special Educational Needs Panels who discuss the full extent of difficulties being experienced by children. This includes consideration of social, emotional and physical development, behaviour, sensory and physical impairments, how much children can attend to their personal needs, communication and language skills. The representation of Panels usually comprises members of the statutory Special Educational Needs team, an educational psychologist and SENCOs; on occasions, there may be other professional roles represented, with local authorities having their own specific composition. The range of professional experience will vary from those new to post to those of senior level and, in accordance with their particular professional role, will bring divergent perspectives, knowledge and experience to the discussions. Panels examine the whole picture presented by children, including the severity and range of difficulties experienced, and the needs that arise from them; from this information decisions are taken regarding whether needs can only be addressed through statutory provision.

Refusal to Assess

There are many valid reasons for local authorities refusing to undertake Statutory Assessment, such as:

- The child may present with difficulties that should easily be managed with appropriate teaching strategies and within existing school resources.
- The child's difficulties are not sufficiently severe enough.
- The school has sought a Statutory Assessment on the pretext of having insufficient resources to meet the child's needs and is basically seeking extra funding.
- Schools may have encouraged a parent to apply for Statutory Assessment in the hope of securing extra funding, not specifically because of the needs of the child, nor their inability to provide for those needs. Parents should not be used as political pawns in relation to schools applying for additional funding.
- When parents have requested Statutory Assessment but the school does not support the request as they consider they are adequately meeting the child's needs, an assessment is unlikely to proceed.

- Schools have failed to adequately address difficulties through appropriate strategies and existing resources. Schools must demonstrate they have explored all options.
- Strategies adopted by schools are not supported by documentary evidence so it's impossible to verify whether children have progressed or deteriorated in their performance. Local authorities must have evidence of strategies and monitoring as this informs their decision-making.
- Schools submit incorrect or incomplete documentation which prevents requests being processed.
- When schools fail to access specialist services they have not tried every option. Local authorities require evidence of involvement by specialist services and that schools cannot do more within existing resources.

When a request for Statutory Assessment is refused, local authorities advise parents of their right to Appeal against the decision – a legal process that involves the First-tier Tribunal (SEND). In my experience, some of the most successful applications for Statutory Assessment have been when schools and parents have worked together, towards the common goal of gaining evidence of difficulties and documenting every strategy and learning resource that has been tried, with a record of monitoring that demonstrates what a child can and cannot do. This is supported, of course, by up-to-date reports from any medical specialists involved in monitoring or providing treatment or care, with a clear diagnosis (or suspected diagnosis) with specific details about how the condition affects the child in every-day life, with some indication of severity. This process may take several months but does tend to strengthen requests for assessment and helps local authority decisions to be made with the best possible information.

Assessment Going Ahead

Assuming a request for Statutory Assessment has been accepted, the local authority will proceed to obtain as much information as possible about the difficulties being experienced by the child. Professionals from health, education, educational psychology and social care, involved in supporting the child, will each be required to submit a report on the child's difficulties. Information must be current, so if the child has not had a recent appointment with their particular specialist services (such as a speech and language therapist or paediatrician), they will usually need to be re-assessed; without this information, the local authority may be hindered in being able to make a decision about whether they should issue a Statement of Special Educational Needs. Parents will be invited to submit a written statement, explaining their child's difficulties, including details from birth to the present date, in order to further inform the local authority decision-making process.

Changes under Reform: Statutory assessment will become known as EHC Needs Assessment whilst Education, Health and Care Plans will replace Statements of Special Educational Needs *(DfE 2013: 27).*

Statement of Special Educational Needs

A Statement of Special Educational Needs is a legally binding document in that all educational provision written into the Statement *must* be provided. The *SEN Code of Practice (2001)* clarifies the component parts of Statements which, overall, should include information regarding the difficulties experienced, support provided by education, health and (sometimes) social care services and the named school *(DfE 2001: 100-101).* Parents should be aware that professional reports, which underpin provision written into a Statement, should always be explicit about the type, frequency and amount of support or therapy that is required to help children progress, including who is responsible for the activity. For example: speech and language therapy - should be specific about the type of regime.

> Conducted by: teaching assistant (or therapist)
> Frequency: twice a week.
> Time period: 30 minutes each session.
> Duration of programme: 6 weeks.

If reports omit this type of information, parents have the right to request its inclusion. Reports that simply refer to *'frequent'* or *'regular'* programmes are inadequate as such words represent different timescales to different people – they need to be explicit. Also, if therapy will only take place over a specific period of time, such as six weeks, then this should also be stated in the report.

Appeals

Parents may apply to the First-tier Tribunal (SEND) regarding lapses in provision of the educational aspects of a Statement and there will be continuity under Education, Health and Care Plans (applicable from 0-25 years of age). The system for addressing lapses in health and social care provision will be explained in the new Code of Practice. Parents will be invited to approve Plans in the same way they already do for Statements. The *Green Paper (DfE 2011: 47)* advised that parents will have the option of being in *'control'* of personal budgets, with respect to educational provision written into their children's Education, Health and Care Plans and this will be explored in Chapter 9.

Annual Reviews

Children with Statements have an Annual Review each year. Local authorities advise headteachers about which children have forthcoming Annual Reviews, approximately two weeks before they should take place. Headteachers then schedule the Review with parents, teachers and other professional staff who have been supporting the child. Annual Reviews provide an opportunity to assess a child's progress over the previous year, and evaluate the extent to which Individual Education Plan targets have been achieved. Progress and concerns will be discussed and Next Steps agreed with respect to any changes in provision.

Occasionally, a child will have made sufficient progress to no longer justify maintaining the Statement and the Annual Review will provide the local authority with the opportunity to inform parents of their intention to withdraw the Statement, which will subsequently be confirmed in writing. Parents will not usually be surprised as they will obviously be aware of any improvements in their child's capabilities. If parents anticipate any differences of opinion at meetings, they can seek support from their local Parent Partnership Service, where a representative may be able to accompany them, providing sufficient notice has been given. At the very least, parents could receive telephone support, which would provide an opportunity to air their concerns and be advised on how to approach the meeting. Equally, parents may be accompanied by a representative of another professional organisation, family member or friend, if they so choose. Reports following Annual Reviews are sent to the local authority and parents will subsequently receive their own copy. When Statements are being withdrawn, the local authority will write to parents, giving notice of their intent and inform them of their right to Appeal against the decision. Parents have two months from the date of the letter, in which to submit an Appeal, if they disagree with the decision.

Changes under Reform: In an effort to reduce bureaucracy, the Government is introducing an Annual Review Form to replace lengthy reports submitted by headteachers. Parents are already entitled to Appeal to the First-tier Tribunal (SEND) following an Annual Review, if requested changes are not made. Under the *Children and Families Bill (2013)* parents will be asked to consider mediation before being permitted to submit an Appeal, although they have the right to refuse. If mediation is rejected, an Adviser will then issue a certificate that enables parents to submit an application to the First-tier Tribunal (SEND). Alternatively, parents may participate in mediation and have their concerns resolved amicably whilst others may be less fortunate and be unable to reach agreement with the local authority; in other cases, the local authority may commit to specific actions, which subsequently remain unfulfilled. In such cases, parents may still be able to formally Appeal, providing the time period for lodging an application has not lapsed *(DfE 2012: 27)*. This process also applies to young people, who can submit an application in their own right.

Legal Protection and Notes In Lieu

The greatest incentive for parents in obtaining a Statement of Special Educational Needs for their children is that educational provision is legally enforceable. Parents are, quite rightly, often keen for a Statement to be issued even when there is no additional funding attached to meet those needs simply because there is a system of redress, if those needs are not met. When local authorities refuse to issue a Statement of Special Educational Needs, they currently issue a Note in Lieu, which is similar to a Statement in that it will detail the difficulties experienced by a child and the strategies that should be implemented by the school to address them. In many respects a Note in Lieu is equivalent to a Statement with respect to detailing provision, but parents must be aware, that unlike a Statement, this is *not* legally enforceable and parents cannot lodge an Appeal with the First-tier Tribunal (SEND) if schools subsequently fail to implement the necessary support. Once a Statement has been refused, parents must wait six months before they can reapply for reassessment, so an initial refusal does not necessarily mean the chapter is closed. Special Educational Needs and disabilities are not fixed - they change over time, and with new evidence to support children's difficulties, future applications *may* be more favourably received, resulting in a different outcome. I emphasise that a second (or subsequent application) may be viewed differently, but there is no guarantee.

Changes under Reform: There is currently no indication of an equivalent system under reform *(DfE 2013)*.

Support and Protection for Disabilities

Reasonable Adjustments: Under the *Disability Discrimination Act 1995*, schools and local authorities were charged with the responsibility of eliminating discrimination and promoting equality of opportunity for disabled pupils and other people who used their services. The Act enforced the application of *reasonable adjustments* in respect of pupils and adults with disabilities. This duty is anticipatory in that strategies and systems should be in place, in advance of actual need, wherever possible. For example, school buildings may be modified to facilitate access of children with physical disabilities to enable them to independently manoeuvre around the site. Anticipatory duties equally apply to *'hidden'* disabilities where teaching staff may implement specific strategies for managing aspects of behaviour in advance of their occurrence. The *Equality Act 2010* has now superseded earlier legislation, retaining the need to apply *reasonable adjustments*. The application of *reasonable adjustments* does not mean that all children with particular disabilities need the same type of provision being made for them, although awareness of specific disabilities may help professionals consider the range and type of adjustments that might be necessary. The needs of each child must be addressed individually as disabilities will present differently in terms of their severity and the prevalence of symptoms. Often the best way of supporting a child is to ask them what type of help they need. When schools take the lead and implement what they consider to be *reasonable adjustments* without first discussing this with pupils and their parents about what type of support would be most useful, they may subsequently find their efforts have been inappropriate and unhelpful. This will require the matter to be revisited because as far as that pupil and their parents are concerned they are not being supported.

Schools need to ensure that any *reasonable adjustments* aimed at supporting pupils with disabilities do not inadvertently segregate them as inclusion with their peers and the rest of the school community also contributes to a child's well-being. Responses to disability through the application of *reasonable adjustments* might look like this:

- Pupils with mobility difficulties may require additional time to reach classrooms when there is a change over between lessons.
- Teaching strategies and methods of communication may need to be adapted for children with *'hidden'* disabilities and those with health concerns such as depression or myalgic encephalomyelitis (ME), when there may be significant issues with respect to tiredness, lack of energy and difficulties with concentration and processing information. Children may additionally require a restricted timetable or attend school part-time for a limited period.
- Pupils with conditions along the Autistic Spectrum may require teaching staff to modify their approach with respect to behaviour management.
- Lessons may need to be re-located to ground floor classrooms to accommodate pupils in wheelchairs, unless there are other appropriate means of enabling them to reach first floor classrooms.

Having supported parents, I have become aware of the extent to which *'hidden'* disabilities can present difficulties for schools, parents and children. With respect to disabilities that pre-dispose children to unpredictable behaviour, it may sometimes be difficult for educational staff to develop sufficient sensitivity and knowledge in order to assess whether behaviour patterns are a result of the disability or due to rebellion. As it may take some considerable time before a diagnosis is confirmed, pupils may be unjustly punished for behaviours that they cannot control, due to negative assumptions by staff; it may not occur to them there could be a legitimate reason for such behaviour. Without considering the possibility of legitimate causes of disruptive behaviour, teaching staff effectively preclude children from access to *reasonable adjustments* which may benefit their learning and behaviour. As a consequence, children's behaviour may deteriorate due to the frustrations caused by their disability and their inability to learn; so poor behaviour caused by disability may be exacerbated by frustration and anger. This then becomes a negative spiral as children are punished for misbehaviour which further masks the disability, and may lead to either fixed-term or permanent exclusion from school. Whilst supporting parents, I became aware that teaching staff would sometimes disregard children's disabilities, even when parents had advised them of *'suspected'* conditions whilst awaiting a formal paediatric diagnosis. Unless schools received a paediatric diagnosis in writing, staff discounted parental information and failed to implement *reasonable adjustments*.

So herein lies a dilemma - on the one hand, teachers may lack the skills to identify the characteristics of *'hidden'* disabilities and therefore, not implement appropriate *reasonable adjustments* in order to help children. Secondly, we have teachers refusing to believe what parents tell them, which is neither conducive to working in partnership nor respecting parental knowledge. Thirdly, even with a paediatric diagnosis, this is not necessarily the end of the matter; parents have sometimes reported that teachers refuse to accept the existence of some conditions, not only within specific children, but in general and, as a consequence, they continue to punish children for behaviours associated with the condition, and still refuse to implement *reasonable adjustments*. Fortunately, this doesn't apply to all children with *'hidden'* disabilities, but such experiences can be detrimental to the mental health and well-being of those who do.

Discrimination: If parents and their children believe they have been discriminated against, they can seek redress through the First-tier Tribunal (SEND). As already mentioned, children with disabilities are afforded protection under the *Equality Act 2010* if they are subjected to discrimination because of their disability. Under this Act, discrimination arises when an individual is treated unfavourably because of their disability or when their treatment cannot be justified by a *'legitimate aim'*. However, it is not discriminatory when an individual is treated unfavourably when the other party had no knowledge of their disability; therefore, for someone to benefit from protection under the Act, they must advise schools or employers of their circumstances.

Anecdotally, schools usually modify their approach to children, when parents (or a support service) have informed them of requirements under the Act. Unfortunately, the new approach is not always long-term and sometimes previous approaches and attitudes held by staff re-surface. Fundamentally, professionals need the *'right heart'* to work appropriately with parents and their children and some struggle to demonstrate this.

Systems of Redress

Most parents of children with Special Educational Needs and disabilities have a lot of contact with teaching staff, sometimes even on a daily basis, presenting an opportunity to discuss any concerns in an informal manner. Sometimes, over time, more significant concerns become apparent, requiring specific actions to be taken by teaching staff to remedy them; as a result, parents will keenly be waiting, observing and seeking reassurance that the issues causing concern are being addressed. A general outline of the complaints system might help parents in these circumstances. This is not to encourage parents to formally complain, but will inform them of the options available if previous efforts failed to achieve positive results.

Complaints about the School: When parents are dissatisfied with some aspect of their children's education, they are entitled to speak to their children's class teacher. Quite often this approach will be sufficient to bring about any improvement although some parents may find it necessary to repeatedly see their child's class teacher, either due to unresolved difficulties or new ones being presented. In order to resolve matters, teachers may agree to specific follow-up actions which are subsequently followed through; others may undertake some of the actions, and a few will do nothing at all, having had no intention of taking any action in the first place. I have supported parents who have experienced all of these scenarios, but parents don't have to leave things there as they are entitled to a copy of the school's Complaints Procedure.

Some parents give up, being resigned to their concerns remaining unresolved whilst others will persist until they achieve some form of resolution. The next stage will be for parents to take their concerns up the hierarchy; for primary schools, this will most likely involve a meeting with the headteacher, whilst at secondary school, meetings may be with staff holding *Head of Year*, or *Head of House* positions, depending upon how the school is organised. If concerns at primary school remain unresolved, the next stage in the complaints procedure would involve writing a letter to the Chair of the school's governing body, whilst the secondary school system would involve meeting with the headteacher before any approach to the governing body should be made. Many schools have converted to Academy status, meaning they are independent from local authority control. The Department for Education provides some general advice on its website regarding what parents may do in relation to specific concerns. If they remain unable to have their concerns addressed, having explored every other route, the final recourse is to write to the Secretary of State for Education. For schools which remain under local authority control, parents may complain to the local authority, who can act as an intermediary in resolving difficulties between parents and school. In my experience, few parents take their concerns beyond meeting with headteachers, irrespective of the strength and justification of their complaints. They may spend considerable time unburdening their concerns to a helping professional (such as Parent Partnership Service representative or other organisation), but when advised about their right to complain, the majority prefer not to pursue the issue further, sometimes in the hope that the matter will *'blow over'*.

Complaints are stressful for all family members; children will be aware of the actions being taken by their parents, whilst parents will be anxious about achieving good outcomes for their children, at the same time there may be a certain amount of trepidation in making a formal complaint as parents are usually worried that teachers might seek retribution through their children. So this is a significant deterrent for parents, however strongly they may feel about their children's treatment and provision at school. Such concerns highlight the power imbalance of parent-teacher relationships, with parents acknowledging the power that teachers have over their children and, indirectly, over them, resulting in them being maintained in a submissive position. Complaints procedures are not a *'quick fix'* either and may take months before some sort of conclusion is reached.

There are other options for parents – some choose to move their children to new schools and resign themselves to the inconvenience this often entails; new schools are often further away from their home and may involve additional travelling expenses as well as extra time for the journey. In addition, local friendships may be broken and children may no longer have friends close to home, which could result in significant emotional upset. Other parents simply resign themselves to unsatisfactory situations at school and bide their time until their children move up the school system or leave education altogether. If parents find themselves in this situation, only they can make the decision about what they and their children can cope with, and what is the right decision for the family.

Appeals: The Appeal process is quite different and relates specifically to statutory processes and claims about Disability Discrimination. Parents currently have the right to Appeal to the First-tier Tribunal (SEND) in relation to the following:

- The local authority refuses to carry out an assessment of Special Educational Needs.
- The local authority refuses to issue a Statement following Statutory Assessment.
- More than 6 months have elapsed and the local authority refuses to re-assess a child.
- The local authority decides to withdraw a Statement.
- The child has had an Annual Review and parental requests for amendment have been refused.
- Changes have been made to the Statement and parents disagree with the content.

These reasons will also apply in relation to EHC Needs Assessment and Education, Health and Care Plans, as published in the *Children and Families Bill (2013: 35)*. The Appeals process is part of the legal system and has a judge presiding over hearings. As a legal process, its primary purpose is to make objective decisions regarding how children's difficulties can best be addressed. The speed at which Appeals are heard is determined by the quantity of applications being processed in the local area but it's not unusual for parents to wait several months before the actual hearing takes place.

A brief Overview

To summarise key points, children with short-term difficulties that are resolved through short-term intervention are not considered as having Special Educational Needs. There are a number of methods used by educational practitioners to ascertain whether children have difficulties, which include comparison with their class peers as well as against national indicators. The presence of procedural guidelines for the identification, assessment and monitoring of children does not guarantee that all children will have their difficulties identified or that they will be acknowledged as early as they could be.

When parents express concerns to teachers regarding aspects of their children's behaviour or other difficulties, these are not necessarily given their due regard, especially if concerns involve behaviour that is not witnessed in the school environment. The approach adopted by educational professionals may contribute significantly to both the educational success and emotional well-being of their pupils. Parents are entitled to complain or appeal against local authority decisions but there are *'hoops to jump through'* and the processes are not for the *'faint hearted'*.

Some Good News

Whilst SEN reform may be construed as radical, there *is* some continuity in provision, with only minor modifications (albeit important ones) to some aspects. Comparison between the existing system and that incorporated into the *Children and Families Bill (2013)* indicates continuity in the following areas:

- Reasons for right of Appeal to Tribunal.
- The definition of Special Educational Needs.
- Local authorities retain responsibility for children with Special Educational Needs, or those suspected of having SEN.
- Local authorities retain their responsibility for maintenance of Education, Health and Care Plans (as they do for Statements now), ensuring that Annual Reviews take place, irrespective of the type of educational setting attended by children.
- The process will remain broadly the same with respect to Annual Reviews and ceasing to maintain Education Health and Care Plans (as for Statements now).
- The Government retains its emphasis on inclusion and children without Education, Health and Care Plans are to be educated in maintained nurseries, schools and post-compulsory education settings (or equivalent schools).
- Local authorities continue to provide services for parents (and their children) that offer information, advice and support.
- Furthermore, children with disabilities are viewed as having *'protected characteristics'* under the *Equality Act 2010* and can expect *reasonable adjustments* to be implemented in educational settings.

Hopefully, this news will allay some concerns for the future.

Chapter 4
Support for Parents

Introduction

Parents of children with Special Educational Needs and disabilities may require support in navigating the educational system - to understand the processes and procedures associated with Statutory Assessment (soon to be replaced by Education Health and Care Needs Assessments) and in knowing the most appropriate way to address their concerns when they are in dispute with schools and/or the local authority. *The Warnock Report (1978: 152)* was responsible for many of the foundational principles under which the Special Educational Needs system now operates and was first to acknowledge that many parents were confounded by the complexity of the system and that they required information and advice whilst their children were undergoing Statutory Assessment. The report introduced the concept of the *'Named Person'* as being a person who could inform parents about services and provide advice, acknowledging this function could be undertaken by different professional roles during different phases of children's development. For instance, for pre-school children this could be health visitors whereas headteachers or social workers might fulfil this function for school aged children *(Warnock 1978: 158)*. This role can additionally be undertaken by local authority officers, in statutory Special Educational Needs teams, with responsibility for case management of children with Statements. As the education system has become more complex, with new professional roles now involved in children's care, it's possible that several professional roles could be construed as the *'Named Person'*, at the same time, although this obviously wasn't the original intention.

Parent Partnership Services

Parent Partnership Services evolved directly from the recommendations of the *Warnock Report (1978)* with the purpose of providing information, advice and support to parents of children with Special Educational Needs. Originally developed around the time of the first *Special Educational Needs Code of Practice (1994),* Parent Partnership Schemes (as they were originally known) were established on an ad-hoc basis until 1997. Due to local authorities having no absolute requirement to provide such services, centralised funding was withdrawn for a year, only to be reinstated a year later, which resulted in further services being developed around the country, fulfilling Warnock's requirements that the role should be undertaken by professionals who were not employed by the school system *(Warnock 1978: 158; Stone 2004)*. Eventually, under the *Special Educational Needs and Disability Act 2001*, it became a statutory requirement that each local authority should provide a Parent Partnership Service for parents and this requirement has been carried forward in the *Children and Families Bill (2013: 24)*. However, it should be noted that services provided in each local authority may be known by slightly different names, but their statutory functions remain the same.

Organisation and Delivery of Services

A brief resume', based upon my own professional experience, will explain some of the operating principles of Parent Partnership Services. There has always been flexibility in how services are delivered, with each local authority making its own arrangements from options that include in-house services with local authority staff, services out-sourced to the voluntary sector or combined models using both local authority and voluntary sector resources. However delivered, all services are confidential, free and operate from an impartial position, meaning that service representatives must not take sides, but through recourse to legislation and national guidance can support parents in fighting for improved educational provision for their children (which can, at times give the *impression* they are taking sides, but that's the nature of the role). There is a duty to both advise parents of their rights and responsibilities and to empower them in their pursuit to having their children's difficulties resolved, wherever possible, whilst also to advise educational professionals (local authority and schools staff) if their actions are not compliant with national guidance and legislation.

In-house services always operate at *'arms' length'* from the local authority, walking that careful *'tightrope'* of being local authority employees whilst sometimes having to advise parents that it's in their interests to pursue an Appeal against their employer in relation to procedures under statutory provision. Parents may receive practical assistance in completing documentation to submit an Appeal to the First-tier Tribunal (SEND) and representatives may accompany them (as supporters) to the actual hearing. As a result of the *Lamb Inquiry*

(DCSF 2009) Special Educational Needs and Parental Confidence, there has been an increase in the number of Parent Partnership Services that are out-sourced to the voluntary sector, as a means of further demonstrating their impartiality. Outsourced services operate under Service Level Agreements issued by local authorities and are located in separate premises; as a result, parents may *perceive* services as being more impartial than in-house provision although they remain accountable to their local authority and usually demonstrate service effectiveness by anonymised statistical data reporting.

An Evolving Service

As a former service manager, I experienced the continuous quest for service improvement with respect to accountability and measuring service deliverables. In recent years, the National Parent Partnership Network, the Council for Disabled Children and government departments have collaborated to develop greater consistency between services and raised professional standards through the introduction of legal training and precise and measurable service standards. Whilst minimum operating standards are published in the *SEN Code of Practice (2001),* regional networks devised their own Regional Standards which elaborated upon this framework. Subsequently, professional standards and operating practices were enhanced by publication of the *Exemplification of Minimum Standards (DCSF 2007)* which provided services with a stringent measurable framework for professional practice. This was followed by additional requirements *(NPPN 2010)* as a result of the *Lamb Inquiry's (2009)* recommendations that service staff should receive basic training in education law, prompted by the Labour Government's drive to improve standards, although actual implementation was effected under the Coalition Government.

Accountability is evidenced through the need for services to have multi-agency management teams which are known as Advisory or Steering Groups, with the fundamental purpose of ensuring that services meet or exceed the operating standards required. Annual Reports are produced each year and are available to the public; services are encouraged to have such reports published on their websites, or in the case of in-house services, on the relevant section of their local authority's website. Parents may request paper copies of reports or large print versions, if required. In-house services are accountable to local authority senior management through anonymised data reporting whilst statistical data is provided for national benchmarking which enables comparison between services. For a period of time, under the Labour Government, services were supported by *'critical friends'* which meant that neighbouring services would meet to assess professional practice against a rating scale and shared *'best practice'* and service reports were submitted to government representatives. It should be evident from this basic background that Parent Partnership Services operate as *'tight ships'* with the requirement to demonstrate professionalism at all times, both through their interactions with parents, their children and other agencies.

Parent Partnership Services have evolved since *Warnock's (1978)* original inception of the need to support parents in connection with Statutory Assessment as services often support parents when *'things have gone wrong'*. This could involve supporting parents regarding their children's educational provision – from the time their first concerns are being raised through to supporting parents at Annual Reviews, transition planning or when Statements are not being fulfilled. Parents might be in dispute with the local authority or their children's school especially in relation to matters of school discipline, there could be concerns about children being bullied or cases of Disability Discrimination or parental concerns may have been disregarded by school teachers and they require advice about what to do next. Headteachers sometimes approach services with the request they facilitate informal mediation to help resolve disputes between them and parents. For mediation to go ahead, both parties must be willing to participate in the process, with the understanding that compromise is likely to be necessary. There are innumerable reasons parents might seek support from Parent Partnership Services, which support parents of children and young people from 0-25 years.

To clarify who can access support - parents may suspect their children have difficulties (even if subsequently proven unfounded), children may already have known difficulties and be receiving school support; they may have Statements (or Education, Health and Care Plans) or they might not. Parents may also seek support with respect to their children having fixed-term exclusions or being permanently excluded.

Accessing Support

Parents can self-refer to services; occasionally referrals may be accepted from other professionals (with parental knowledge and consent), although individual services will have their own procedures regarding this. Advice may be given over the telephone in single contacts or multiple (when the latter is known as *'casework'*), in one-to-one meetings which can take place in a variety of settings such as offices, libraries or children's centres, according to the circumstances of those seeking support. Parents can be supported at meetings, and receive assistance in putting their point of view across and they can be assisted in completing forms or writing letters (depending upon their needs). Sometimes parents simply want some procedural advice or to check on an aspect of education law and once such information has been provided, they are able to pursue their concerns without further support. As services are parent led, representatives can only advise parents of the options available to them, with parents always making the final decision.

Support from Volunteers

The majority of Parent Partnership Services will have a team of volunteers, known as Independent Parental Supporters, who have been trained in relevant aspects of Special Educational Needs provision to enable them to support parents. Volunteers serve a valuable role in supporting parents and overtly demonstrate the impartiality of Parent Partnership Services by not being employed by local authorities or schools. Although volunteers are unpaid (excepting for basic expenses), their recruitment follows a similar format to that of paid employees as references are sought and Disclosure and Barring Service (DBS) checks are made. Volunteers are supervised and attend regular training updates in order to maintain and improve their knowledge over time. The content and duration of training programmes varies from service to service, but general topics of training include: SEN legislation and procedures, local policies, Disability Discrimination, how to work with parents, confidentiality, Data Protection and Health and Safety.

Training, advice and support

Services are required to provide training events for both parents and professionals: parents may be trained on aspects of Special Educational Needs and types of disability, as well as the procedures involved in the Statutory Assessment process (soon to be known as EHC Needs Assessment). Services may offer training, as part of their Parents' Forum programme or organise separate workshops. Professionals may be advised on how to work more effectively with parents as well as how the service supports parents and the type of work undertaken. Services will offer training according to local needs and the particular interests of the service manager. For example, some services may offer training on tackling bullying with teachers being taught strategies to manage episodes whilst parents can learn strategies (to pass onto their children) on how to deflect bullying. Parents might want to investigate whether Anti-Bullying training is available in their local area if their own children are victims of bullying; if their local Parent Partnership Service is unable to help, they may be able to signpost them to another service which can.

Informing policy and local practice

Parent Partnership Service Forums usually meet several times over the academic year; the composition of such Forums varies between services and may comprise parents only, or have a combination of parents and professional representatives from education, health and social care, attending events. All service Forums are expected to be used for consultation purposes in respect of local authority planning of services for children with SEN and disabilities, although the extent to which this occurs can vary within a single service as well as between services. Parent Partnership Services may also use their own Forum to consult on aspects of their own service delivery both to ensure they are meeting parents' needs and as a means of improving service quality.

Service Individuality

All Parent Partnership Services must comply with legislative requirements, but the manner in which these are undertaken will vary between services, with each having their own *'local flavour'* with respect to how they undertake their responsibilities. Each service will implement their own innovative practices, in accordance with their geographical area, the needs of their service users and the resources available to deliver them. One consistent aspect between services is that all representatives will advise parents in relation to national legislation and guidance, being mindful that local procedures are not always fully compliant. As service representatives must have a sound knowledge of SEN and disability legislation, plus any other legislation that impacts upon provision for children with SEN, they are able to advise parents in relation to their children's educational provision as well as their entitlement to be involved in their children's education.

Disability Specific Organisations

There are a significant number of national and regional organisations which can provide parents with information, advice and support. Some provide on-line forums, or have local branches that facilitate their own Parent Forums to provide opportunities for networking, giving and receiving informal advice as well as the possibility of becoming involved on a more formal basis. In addition, there are independent Parent Support Groups, relating to specific disabilities (such as Tourettes or autism) that provide information, advice and training to aid parents' understanding and empower them in their interactions with schools and local authority professionals. Information regarding specific types of local support should be available through the local authority Family Information Service, libraries and Parent Partnership Services.

Miscellaneous Support Services

The Labour Government introduced significant changes to services for children and families which are summarised as follows:

- *The Children's Act 2004* – introduced the role of Children's Commissioner to champion the views of children and young people and made it a requirement that agencies cooperated with each other in the delivery of services; local authorities had to produce Children and Young People's Plans, appoint Directors of Children's Services and Council Lead Members.
- *Every Child Matters: Change for Children (2004),* provided the new framework for delivering children's services. Extended Services became available in schools although some were provided on a school cluster basis, offering breakfast clubs and a variety of after- school care and activities.
- *The Children's Plan (DCSF 2007)* emphasised the importance of the parenting role when it acknowledged the need to support parents as a means of improving their children's outcomes.
- *The National Service Framework for Children, Young People and Maternity Services (2004),* promoted early intervention so that parents receive information and services necessary to support their children's physical and emotional development.
- The *Childcare Act 2006* placed a duty upon local authorities to increase the scope of information available to parents in order to help them fulfil their parenting role.

- *Parenting Support: Guidance for Local Authorities in England (2006),* advised local authorities and children's trusts on how to deliver a continuum of support for parents.

Models of Service Delivery

These changes resulted in further development of co-located teams. Whilst they already existed, to a limited degree, multi-agency teams became established in new settings in an endeavour to make attendance more accessible to parents and their children. Such teams were often located in many of the newly created Children's Centres, which significantly increased in number, under Labour Government initiatives. Since then, services have been routinely categorised according to access routes and complexity, with some variation in approach between local authorities. A rough guide to the model is illustrated below:

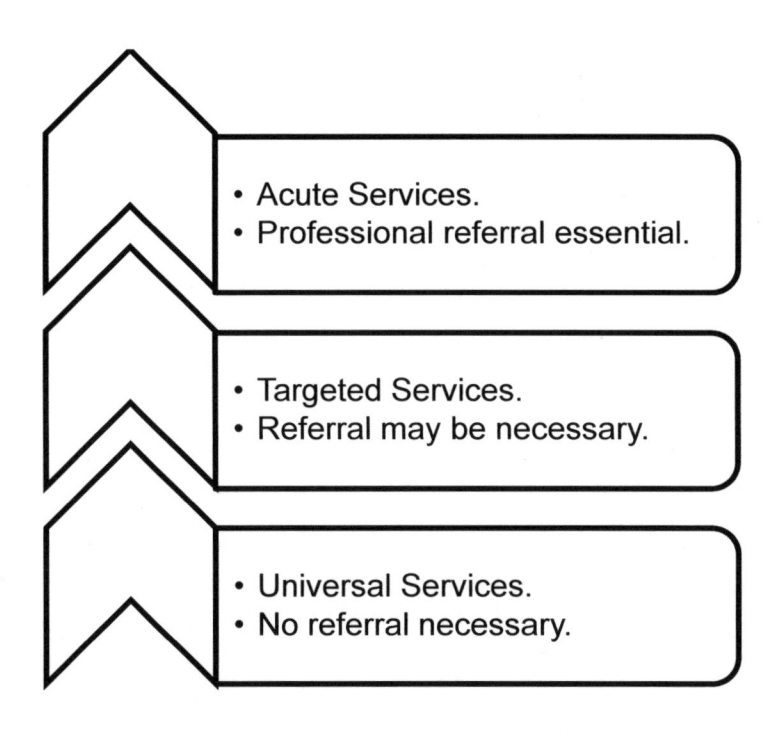

- Acute Services.
- Professional referral essential.

- Targeted Services.
- Referral may be necessary.

- Universal Services.
- No referral necessary.

Examples of the type of service under each category are shown below.

Universal	Targeted	Acute
• Children's Centres • General practitioners • Health visitors • Schools' Extended Services • School nurses • Education services • Children's activities • Benefits advice • Ante and Postnatal Care • Family support workers	• Counselling Services • Mental Health services for Adults • Educational Psychology • Speech & Language Therapy • Specialist nurses • Specialist Educational Support Services • Education Welfare • Family Support packages, • Parent Partnership Services	• Social Care Child Protection Services • Child and Adolescent Mental Health services • Residential schools • Youth Offending teams • Disability teams • Multi-agency teams dealing with complex needs

Support and guidance is available for parents, including evidence-based Parenting Programmes which can help parents manage their children's behaviour. Parents may access such programmes through referral or may be able to enrol themselves, depending upon local arrangements. Targeted services such as speech and language therapy or psychology clinics may be offered at some Children's Centres without a referral whilst in neighbouring areas, a referral will be necessary. As geographical areas vary in how they organise provision, parents are advised to check their local arrangements either through their children's pre-school setting or by contacting their local Family Information Service.

Children's Centres

Under the Labour Government, approximately 3,500 Children's Centres were created, with many of them being developed as part of the *Every Child Matters: Change for Children (2004)* programme. There was particular emphasis on delivering *'preventative and protective'* programmes for families, with some centres being located in more affluent neighbourhoods which attracted a wider range of service user. It could be construed this approach might have erased some of the stigma associated with the original Sure Start Local Programmes launched in the late nineties.

However, since the Coalition Government's *Comprehensive Spending Review (2010),* priorities have become refocused on disadvantaged families, especially in relation to offering free child-care to three and two year olds, as well as a range of other support systems to help such families. Recently, the media have reported that a number of centres have closed and services have either been *reduced* or become chargeable, when they were previously free at the point of delivery *(Butler 2013; Ellis 2013).* This is obviously a sign of the economic times in which we live, but there is a risk that such policies could have the opposite effect to that desired. As a result, Children's Centres could become re-stigmatised and chargeable services may result in such provision being prohibitive to families which are already financially stretched. By reducing the type of services offered at local centres, families may have to travel further to access essential provision, thereby incurring additional costs; all of which have the potential to reduce accessibility to those families most in need of services. Parents will need to check their own local arrangements, as before.

Parent Support Advisers

Parent Support Advisers (PSA) were introduced in 2006, under the Department for Children, Schools and Families, through the Training and Development Agency for Schools. After piloting the service for two years, the role became embedded between the years 2008-2011 through central government funding, although funding ceased after this period with the expectation that schools would directly fund their own posts. As a consequence, Parent Support Advisers were either employed directly by schools or through school cluster arrangements, although in some areas the role could not be sustained. This has resulted in a reduction of Parent Support Advisers although this varies between areas. Some PSA responsibilities have been incorporated into other roles such as Parent Liaison Officers. School newsletters or websites will inform parents about which member of staff is available to support them.

Function of PSAs

The original purpose of Parent Support Advisers (PSAs) was to undertake preventative and early intervention work, especially in relation to managing children's behaviour and attendance. By working with families, they could help resolve difficulties before they became intractable and could support children in returning to school. Now, this function is often undertaken by Attendance Officers (or similar roles). Where Parent Support Advisers continue to exist, schools or their cluster arrangements will determine the specific responsibilities of the posts and parents will be advised about what support is available. Generally speaking, PSAs might work with families on a range of issues and they can act as intermediaries to gain access to other services *(TDA 2008)*

Qualities of a Helper

Whenever parents seek support and advice, they are likely to have some notion of the qualities they expect from a *'helper'*, even if only at an unconscious level. Often the needs and motivations of parents will influence the type of support they seek and from whom; their priority may be to access someone with professional expertise (vital for some concerns) whilst others may prefer to speak to someone who has had similar personal experiences, or a combination of both. *Warnock (1978: 155)* noted that aside from training, not all the qualities of helpers can be taught. From my own professional experience in supporting parents, I believe that *'helpers'* should have qualities that almost instantly put other people at ease, they should be able to understand the other person's perspective and be people that others can easily relate to, especially when discussing matters that are often very sensitive in their nature. Fundamentally, *'helpers'* should have a *'heart'* for helping people, underpinned by relevant personal qualities and training, to be really effective in their role. This will be explored in Chapters 6 and 7.

Chapter 5
Legislation and Promises

Introduction

This chapter will attempt to explore the political journey of parental involvement. This concept originally applied with respect to children's education, but evolved to include how professionals from health and social care also work with parents. In addition, I will highlight some of the key messages from government legislation and guidance concerned with provision for parents and their children due to its influence on services and procedures in operation today. A brief history will help establish the context of proposals originally published in the *Green Paper, Support and aspiration: A new approach to special educational needs and disability (2011)*, which has subsequently been incorporated into the *Children's and Families Bill (2013)*.

An examination of legislation and policy will attempt to determine the true position with respect to the role of parents, who have, at different times been positioned as *'partners'* and *'consumers'*, considering whether parents ever genuinely inhabited such roles and will consider their position today. Most parents of children with additional needs will have some awareness of government initiatives (if not legislation), whether through contact with Children's Centres, Early Support or pre-school and school settings, as well as from reading national newspapers and hearing the news on radio or television. Parents will probably have some knowledge of how successive governments have prioritised education, especially in relation to children with Special Educational Needs when new legislation and policies have attempted to ensure that such children receive the additional help and support they need to help them lead productive and useful lives.

The position of parents with respect to the Coalition Government, will bring the evolving picture up-to-date and help us consider whether the concept of *'working in partnership with parents'* has become further embedded in practice or whether, in reality, it's being stealthily eroded, as demonstrated through language and changes to policy and practice, revealing the true position of parents today.

The Historical Journey

The Plowden Report (1967) introduced the concept of *'partnership'* in an effort to reduce class inequalities and social disadvantage. Teachers were expected to interact with parents in order to positively influence their values with respect to their children's education. It had been noted that developmental delays with respect to children's vocabulary and reading skills resulted in some being educationally disadvantaged and this, in turn, affected their ability to secure paid employment, with its inevitable impact upon the economy. The strategy to address this problem was that parents and teachers should become partners in education, with joint responsibility for children's education and that through such partnership, it was hoped that those from disadvantaged families would remain at school longer and that the gap between them and more affluent families would close. It was further noted that parental attitudes and aspirations were particularly significant with respect to their children's achievements with those who valued education having more contact with their children's teachers than parents who didn't share this ethos. Therefore, teachers were responsible for fostering cooperation from parents who usually had little contact with their children's school; strategies to engage parents included encouraging them to hear their children read and visiting their children's school to view work on display. Meanwhile, the expansion of nursery school provision enabled mothers to undertake paid employment whilst permitting earlier contact with educational settings. This presented additional opportunities for school values to influence those of the home environment, with each family being expected to subscribe to the norms and values of the school. Additional influences of *Plowden (1967)* included:

- Parent Teacher Associations (PTA's) created *'partnership'* through fundraising activities by parents.
- Headteachers and staff demonstrated *'partnership'* by welcoming parents at school gates or walking around playgrounds. This enabled staff to get to know families informally.
- *'Partnership'* was demonstrated by schools producing a prospectus, informing them of their children's progress and by advising parents how they could support the school. (*CACE 1967: 37-42*).

The Warnock Report (1978) was responsible for changing the language of special education by introducing terms such as *'learning difficulties'*, *'Special Educational Needs'* and *'integration'* with the latter term eventually becoming known as *'inclusive education'*. Children with Special Educational Needs and disabilities were expected to be educated in mainstream schools, wherever possible, resulting in the demise of many special schools. Warnock noted the value of parents in respect to the assessment of children with Special Educational Needs, due to their personal knowledge and expertise on their children which helped inform professional decisions about provision. Furthermore, as some parents were *'out of their depth'*, struggling with SEN systems and processes, it was proposed that flexible services should be available to provide them with different kinds of support, including short to long-term assistance. The concept of *'Named Person'* was introduced where parents could access information, advice and support from specific people during different stages of their children's development. To further the concept of *'equal partnership'*, educational professionals facilitated parent workshops, *'transplanting'* their knowledge about reading systems or mathematical processes so that parents could effectively support their children at home. Portage schemes[1] still operate under these principles, where specialist staff make home visits and teach parents of pre-school children a range of activities to be practised daily with their disabled children. Whilst of significant benefit to parents, these systems uphold the position of professionals as *'experts'* to whom parents defer. *'Partnership'* gained further momentum through the role of Parent Governor where elected parents could influence school policies, as members of the Governing body (*Warnock 1978: 32,37,43,151,153,157*).

The Children Act 1989 refers to children and their welfare within the context of family matters where married parents both have equal *'parental responsibility'*, under the Act. When children are born to unmarried parents, *'parental responsibility'* automatically falls to the mother unless the father has made a court application. With respect to children in care, parental responsibility may apply to both the local authority and the children's natural parent(s). *'Parental responsibility'* means that adults have the right to make decisions regarding their

---

[1] Portage schemes provide home teaching services for pre-school children with Special Educational Needs.

children and their property. Legal Guardians have the same rights as parents but adults who simply care for children can only take actions that keep them safe and promote their welfare.

The Education Act 1996 defined Special Educational Needs and permitted parents of children with Statements to select their *'preference'* regarding which school they wanted their child to attend and to have this named in their Statement, allowing for valid exceptions to apply. The *Children and Families Bill (2013)* has repealed Part 4 of this Act, but has carried forward key principles, under SEN reform.

Green Paper: Excellence for all Children Meeting Special Educational Needs (1997) established the Labour Government's educational strategy with respect to children with Special Educational Needs. Parents could influence and contribute to their children's education, *'working in partnership'* with schools, local authorities, other statutory services and voluntary agencies. Inclusion continued and local authorities were required to develop strategies for managing behaviour, in an effort to reduce school exclusions. There was a greater reliance upon teaching strategies to reduce the number of pupils categorised with Special Educational Needs whilst early identification of difficulties was viewed as the route to improving standards. Government funding accelerated the expansion of Parent Partnership Schemes *(DfEE 1997: 8-10)*.

Special Educational Needs and Disability Act 2001 further developed the concept of inclusion for children without Statements whilst those with Statements could attend mainstream schools unless their education was incompatible with their parent's wishes or their presence would affect the provision for other children. Under this Act, local authorities were required to provide Parent Partnership and independent Disagreement Resolution Services for parents. Schools were expected to inform parents of additional support being provided to their children and parents could choose to send their children to independent schools, but were expected to meet their own costs.

The Special Educational Needs Code of Practice (2001) is the practical guidance for professionals on how to implement statutory provision under the *Special Educational Needs and Disability Act 2001*. The *Code* promoted the benefits of agencies working in partnership with parents, under Section 2, *Working in Partnership with Parents,* especially in relation to Parent Partnership Services, where their fundamental operating principles are stipulated *(DfES 2001)*.

The Children Act 2004 reformed children's services in England with specific emphasis on preventative services and strategies to *'improve parenting'*. Universal services became available through Children's Centres whilst joint commissioning of services between education, health and social care resulted in more effective use of resources and closer working relationships between agencies.

Every Child Matters: Change for Children (2004) provided the practical framework for the delivery of services to children, young people and their families under *the Children Act 2004*. The Labour Government introduced an Outcomes Framework which was considered crucial to children's development, well-being and later life. Services delivered to children and families were underpinned by Five Outcomes, as follows:

- "Being healthy
- Staying safe
- Enjoying and achieving
- Making a positive contribution
- Achieving economic well-being".

(DfES 2004: 9)

Health service obligations towards children and young people were fulfilled under the *National Service Framework for Children, Young People and Maternity Services (2004)* which also contributed to the achievement of these Outcomes. The introduction of Extended Services enabled more parents to undertake paid employment whilst providing opportunities to raise concerns during *'drop-off'* or collection times *(DfES 2004: 4-5)*.

The Common Assessment Framework (CAF) developed integrated service provision for children's needs, with the formation of multi-agency teams, known as the *'team around the child' (DfES 2004: 19)*. The *Every Child Matters (2004)* agenda valued parents for their supportive role with respect to their children and government initiatives supported them in achieving these aims. Under this programme, parents were being *'helped'*, *'informed'* and *'supported' (DfES 2004: 13)*.

Higher Standards, Better Schools For All (2005) introduced new freedoms to schools and changed the function of local authorities to *'commissioners of services'* and *'champions of pupils and parents"* *(DfES 2005: 11)*. Parental power and influence was extended through their rights to establish new schools and Parent Councils *(DfES 2005: 1)*. Parents retained their right to *'choose'* their children's school and the role of Choice Adviser was created to support parents in making their selection. Additional information was made available to parents such as Ofsted reports and other data to help inform their decisions *(DfES 2005: 4)*. Whilst parents *'rights'* were developed, their responsibilities were emphasised through the introduction of Parents' Agreements and sanctions applying under Parenting Contracts and Orders, in relation to managing their children's behaviour. *'Working in partnership'* was a priority, with the emphasis (again) on parents being co-educators and Ofsted incorporating the quality of school's engagement with parents as part of their inspection criteria *(DfES 2005: 11, 29-30, 109-110)*.

The Children's Plan (2007) developed strategies detailed in *Every Child Matters: Change for Children (2004)* and asserted that *"partnership with parents is a unifying theme of the Plan"* *(DCSF 2007: 8)*. Schools provided further information for parents and an identified *'named person'* at school became their point of contact *(DCSF 2007: 8)*. In addition, Parent Forums were encouraged to permit parental involvement in strategic local authority decisions regarding children's services whilst personal budgets were introduced to enable parents to manage their children's Special Educational Needs provision. There were commitments to increase the number of Parent Support Advisers and to extend childcare provision to two year olds *(DCSF 2007: 6,8,22-23,26)*.

The Lamb Inquiry (2009) addressed parental confidence in the Special Educational Needs system. The Inquiry primarily focused on services for parents and the expertise of those delivering such services, including Parent Partnership Services. The report established requirements for specific professional roles *(DCSF 2009: 4)*.

Green Paper: Support and Aspiration: A new approach to special educational needs and disability (DfE 2011) referred to parental *'control'* and *'choice'*, in relation to personal budgets and stating school preference *(DfE 2011: 47,51)*. This paper has been superseded by the *Children and Families Bill (2013)* which is discussed in Chapter 9.

What are Parents?

This was the question raised at the beginning of this Chapter – whether parents are (or have been) *'consumers'* or *'partners'* in their children's education. An examination of government policy has revealed the following recurrent themes:

a) There are distinct benefits to children's education by having parents *involved* in their education.
b) The *'deficit'* model of parenting perceives parents as *requiring help* and *support,* especially with respect to their children's learning and managing their behaviour, as evidenced by curriculum workshops, parenting courses and the existence of official roles that support *'Parenting'*.
c) Through having contact with parents, schools can influence family values, where necessary.
d) When school and family values are similar, children are more likely to benefit educationally, thereby enhancing their employment prospects and improving their contribution to the wider economy.

The existence of *'partnership'* will now be explored in an effort to determine when and if partnership actually occurs.

Partnership – On What Terms?

Consultation and research usually underpin government policy, especially in relation to helping children learn, knowing what support parents need to help their children and how educational success benefits individuals economically, as well as society as a whole. *'Partnership'* with parents is vital to maximising educational achievement and benefitting society, but it's *'partnership'* on professional terms *(Roffey 2002: 16)*. Educational professionals determine how parents may be involved at school – welcoming some types of activity but not others, encouraging some parents whilst discouraging others *(Vincent 1996: 94-95)*. Preferred activities are often those which are professionally *'controlled'* such as workshops for parents, information sessions and coffee mornings for parents of children with Special Educational Needs or other similar types of activity, which reinforce the role of professional as *'expert' (Cunningham and Davis 1985 cited in Hornby 1995: 19)*. Whilst these arrangements are beneficial to parents, they are simply *'participating'* in events and cannot be perceived as *'partners'* in any real sense, no matter how convivial such occasions may be. This equally applies to formal meetings often attended by parents, such as Annual Reviews or Parent Consultations – two-way communication does not necessarily indicate *'partnership'* unless equal weighting applies to the parental contribution and they influence decisions *(Roffey 2002: 15)*.

We can generalise about the type of occasion when parents may be *'partners'* in education, but perhaps it's more subtle than that – instead of being about occasions or activities, it's more to do with personal dynamics between parent and teacher, who through informal interaction and establishment of rapport, develop a way of working together that benefits them both. So *'partnership'* can and does exist, but is not necessarily achieved through the type of activity undertaken, nor can it be generalised in relation to meetings with school, local authority and other professionals.

Overall, few parents can exert any real influence and it's, therefore, questionable as to whether *all* parents can be considered as partners in education. It would be more accurate to state that parents *'have an opportunity to work in partnership'*. To further explain - some individuals work as company directors, but we don't generalise and say that every adult who works is a *'director'*; in the same way, not all parents work in partnership with professionals, whether by choice or circumstances.

Many parents are simply concerned about whether they are perceived and treated as partners, on a one-to-one basis, each time they meet with an educational professional and whether their concerns are taken seriously and acted upon. A statement by a parent illustrates the frustration experienced when not treated as a *'partner'*.

"Sometimes you come out from a meeting, thinking, have I actually achieved anything, will anything ever happen?"
(Attwood 2007:74)

The reality of educational interactions is that partnership cannot apply in all situations, even if it was desired, especially in relation to matters of school discipline. As one Headteacher stated:

"If it were appropriate for parents' views to have equal status, the demonstration would be through the minutes of the meetings and the action that then happens. However, the kind of meetings in which the parents' views would have equal status, in terms of actual influence, I'm trying to imagine

what kind of meeting that would be, because a lot of the time, I don't think schools should be pretending to offer power to parents that they cannot have..."
   (ibid: 75)

Partnership Roles: Roles which present genuine opportunities for *'partnership'* include:

- Parent-Governors.
- Parent Council Members.
- Parent Forum Members, especially when connected with local authority strategic groups in which decisions about resources are taken.
- Parents involved in consultation, which may overlap with Parent Forums or Parent Councils, or could be one-off occurrences.
- Parents involved in the establishment/operation of Free Schools.

Equal partnership can only be said to occur when parents hold influential positions such as that of Parent-Governor or Parent Council member, due to their opportunities to influence school policy *(Vincent 1996: 44)*. However, even when parents are elected to positions of influence, not all have the confidence or assertiveness required to effect change, resulting in their presence sometimes being merely tokenistic. However, those parents involved in the development and operation of Free Schools have the opportunity to be *'lead partners'* in such processes and enter into real *'partnership'* with collaborators and professionals employed in their schools, but such opportunities are limited.

The Language of Partnership: In an effort to more accurately represent the nature of the relationship, schools sometimes adopt a variety of words to signify the extent and type of parental involvement, using terms such as *'participation'*, *'collaboration'*, *'cooperation'* or *'community'* *(Attwood 2007 Appendix G2: 15; Pinkus 2003: 132)*. Others may adopt one term for parental involvement and another for their pupils, according to the type of activity. Examples of terminology and meanings are illustrated below:

"I think we use 'partnership' quite a bit and the meaning we attribute to that is working together with parents on strategies that we need to employ with pupils in school; 'collaboration' is also a word that we use and again, it's about working together with other people and agencies to effect positive change or

provision for pupils. We also use 'cooperation', particularly with pupils when we put different things in place ..."
School Support
(Attwood 2007 Appendix D10: 53)

"I think 'partnership' probably is the word we want to use; that's one of our slogans, 'working in partnership in the interests of young people'. 'Cooperation' to me has a smack of cooperating with what the school is and what the school dictates, whereas 'participation' is more of an inclusive word with both participating in the education of this young person, of every young person which we are privileged to be given a responsibility to do. When you collaborate, you are working with somebody, but it's got a slightly negative vibe to it and I wouldn't tend to use that word."
Deputy Headteacher
(ibid: D16: 87)

"I think our school wants to be seen as a school that 'works in partnership with parents', but then 'cooperation' springs to mind because they have got to be cooperative. We do use 'collaboration' and 'participation', but the other two are directly linked to the parents; they are the sort of words you would see on letters, or within policies."
Class Teacher
(ibid: D15: 81)

Information and Parents: There have been significant strides with respect to the availability of information for parents, concerning their children's progress, school performance and services available, with this continuing to be developed under SEN reform. This, of course, is valuable information for parents, helping many to make informed decisions, but not all parents are able to take advantage of such information, depending upon a range of factors, including language difficulties or any Special Educational Needs and disabilities that parents themselves may have. Generally, however, information does contribute to parental *'choice'* and may indicate a degree of *'partnership'* through a one-way directional flow of information, but this cannot be construed as *'equal partnership'*.

Consultation and Partnership: Consultation with parents is often used as a mechanism to demonstrate *'partnership'* at both national and local level and can be of immense value. However, there are occasions when the process may have limited value and not provide the *'true'* picture. For example, questionnaires with *'closed'* questions restrict responses and may prevent valuable information being shared, there is the potential for questions to be *'skewed'* to influence favourable responses or participants may have been *'chosen'* specifically to report upon, what are already known to be, positive experiences. Alternatively, response options on multiple-choice questionnaires may not truly reflect a person's perspective which can then appear more favourable or negative than was actually experienced. There is the potential for these situations to occur, which then affects reporting of the lived experience.

Services are supposed to be realigned as a result of consultation, but the extent of improvement can, at times, be minimal. In some circumstances, the process may be of more significance than the result – so that parents *'feel'* they have contributed and that their responses matter. Strategists are not necessarily averse to creating *'warm, fuzzy feelings'* from their target audience, with the focus being on the emotive experience rather than the *actual* lived experience, supported by results. As long as parents *'feel good'* that may be all that matters in relation to their experiences.

Support for Parents: Many services *'support'* parents. By using this term, professionals are technically placing themselves in an elevated position to that of parents, unless they willingly relinquish their power *(Vincent 1996: 3)*. This is the position taken by Parent Partnership Services, which being parent-led, are required to place parents at the helm of all services provided. Once appropriate advice and information has been given, parents are then empowered to make informed decisions. Of course, there are other services which operate under similar principles, but for *'partnership'* to be equal, one party must relinquish some power whilst *giving* power to the other party. However, not all parent and professional relationships can operate under these principles and sometimes the only way in which parents are equal is through respect being demonstrated and the manner in which communication takes place, whilst professionals retain their *'expert'* knowledge and the power that goes hand-in-hand with such roles *(Hornby 1995: 18)*.

'Consumerism', 'Choice' **and** *'Control'*

A wealth of information is already available to parents regarding local schools and services, to help inform their decision making regarding school choice and access to services. Under reform, this is being further enhanced through parents having the option of Personal Budgets in respect of children's Education Health and Care Plans whilst the new *'Local Offer' (DfE 2011)* provides them with additional information about services that should be available in their local area. Such information enables parents to exercise some *'choice'* and *'control'* in respect of their children's education.

Parents are viewed as *'consumers'* in relation to *'choosing'* their children's schools. However, in the real market place, when goods are chosen, they are purchased and taken home, but with respect to school choice, it's a competition with other parents, under a range of selection criteria, and there is no guarantee that the *'preference'* stated on their application will result in a place being offered. As *'consumers'* parents are placed in the driving seat, accessing professional advice and information, as needed and are considered as *'experts'* in relation to their children *(Hornby 1995: 23; Vincent 1996: 32)*. Parents are certainly *'consumers'* when they access Parent Partnership Services (or similar services that offer advice and information) as once they have received information regarding the options available, they are at liberty to decide whether to act upon such advice or reject it. Parents are also experts in relation to their own children, but even though political rhetoric promotes this in government publications, the actual *lived* experience in having this acknowledged on an everyday basis, when parents interact with professionals, can be somewhat different.

With respect to Personal Budgets, parents may *'choose'* to become budget holders, or at least participate in decisions regarding SEN provision for their children – creating a further opportunity for them to become *'consumers'* in relation to educational provision. However, whilst the *Green Paper (2011)* alluded to parental *'control'*, the *Children and Families Bill (2013)* refers to parental *'involvement'* which isn't nearly as influential; parents will also be supported by key workers, which may further diminish their influence in processes concerning their children's educational provision. Only time will tell if parental influence is enhanced under the new system.

A Final Note

The Coalition Government's preferred language in relation to parental involvement has been *'choice'* and *'control'*, with little, if any reference, being made to *'partnership'* and parents as *'consumers'*, although aspects of their policies position parents as *'consumers'*. *'Engagement'* is being used in some contexts in relation to parents *(DfE 2013)* and this may be more representative of their true position.

Overall, when governments promote their policies, in their efforts to generate public interest and excitement, it appears they sometimes over-state their case. This can lead to expectations that are subsequently unfulfilled for the majority of the relevant sector, with only a few benefitting to the fullest extent possible. Perhaps language that is truly representative of parent and professional relationships and their choices within the educational arena are on the horizon.

Chapter 6
Communication with Parents

Introduction

This chapter will examine communication from a variety of perspectives with a view to helping readers understand their motivation for instigating communication with professionals and how the approach they adopt is likely to influence the reactions of other people towards them. Professional motivation will also be explored, emphasising that their approach and reasons for instigating communication are likely to be at variance from that of parents. Whilst the topic will be addressed within the arena of Special Educational Needs and disabilities, and in particular, will relate to meeting educational, health and social care professionals, the chapter will invariably contain information that can be generalised to other types of communication such as that with friends, family, acquaintances and business contacts.

'Communication skills' is a subject in its own right, with many books that specifically cover the subject in depth. However, the purpose of this chapter is to draw upon some broad principles from communication and psychological theories, my own research and anecdotal experience from supporting parents. I hope to empower parents in their communication with professionals and provide some insight into the different perspectives taken by parents and the professional workers who support their children. Good communication can result in getting what you want, in a way that doesn't upset or belittle the other person whilst poor communication can cause the other person to close down, resulting in total relationship breakdown, where nobody feels good about the outcome *(Phillips 1978 cited in Hargie 2006: 10).* Broadly, this chapter will cover:

- Assumptions about communication.
- Motivation and differing perspectives.
- Psychological explanations for misunderstandings.
- Critical communication.
- Language and listening.
- Some research findings.

What do we mean by Communication?

Communication is essentially the transmission of information from one person to another or any number of people and may take place in a variety of situations and through a number of different methods. It usually involves a two-way exchange, with one person initiating contact and the other(s) responding; the content of communication will usually depend upon the context and type of relationship with the other person. Broadly speaking, communication may include giving instructions, clarifying instructions, stating courses of action, clarification of the message received, discussing ideas and plans of action or may be more emotionally intense through the sharing of *'life stories'* and experiences that reveal intimate thoughts and feelings.

Face-to-face communication is known as *interpersonal communication*, and is often viewed as a skill that has to be learnt *(Hargie 2006: 8)*. If this is the case, we can assume that we are not all equally skilled as each other. Our abilities in this area, will be influenced to a large extent by our social learning experiences as young children and whilst growing up *(Mead and Heyman 1965: 82)*. Even as adults, we can still be influenced by our observations of others, adapting our style to suit that of friends or work colleagues. Furthermore, if the behaviour of *'observed subjects'* has been argumentative, confrontational, passive, abrupt, bubbly or friendly, it could influence our own manner of communication when interacting with others. The family of origin may have adopted a style of communication which was crystal clear, unambiguous and possibly even blunt, which wider society may or may not admire. Alternatively, family members may never have addressed matters explicitly, preferring instead to dance around subjects, in an attempt to avoid causing offence, but through this approach never really resolving issues, with resentments simmering just beneath the surface.

Style and use of language may affect whether we are viewed as socially skilled communicators. Our families and the communities in which we live will contribute to our language and communication skills and whether we are able to communicate effectively and be understood by others in a wide range of social situations. Added to this are our own temperaments that will affect our desire to communicate in a particular way such as whether we are polite and measured in our approach or loud and aggressive, with frequent use of expletives, or something in between. The manner in which we communicate is not fixed, but will be influenced by different social situations and by the circumstances taking place in our own lives, although we may not acknowledge how we behave and communicate differently on different occasions. A normally calm and pleasant individual may become brusque and intolerant if they are experiencing stressors in their lives although *Hargie (2006: 43)* asserts that mediating factors affect the extent to which inner turmoil may be displayed in any given situation. For example, individuals are likely to be less brusque with their employer or a client than with friends and family.

Some people are naturally adept at communicating appropriately in all situations, whilst others may need to modify their approach in order to become socially skilled in those areas. Individuals may be unaware that they lack appropriate communication skills until somebody, such as their employer or a family member, alerts them to the inappropriateness of their communicative style and suggests an alternative approach. *Hargie (2006)* believes that the acquisition of new skills is a four-staged process. This will usually necessitate un-learning previous, inappropriate behaviours and forms of expression whilst adopting new techniques, taking the individual from a position of oblivious incompetence through to where new skills have become embedded and they are being applied without having to think consciously about their approach *(Hargie 2006: 17)*. Some individuals, despite having the knowledge and ability to communicate effectively, may consciously and deliberately choose not to apply their skills. This could occur for any number of different reasons, known only to them, but the effects of poor communication, in both professional and personal contexts, may be particularly upsetting and harmful, with long-term repercussions.

Methods used to Communicate

In this highly technological age, there are many ways in which we can communicate with others, for example, mobile telephones and text messaging, computers allow access to e-mails and social networking sites such as Twitter and Facebook and there are web pages with information. There are multiple forms of written communication such as notes, letters and cards, (whether handwritten or typed) and messages conveyed through symbolism and non-verbal communication (NVC) which encompasses body orientation, gestures, posture and proximity in relation to the other person *(Hargie 2006: 5, 80-83)*. Added to these are intonation and phrasing of words spoken, as well as the literal words that come out of our mouths. The primary focus of this chapter is interpersonal communication, the significance of non-verbal communication and the effects of actual words spoken.

Reasons for Communication

Reasons are many and varied and include the pure pleasure of social interaction with another human being. Discussing the weather can produce a warm glow in someone who simply wants to *'connect'* with another person, to have a feeling of acknowledgement and acceptance from another and sometimes, in return, to affirm them – giving compliments or simply conveying that the other person matters. Businesswise, communication fulfils a myriad of purposes, for example, from selling and advertising products, dealing with customer service queries, giving and receiving information, presenting ideas and promoting the effectiveness of services offered, and so on. With respect to professionals and parents, the reasons for communicating with each other are usually more restricted and focused. We will now examine the differences.

Parents: When parents meet with professionals, they will be approaching any discussion from a different standpoint to the professional, despite their common focus being their child or children. Parents, naturally, will focus on their own children's difficulties and needs, whilst school and local authority professionals will consider the specific children being discussed *and* the wider context of the class and school environment, including resourcing issues and any potential impact upon other children. Unrealistic expectations from both sides can be a contributing cause of friction between parents and professionals *(Hanko 1999 cited in Roffey 2002: 18)*. The following statement by a parent supports this assertion:

"For the parent their child is the most important one and for the school and local authority, the child is one of many. They are not really on the same side, but might be sometimes."
Parent
(Attwood 2007 Appendix G6: 42)

Frequently, parents will seek information, advice and support regarding some aspect of a learning difficulty, behavioural problem or management of a health issue. Parents will want to know what is *'wrong'* (possibly requiring a diagnosis) and what can be done; what will happen next, who will do what and when it will take place *(Attwood, 2007 Appendix G6: 40)*. Subsequent to identification of a learning difficulty, disability or health problem, parents will often seek both short and long-term prognoses and reassurance that they will be able to cope and where to go for further support and information. How this is handled by professionals will be dependent upon their personalities as well as the structural and time constraints under which they work, as expressed by the following parent:

"I think that some individuals are more understanding and supportive than others, probably from their own personality and experience, not necessarily training, but actually, it's really important to feel at that time that they have got time and want to be positive, but realistic and looking at what they can do to help and support the individual."
Parent
(ibid: C8: 56)

As situations change over time, parents may occasionally require professional counselling to help them manage their emotional responses and develop strategies for coping, even if they didn't require such support upon first being advised of their children's difficulties. Some parents may seek support from specific organisations that provide information and resources on their own children's particular difficulties or may approach local and national support groups or helplines, as and when needed. Other parents will approach their children's class teacher, speaking to them on a wide range of issues. They might divulge intimate, family information which is not always directly relevant to their children's education, but teachers are approached simply because of an existing rapport between them and because parents believe they 'know about such things', as the following statements indicate:

"... we are not just dealing with the child and if the parent is distressed for whatever reason through work or family issues, then I will spend quite a lot of time with parents as well, talking about their own issues and their own problems, because I think at the end of the day, that's going to benefit the child and it's worth doing."
Teacher
(ibid: D4: 19)

"...and just listen to what they have to say, because they are obviously worried about something otherwise they wouldn't have come to see you, so listen to what they are saying. And accept that outright; accept that they are obviously upset about something or concerned about something..."
Teacher
(ibid: D5: 20)

"I think you have to be sensitive towards the parent. You always have to be there, you always have to be a sounding block. They have to feel comfortable with you; they have to be able to rely on you. You also have to give them a sense that you are there to help, not just them, but their child, and you are always there to listen and support them, and you have to make them feel quite important."
Teaching Assistant
(ibid: D3: 10)

Teachers' professional commitments may result in limited capacity for having extended or frequent conversations with parents; additionally, some will feel uncomfortable being approached about personal matters and may lack the experience and skills for managing such conversations. Teacher training courses sometimes contain little modular content on working with parents and, from my professional experience and research, there is a significant lack of training within schools on how teachers should work with parents, establishing rapport and managing such relationships *(Attwood 2007: 85)*. Even though communication with parents has become an integral aspect of their professional role, some teachers are ill-equipped for this responsibility although a few schools do operate mentoring schemes for Newly Qualified Teachers (NQTs), who are observed when they first meet with parents (usually within the context of formal parent consultations). The effectiveness of such schemes will be largely dependent upon the skills of the mentor and their own approach to working in partnership with parents. Many conversations with parents require the application of counselling skills and unless individuals have undertaken basic counselling training, they may lack the skills necessary to manage sensitive conversations. Educational professionals might assume that because they possess effective communication skills for teaching pupils that they can also appropriately engage with parents and, therefore, reject the need to prioritise training on *'working with parents'* during staff development sessions *(Attwood, 2007: 96,99)*. Teacher-pupil interaction requires a different skill set to that which is necessary for meeting with parents. Professionals should be mindful that the approach they adopt can have a positive or negative long-term impact upon parents which can influence the whole family *(Pinkus 2005: 185; Attwood 2007: 81)*.

Professionals: Professional relationships with parents are primarily instrumental in nature, being significantly influenced by the *Warnock Report (1978)* which viewed parents as an *'information source'* from which professionals can make decisions regarding support. Information required from parents may include details about family circumstances, health problems and how *'hidden'* disabilities affect particular children, including their sensitivity with regards to changes in routine. Furthermore, parents are expected to inform teachers of any difficulties their children are experiencing in the home environment that may impact upon their ability to learn and affect their behaviour in school. By having such information, teachers are better equipped to manage children appropriately at school; this may result in more observations taking place and the adoption of different teaching strategies to aid the learning experience or to manage behaviour. Teachers have a statutory duty to inform parents when their children are placed on the Special Educational Needs register at school and are receiving either *'additional'* or *'different'* support to help them with their difficulties *(DfES 2001; DfE 2012)*. At times, educational professionals may adopt an authoritarian stance when they need to inform parents of their children's behavioural difficulties and other discipline matters, when the expectation is that parents will cooperate with the school in managing the difficulties, as shown by the following statements:

"I have one boy and I have to comment on his behaviour and there are consequences for him at home, if he doesn't behave at school, and equally the other way round, there are consequences in the school. To see a link —you have to behave the same — what we expect at school is what you should be doing at home and vice-versa sort of thing."
Secondary school Head of Year
(Attwood 2007 Appendix D5: 21)

"The school is the arena that the pupils play out their difficulties, so it's really important that you have that liaison and relationship with parents so you can actually be working together to manage their whole day and their whole experience because so many of the issues with pupils with Special Needs have arisen outside of the school, and we have a big responsibility to manage those

needs within the school day. It's really important that you have a good relationship with parents, so we are both actually working together on that and I think that's a really important message for the young person to be aware of – that actually they can't collude or manipulate or come between the school and the parents."
SENCO
(ibid: D9: 46)

Assessments undertaken by health professionals usually focus on the negative attributes of children, through the adoption of a *'deficit'* model which ascertains *'what is wrong with the child'*, with particular focus on their limitations and little acknowledgement of their attributes. For example, paediatricians, during assessment, will ask parents about their observations and the difficulties experienced by their children, both at home and at school[2] in order to arrive at a diagnosis or determine the next course of action. Children are often present throughout such consultations and, therefore, hear negative things spoken about them, with respect to their difficulties, which can be difficult for them to deal with, as supported by Mrs B's story in Chapter 8 and another parent's statement:

"I think it is good that he is there all the time, although sometimes I would value an opportunity to say some things when he isn't there because he is very loath to allow anybody into his world. And if we say things that we believe are quite important, he is either embarrassed or he will say it's not an issue, but it is. Sometimes, I then have to phone up afterwards and say, I have something that I'd like to add."
Parent of secondary school child.
(ibid C1: 6)

Social care conversations with parents will be influenced by the reason for social worker involvement; interactions are likely to be helpful and constructive for parents when contact is associated with arranging Short Breaks or the acquisition of wheelchairs for their disabled children, whilst meetings associated with child protection matters are likely to be more stressful, but still constructive for parents. These basic examples should provide a flavour of how parents are used as an *'information source'* in order to help improve their children's outcomes. Whether discussions are simple or complex, informal or formal, parents are their

---

[2] Schools are usually required to supply separate information to paediatricians.

children's advocates and are expected to impart information about their children, to professionals who are involved in aspects of their care. Professional and parental relationships are reciprocal, with each wanting something from the other.

A further reason for educational professionals to initiate contact with parents is to exert influence; this has been a recurring theme since the *Plowden Report (1967)* when teachers were required to impart school values to parents. Schools now employ staff with responsibility for tackling behaviour and attendance issues and whether this function is undertaken by Parent Support Advisors, Family Liaison Officers, or individuals holding similar roles, they will work with families to help resolve difficulties, with the specific goal of getting children back to school and maintaining their attendance. Much of this will be achieved through practical support and by influencing family attitudes and values. *The Warnock Report (1978: 153)* acknowledged the reciprocity of relationships between parents and professionals and the need for professionals to adjust their communicative style in accordance with parental understanding as a means of improving children's outcomes.

Overcoming Assumptions

Parents are frequently on the receiving end of communication from professionals who believe that because of their role, training or qualifications, they are automatically effective communicators with parents, as the following assumptions illustrate.

- **Teachers** – *'of course, we know how to communicate with parents, we teach don't we?'*
- **Educational psychologists** – *'of course, we can communicate effectively with parents; we understand psychology and know how the mind works.'*

These assumptions usually arise from the belief that because professionals are trained to work with individuals in specific contexts where a particular style of communication takes place, it means they have the skills necessary to communicate effectively in *all* situations. These examples are merely being used to illustrate that it doesn't matter how highly qualified and experienced someone is, anyone can communicate inappropriately or ineffectively on *some* occasions. Effective communication is more than just speaking to another person politely and responding appropriately to what they say. Communicators should take into consideration the impact of the words spoken to another person and the messages that will be taken away from any discussion, which can remain with individuals for many years. My own research *(Attwood, 2007)* and subsequent anecdotal experiences, acquired in my professional capacity, support the view that whilst there are many professionals who communicate well with parents, there are others who simply lack the required diplomacy and sensitivity required for some conversations, as the following quotations illustrate.

"I was approached by the educational psychologist, who had seen my son at school that morning and they came to see me, and terrified me. Some things said to me were probably the most scary things that I have ever heard. I didn't quite know what to do with myself when they left, and that was pretty horrible, and I don't think I will ever forget that. The educational psychologist had contacted the hospital and I was just left waiting, in panic, to see somebody there."
Parent
(ibid C6: 37)

"… to be asking for something that you know your child needs, but you've got no evidence and no professional back-up; it is just your feeling, your gut feeling, your knowledge of your own child because you know them really well. There were three people who said, 'in our expert professional opinion of …' and they would say a time, like one said ten years, one said seventeen years and I felt like I was being very firmly put in my place."
Parent
(ibid C6: 42)

The Coalition Government is propelling forward a range of initiatives to improve teacher skills in the area of Special Educational Needs and disabilities. However, it's unknown whether they will take forward any of the principles from *The Common Core of Skills and Knowledge (2005)* that were developed by the *Children's Workforce Development Council* as part of the *Integrated Qualifications Framework* for professionals working with families, implemented under the Labour Government's *Every Child Matters: Change for Children (2004)* agenda. Whilst there had been no requirement for teachers to undertake such training, this model was promoted for other sectors as providing the foundational principles for their work with particular client groups. Meanwhile, Parent Partnership Services continue to have a remit to provide training to schools and local authority professionals on working effectively with parents although take up has always been voluntary, with some schools commissioning whole school training, whilst for others it never features on the agenda. Parents of children with Special Educational Needs and disabilities tend to have more contact with a range of professionals and yet, on occasions, professionals from health and education can demonstrate a significant lack of skill and understanding in relation to their communication with parents. For example, professionals can blame parents for their children's responses when they are, in fact, representative of specific disorders or a prognosis might have the effect of crushing all hope. Nevertheless, they are not always correct in their assessments, as case studies in Chapter 8 will illustrate. Professionals have a responsibility to parents, as well as the children in their care, and should ensure that what is said to them does not exacerbate existing feelings of distress and concern about their children's well-being and educational progress. Clearly messages that convey judgemental attitudes or *'doom and gloom'* are hardly encouraging for parents. Of course, parents want to hear the *'facts'* but whether these are conveyed by medical or other professionals, there is always the possibility of being wrong or the prognosis not being as dire as originally anticipated. Furthermore, it shouldn't be difficult for parents to *'prove their case'* with respect to their children's abilities (whether they are progressing well or experiencing difficulties), nor should they be subjected to blame when their children have *'hidden'* disabilities and other difficulties, whether overtly stated or inferred. *'Sweeping statements'* are not necessarily helpful or accurate and such comments remain with parents long after the original words were spoken, as illustrated by case studies in Chapter 8.

Parental Responsibility

Parents share responsibility for maintaining communication with professionals, even when the circumstances connected with their meetings generate feelings of anger, frustration or sheer despair. Of course, there will be occasions when parents display emotion when discussing their children's difficulties or because of long-term stressors they have experienced, but what can be difficult for professionals to manage is when they vent their frustration towards one individual for all the negative experiences of the past, which may span several years, simply because they have encountered a professional who is willing to listen to them. Whilst such reactions are understandable, they can sometimes be directed at the person who is most in a position to help them, and this can be a hindrance to some helping relationships. Not all individuals can distinguish between *'a general outburst'* and that of personal attack. An educational psychologist asserted *'successful'* communication is:

"... in the context of my work, it would mean getting across what I intended to get across and hearing what the other person intended to get across, and each person being appropriately assertive, and departing on good terms, with no issues hanging over them."
(ibid E1: 1)

To clarify this statement, it's about person (1) achieving their purpose in communicating with person (2), without causing offence or denigrating them; it's a reciprocal exchange in that person (2) will expect to achieve their own objectives from the communication, without causing offence or denigrating person (1). Each person must conduct themselves in a socially acceptable manner, for the exchange to be considered successful.

We will now look at some situations where professional communication skills may have a significant impact upon parents and/or their children. This will take into consideration the social environment and the manner in which information has been conveyed to parents, where the outcome from such communication may be life-enhancing or damaging to families.

Critical Communication

Early Diagnosis: Some children will have had their disability identified soon after birth with their parents being unexpectedly plunged into an existence that requires countless appointments that seem to dominate family life. Their newborn child's disability soon becomes the focus of existence, even when there are existing siblings in the family. Some families are stretched even further when there is more than one child with a disability which may or may not be the same as an older sibling's difficulties. It is a traumatic experience for parents when their child is diagnosed with a disability. Initially, they may experience a myriad of emotions, ranging from denial, grief, anger and despair, as part of the grieving process, before they reach a place of *'reluctant'* acceptance. The following statement sums up the experience.

"It's like going through a mourning - what you are not going to get, and realising that there is an angle to life that will never change. We know there is

a chance that he will never leave home. We know that we will always have to be part of his life. If he does get married or has a partner or has children, they are going to need help..."
Parent of a child with Asperger's Syndrome.
(ibid C4: 23)

Parents need time to assimilate information, ask questions and learn about the condition that is affecting their child and its *potential* long-term impact upon both their child and family life. Parents need both practical and emotional support to help them deal with the practicalities of daily living whilst, at the same time, helping them to adjust to a new, unexpected reality.

"We got to know the implications for their longer life and relationships and kids and all the rest of it. I suppose at the time when you are told, you want reassurance that it is not your fault, you know – as parents, you haven't done something wrong, and we asked all kinds of questions."
Parent
(ibid C7: 46)

The way in which professionals first inform parents of their children's disabilities may either add to their despair or in some small way, may help them summon the strength to deal with the situation. Parents are expected to cope with and adapt to the specific demands that orientate around their children's disabilities whilst inwardly wrestling with interminable despair, brought on by grief for the child they expected but would never have, with hopes and dreams for the future dashed. Their idealistic hopes for family life are instead replaced with the tedium of hospital and other appointments and having 'bad news' presented to them at every turn, with anxiety and despair a new companion *(Bruce and Schultz, 2001:8; 2002)*. The following quotations illustrate:

"Meetings have been incredibly time consuming and particularly when my son was little, other parents would be going to parties or the park and we would be off to the hospital again..."
Parent
(Attwood 2007 Appendix C8: 57)

It is unsurprising that parents may struggle to come to terms with a different reality and future to that imagined.

"As a parent, although it is not the end of the world, part of you is devastated really. It's still your baby at the end of the day, and we now feel that we will fight and do whatever we can to help her."
Parent of a child at Primary School.
(ibid C5: 30)

"Our son has always had a very big impact on the family, and the girls to some extent have resented the amount of time he has consumed from us. My husband took an awful long time to accept he had any problems."
Parent of a child at Secondary School.
(ibid C3: 20)

Later Diagnosis: Many parents have their children's difficulties identified or diagnosed much later, with a picture developing as their children grow and develop – sometimes as late as adolescence. Parents may experience *'crisis'* from the moment they suspect that *'something is not quite right'* and despite repeated appointments with school teachers, general practitioners or hospital consultants, children may reach puberty before the cause is identified. In the interim period, the angst of awaiting a diagnosis and having some validation for the difficulties experienced by their children, adds to the emotional turmoil experienced by parents and places additional pressures on their relationships with professionals, who may be unable to provide a diagnosis and therefore, a way forward with regards to coping with the situation *(Rogers 2007: 142)*. For these parents, grief may be hidden, but constantly present, as they attempt to live normally whilst observing their child grow and develop, comparing them with their peers and other siblings, watching intently for *'signs'* that they are different either in their behaviour, development or both. Attempts by parents, more often mothers, at raising concerns with teaching staff may have resulted in them being labelled as *'over anxious'* with them being fobbed off when their children are viewed as 'slow', *'lazy'* or *'naughty'*.

Parents of children with difficulties experience significant frustration when their concerns are apparently belittled, which has the effect of both denying their children the support they need and denying them the *'right'* to grieve overtly due to lack of acknowledgement that something is *'not quite right'*. When, eventually, their children's difficulties and/or disabilities are identified and diagnosed, it may be a relief for parents – a kind of exoneration that they were right all along and they are thankful that their children's difficulties are finally being acknowledged *(Attwood 2007)*. They may consider it a relief to finally have a label that accounts for previous observations and behaviours and to *'know'* that their child will finally receive the help he or she needs to progress through the educational system. Furthermore, following diagnosis, parents will have access to services which were formerly denied them; they will have a specific focus with regards to which organisations to contact for help and support, as shown by the following statement:

"We were never really told – we always thought that he might go to mainstream school and be alright. At one point, it was very frustrating not to actually have a diagnosis because we couldn't link into a group, so we were sort of floundering ..."
Parent of a son with complex difficulties.
(ibid C3: 16)

Breaking News to Parents

'Bad News': This has already been alluded to but now needs to be addressed in its own right. Parents of children with Special Educational Needs and disabilities are likely to become familiar with hearing *'bad news'* from different professional sources. Fundamentally, *'bad news'* is when parents hear something they would prefer not to hear, especially when such news can be life-changing *(Buckman 1994: 11)*. For example, a paediatrician might give *'news'* concerning a medical diagnosis or an educational professional may inform a parent that their child has learning difficulties or is being permanently excluded from school. *'Bad news'*, can therefore, present a new, unexpected reality that must be dealt with. This also includes situations where parents are already aware of their children's learning difficulties or disabilities, but retain the hope that their children can make progress with the *'right'* interventions. *'Bad news'* can follow when there is lack of progress following a period of sustained support, in relation to learning or behavioural difficulties and the number of options are beginning to run out *(Attwood 2007 Appendix D8: 1)*. Further examples follow:

"My role is to support the school, pupil and parents through the difficult processes that may be ahead, such as going down the route of Statementing the child for whatever reason, and that sometimes involves the parent going through a grieving process for the child they now realise they haven't got."
SENCO
(Attwood 2007 Appendix D6: 25)

"If a child is achieving below the national average or ability they should be at for their age, then I think parents need to know that, because they need to be aware that there are other things they could possibly do at home, but also it's worse if you get a surprise and you wait a whole year and then you hand their report and it says, 'they are only working towards what they should be at' and then parents say, 'why wasn't I told earlier; why wasn't something done about it?' So I think it's really important that you are honest about where they are at."

Class teacher
(ibid D15: 79)

"Parents quite frequently ask for results to compare with other children and that's very difficult to do when you have a child with Special Needs ... and to try and put it in a positive way. You don't actually change the results but you show them that it can be worked on."

SENCO
(ibid D12: 61)

Other types of 'bad news' include:

- Children being unable to enter post-16 provision or enrol on their preferred course.
- Frequent criticisms of children's behaviour which cause parents to dread collecting their children from their educational setting.
- Parents being advised that services their children need are not being made available.
- Parents' being informed their children have not been offered a place at their preferred choice of school.
- Perceptions of children differ between school and parents.
- Disciplinary matters, including school fixed-term or permanent exclusions.

(ibid D13-16: 67,74,79,85,93)

Professional sensitivity is required with respect to how 'bad news' is conveyed, although the extent to which this is displayed will be mediated, to an extent, by the type of 'bad news' as well as the communication skills and *heart* of the professional concerned. Whatever the type of news, parents should be given an opportunity to digest the information and respond with any questions they might have before 'next steps' are determined. Many professionals are acutely aware of the devastating effects of 'bad news' upon families both in relation to children's learning difficulties and matters of a disciplinary nature, and will endeavour to manage the situation in a firm but kindly manner, as illustrated by the following statements.

"What is difficult perhaps is the perceptions we have about the child or about a situation at school which may be different from theirs – the fact that perceptions differ; and therefore, it has to be handled with great sensitivity because you may actually be 'bursting a bubble' by trying to encourage a parent to face up to an uncomfortable truth about their child or about a situation."
Headteacher
(ibid D13: 67)

"I think you have to explain why you are taking the action you are taking, and what you are hoping that will achieve and, in particular, how you are going to stop whatever it is that has gone wrong from going wrong in the future, and try to mend the broken situation."
Deputy headteacher
(ibid D16: 85)

In contrast, some headteachers become hostile towards parents with whom they have previously conducted warm and constructive relationships due to some act of disobedience their children have committed. They become cold and distant, effectively punishing parents for the misdemeanours of their children. The *'shutters'* remain down with no acknowledgement that parents are struggling to make sense of an unexpected situation.

'Bad news' in itself is difficult enough to cope with, but compounding this is the manner in which it is sometimes conveyed. Inevitably, parents will experience distress when they are informed their child has a disability, some other major condition or that a behavioural incident is resulting in *'serious'* discipline; these are natural emotions and cannot be avoided. Professionals can exacerbate parental distress through lack of advance planning about how they will break such news. They should consider in advance, the forms of expression and language they will use, as well as their manner and the environment in which information is conveyed. Words carelessly spoken can remain with parents for years and become the focal point of when their lives changed for ever.

Grief may become a constant companion to parents of children with learning difficulties or disabilities. This can be triggered from the point at which parents first become knowledgeable of their children's difficulties, with the trauma of such news being exacerbated by the way in which information has been given. In particular, insensitive words spoken by professionals may be forever remembered by parents even if they previously had their own suspicions of their children having some kind of difficulty. Such events can trigger a form of depressive response which *Bruce and Schultz (2001:8; 2002)* term as *'non-finite'* loss due to its enduring nature throughout life, which can be re-triggered by new events. This assertion can be corroborated from my own professional experience in supporting parents, as well as those who were interviewed for my research. Whilst sharing their *'stories'*, some parents relived the emotional responses from previous events, which in some cases had taken place fifteen years earlier. They recalled the circumstances surrounding events, including words spoken, as if they had occurred only days earlier, even to the extent of remembering the manner in which news had been broken. Parents acknowledged that over the years, contact with professionals continued to re-awaken earlier trauma, especially when derogatory forms of expression had been used about their children further corroborating *Bruce and Schultz's (2002: 11)* assertions.

From my experience, the intensity of feeling experienced by parents in response to derogatory language and terms used by professionals to describe their children can have the effect of outweighing original concerns about educational provision. Insensitive forms of expression have left parents *'stinging'* - due to their loved ones being denigrated during meetings, at which their children were sometimes present.

"He always gets very nervous in advance of meetings. He doesn't like going to them at all and believes it's a criticism of him and we have had to work very hard at that. He doesn't like his life being analysed, which is probably understandable."
Parent of a boy at secondary school.
(Attwood 2007 Appendix C1:7)

'Good News' is 'Bad News': Professionals need to be aware that what they consider is *'good news'*, might, in fact, be *'bad news'* as far as parents are concerned. Teachers may lack comprehension as to why parents fail to display overt pleasure in respect of their children's achievements. However, to parents of children with Special Educational Needs, such news is likely to be a mixed blessing. Whilst there will usually be a degree of pleasure about their children's progress, such news is *'bitter-*

sweet' in the knowledge that their own children will not match the achievements and abilities of those who don't have Special Educational Needs. Consequently, parents will still mourn for what cannot be achieved; knowing there is no possibility of *'catching up'*. Bruce and Schultz (2002: 12) assert this is the *'bad news'* element that professionals might not recognise.

Parents in Denial: This has been alluded to but requires further comment. Some parents respond to *'bad news'* by denial of the circumstances with which they are presented. For example, this may relate to a diagnosis or news regarding their children's behaviour, which they are unable to accept as *'truth'*. These situations are particularly difficult for both professionals and parents to deal with as the extent to which professionals can bring about positive changes can be limited by lack of parental cooperation. I have supported parents who have been in *'denial'*, regarding their children's *'hidden'* disabilities. A late diagnosis can add to the adjustment required by parents, especially if they had no previous indication of any difficulties being present. Until puberty exacerbated symptoms, children's earlier idiosyncratic behaviour had been attributed to other causes, both by parents and school. However, once identified by educational professionals, such parents preferred to attribute the prevailing difficulties as being due to non-medical causes. *'Denial'* by parents can mean they reject working with schools to help address behavioural difficulties, as they refuse to acknowledge any *'real'* difficulties actually exist. Children may be permanently excluded from school, when parents deny there is a problem and, as a consequence, fail to work cooperatively on behaviour management programmes which can effect positive changes that can result in permanent exclusion being less likely to occur.

Professionals and Listening

From my experience of working with parents, substantiated by my own research, the most important aspect of parent and professional relationships is that professionals *'listen'* to parents, as supported by the following quotations:

> "Number 1 – listening. Open-mindedness, but listening, absolutely! It's almost like when I'm talking and I'm looking into their eyes, I know they are thinking about what they are going to say next, and not actually hearing me. I experience that regularly and I always want to say, 'just stop. Just let that go

and just be really open and hear me, please hear me, it is really important'."
Parent
(Attwood 2007:68, Appendix C6: 39)

"I think the main thing is that they listen. You don't necessarily even need their sympathy or anything, you just want them to actually listen to what you are saying. Okay, they understand what you are trying to get across, but I really do want to have someone who listens to your points and can offer any advice and support those things. We just need the professional people to help guide us; that is what we need."
Parent
(ibid C5: 32)

Parents are aware that there isn't always a solution to the problem being discussed, but they do seek validation that their concerns are important, real and justified. Even when professionals hold a different opinion, they should acknowledge the parent's anxiety and not undermine their perspective; they shouldn't take the approach that the problem doesn't exist or is unimportant because to the parent it could be very significant. Parents may have to summon up courage to speak to a professional, simply because of the imbalance of power between them, or they may have fears of hospital or school environments (due to events of the past) and consequently find entering such premises a feat in itself. So when parents discuss their worries, even if professionals *inwardly* disagree that issues are significant, to the parent they *are significant* and they need affirmation that they (as people) and their concerns actually matter.

Counselling Skills Help

When meeting with parents, counselling skills are invaluable and through the application of active listening skills, professionals can help parents establish the main issues of concern, clarify their thoughts and feelings and help them determine future courses of action. *Rogers (1967)* identified essential characteristics for *'helpers'* with respect to person-centred counselling. These attributes include warmth, respect and empathy, being trustworthy, genuine, and non-judgemental whilst accepting other individuals as they are, known as unconditional positive regard *(Rogers 1967: 36-57)*. Whilst teacher-parent relationships are usually not of a counselling nature, many of their conversations will require the use of counselling skills. When parents contact teachers for advice or support, they effectively become *'helpers'* and the characteristics they display will contribute significantly to the establishment of rapport between them and in maintaining responsive and encouraging communication. Over the years, other theorists such as *Egan (1990)* and *Davis et al (2002)* have further developed *Rogers' (1967)* original principles and applied them to specific *'helping'* relationships. These characteristics should be the starting position for working with parents. The principles perpetuated by several theorists are briefly outlined, *(Rogers 1967: 33, 61-63; Egan 1990: 65-71; Davis et al 2002: 58-65),* with some illustrations and examples of *'theory in action'* derived from my own research and professional experience.

There is sometimes a misconception that it's only possible to empathise if the professional has lived through similar experiences to those being reported by parents. However, even if professionals have had similar experiences to some people they are supporting, they are unlikely to have experience of *all* possible scenarios experienced by those who seek help. Whilst similar backgrounds are sometimes a helpful starting point, it's actually a *non-essential* starting point for *'helpers'* as their role is to help another person, applying objectivity, skill and professional knowledge to the situation. *'Helpers'* should attempt to understand the other person's position, where possible, although on occasion they may simply need to state, *'I cannot imagine what this situation must be like for you'* as it's outside their realm of experience and imagination. By making such statements, this is sometimes sufficient to indicate they acknowledge the other person's position and is a form of empathy in itself.

Professionals should present a *'welcoming'* persona, exuding warmth and respect, where parents immediately feel at ease and rapport can easily be established between them. Those professionals who enjoy working with parents are likely to present warmth and caring without consciously making an effort and are more likely to relate to parents on a *'human'* level. In addition, professionals should be genuine and trustworthy towards parents, acknowledging any limitations or restrictions with respect to how they can help, whilst inwardly recognising any ambivalent feelings towards the parent which might be an obstacle to supporting them. When professionals make commitments to parents, stating they will fulfil certain actions, they should always ensure that promises are fulfilled or otherwise inform parents of the reasons why such actions are no longer possible. Both from my own research *(Attwood 2007)* and anecdotal experience, unfulfilled promises are a significant contributor towards parent and professional relationships breaking down. Professionals need to relate to parents as one human being to another, rather than considering them as *'cases'* or simply *'parent'* and should not hide behind a *'professional mask'* when meeting with parents. Whilst this approach may be helpful to professionals – perhaps giving them confidence which they otherwise might not have, it has the effect of creating a barrier between them and parents and affects the extent to which they can appear genuine as people. Parents will always know when someone is not being genuine, even if they cannot quite identify the nature of their perceptions; they are likely to leave meetings feeling that somebody is untrustworthy and may be cautious about meeting with them again. Many professional roles involve evaluation of some sort and making judgements against certain criteria – unfortunately, parents can also be on the receiving end of an approach which is best retained for educational or medical assessments. Forming judgements about someone's circumstances or characteristics is unhelpful in any kind of *'helping'* relationship and aside from this, such views are quite often inaccurate as the following example illustrates.

"The educational psychologist who visited our son at the first school, decided that he was feeding off our negative feelings about school and we shouldn't talk to him about anything negative to do with the school. At no point, was the fact our son has Asperger's acknowledged. The comeback on that was he admitted to his grandmother he was being bullied at school. My mother said, 'you need to talk to your mum about that' and he replied, 'I can't; I can only talk about good things."
Parent
(Attwood 2007 Appendix C4: 27)

Anyone employed in a *'helping'* capacity should suspend their personal prejudices and endeavour to *'draw alongside'* the other person in order to help them objectively *(Attwood 2007)*. The following quotations provide a professional perspective on how to work with parents.

"The teachers go out at the end of the day and they will hand over the children so they are out of the building. They are just being cheerful, being open and honest, being approachable, knowing that they will listen to the parents and it's that sort of culture that we embed."
Headteacher
(ibid D4: 18)

"It's about using a range of listening skills and counselling skills, if you like, to make sure that every party feels that they have been listened to – and that their thoughts and issues have been taken into account and that any solutions that are formed are mutually agreeable."
SENCO
(ibid D9: 49)

"... being friendly and outgoing, and chatting about the good things before you actually have to make the phone call about the bad; trying to develop some conversation so that you have something in common, not only with the child, which is obviously important and you need to talk about the child. But finding out something about them as a person so that they can actually offer the school as much as we can offer to them, so that it becomes very much a two-way thing..."
SENCO
(ibid D12: 65)

"Our business is working with people who are our customers so it's basic customer care. We identified short-comings in some members of staff and their way of dealing with parents – abruptness and things like that. It's worth investing the time with parents because you get lots of dividends back in the school children."
Headteacher
(ibid D7: 35)

Whilst some professionals innately possess effective communication skills, combined with counselling characteristics and have no difficulty in displaying them in their professional capacity, others may need to learn them over time. From my experience, some teachers view counselling skills as an integral part of their skill set, especially when they hold positions that involve counselling pupils, whilst others view the application of counselling skills as being a separate occupational activity.

Active Listening

Being an effective listener is a skill that, for many people, must be learnt. Many counselling theorists have detailed the characteristics of effective *'helpers'* and the skills of active listening, including *Rogers (1967); Davis et al (2002); Egan (1990) and Nelson-Jones (1997) and Jacobs (1996).* Listening to someone's concerns necessitates the *'helper'* being *'active'* during the process, consciously directing their attention on the other person and overtly demonstrating they are giving them attention. *'Helpers'* should demonstrate their attentiveness through conscious application of body language which includes characteristics such as their orientation towards the speaker, their gaze, facial expressions, gestures and even whether they are stood or seated as well as their posture in such positions. All of these help determine the extent to which the speaker feels comfortable and whether it encourages them to *'open up'* or whether they have the effect of closing the conversation down. *'Helpers'* must be receptive to speaker *'cues'* and be attuned to underlying meanings and emotion behind the words spoken *(Jacobs 1996: 27),* whilst noting body language and voice characteristics such as intonation and inflection. As much as possible, *'helpers'* should suspend their own concerns, blocking their thoughts on other matters and give the speaker their undivided attention, although this is sometimes easier said than done! At appropriate points, *'helpers'* should check they have understood the message correctly, usually by paraphrasing what has been spoken. This process has the added benefit of enabling the speaker to clarify their own thoughts, whilst judicious application of questioning through use of *'open', 'closed'* or *'probing'* questions will further help the conversation to move forward, although the extent to which this occurs within an educational context might be limited *(Egan 1990: 108-110; Davis et al 2002: 66-68; Nelson-Jones 1997: 100-143; Jacobs 1996: 13-14).* These skills need to be demonstrated in a genuine way, as the following quotation illustrates.

"... It is about the kind of skills you need as a good counsellor, it's about being a good listener, an empathic listener, being genuine, rather than just going through the motions and bulldozing your way. It's got to be a conversation that is genuine. I know because my own daughter had Special Needs and she had a Statement and I've been into schools and at meetings with teachers, who probably thought they were doing a good job, but didn't listen enough."
Educational psychologist
(Attwood 2007 Appendix E1: 3)

Health and educational professionals may not proceed beyond this point, as having listened to the problem and ascertained they have understood, it may then be their responsibility to suggest what happens next (regarding educational provision or treatment). For situations that involve long term contact with professionals (counsellor, social worker, key worker or other role), parents are likely to be supported through a process that empowers them through the inclusion of goal setting and forming action plans as a way of resolving their difficulties; this is an approach often adopted by Parent Partnership Service representatives *(Egan 1990: 289-308)*.

Listening and Action: Parents will know if their particular *'helper'* is actually listening to them by the careful way in which information has been elicited and responded to. There is another aspect to *'listening'* which is equally as important. From experience in supporting parents, as well as my own research, it became apparent that parents consider that professionals have not listened to them if no action is taken following a meeting during which their concerns about their children's educational provision have been discussed. When no action is taken, parents regard this as an indication that their concerns have been ignored, disregarded and viewed as unimportant – which means they *'didn't listen' (Attwood 2007: 86)*.

Parent and Professional Meetings Preparation: Parents may invest considerable time and emotional energy in preparing to meet with a number of professionals; time may be spent in collecting evidence to support their requests for extra support, they may consider their goals for their children and evaluate the current position, noting difficulties and concerns and deciding what needs attention. Furthermore, they will need to prioritise their concerns and *'rate'* their children's difficulties, whilst preparing any specific requests they might have. Whilst the meeting is in progress, parents will strive to influence professionals in order to have their requests granted, winning them over by their own tenacity and professional approach, which usually means they must remain composed and not overtly display emotion for fear of being perceived as overwrought, overanxious or being mentally unstable *(Attwood 2007 Appendix C6: 40)*. The following quotation illustrates a parent's awareness of how they must behave at meetings with professionals.

"What I try to do is just concentrate on what it is that I want and about treating people with respect and also respecting my own position and my own judgement. What tends to happen is that I spend half of my energy on that and the other half on trying to get people to hear me, trying to make them feel okay

so that I can get what I want from them, and expending energy on making very quick judgements about the situation…"
   Parent with son at secondary school.
   (ibid C6: 41-42)

Setting the Scene: An appropriate setting for speaking to parents is paramount, especially when conversations will contain *'bad news'*. Professional preparation is important and should include consideration of where the discussion will take place (such as a room with privacy and seating arrangements that are not confrontational, with chairs of the same height). In my professional role, parents often reported that an educational professional (usually head teacher or educational psychologist) had *'caught them in passing'* in a school corridor and chosen that moment to divulge some confidential information about their child, whilst a number of other children and adults were passing by. This inevitably meant that conversations were brief and denied parents the opportunity to digest the information and follow-up the news with questions and raising further points. It did, of course, mean the professional could hastily move on after *'dropping the bombshell'*, leaving the parent feeling stunned, dismayed, distressed or angry, with no opportunity to express their reactions in any meaningful way.

Whilst acknowledging the occasional difficulties in arranging formal meetings and that it may be advantageous for parents to hear news at the earliest opportunity, professionals should consider the implications for parents and have regard for the lack of confidentiality associated with public discussions. As already stated, impromptu discussions are likely to deny parents the opportunity to give a measured response: they need time to digest the information they have just received, compose themselves (if necessary) and have the opportunity to ask questions.

Refreshments: The importance of refreshments is often overlooked, especially if meetings of an hour or less have been scheduled, but should be provided, or at least offered, even if only water is available. Obviously, few people would expect refreshments to be available at unscheduled meetings or the sort where parents *'pop in'* to see their child's class teacher. Also, there are logistical and time constraints in being able to offer refreshments at parent consultations, where parents often speak to teachers for a maximum of ten minutes before moving to see someone else, often in a separate room, although providing a *'water table'* at such events could be organised, with a little thought.

Scheduled meetings in which parents and a number of professionals attend are another matter; the number of people attending such meetings will often indicate the importance and/or complexity of the matter to be discussed. Meetings of this type may span two hours or more and parents may become distressed during the proceedings or they may have dashed straight from work to attend an evening meeting. At a basic level, refreshments satisfy a motivational need in that human beings need liquid to remain hydrated *(Maslow 1954 cited in Hargie 2006: 41)*; furthermore, a drink of water or a cup of tea are soothing and often help individuals re-gain their composure during times of stress. Nevertheless, parents have been supported at meetings where, on occasion, educational professionals have brought in their own hot drinks, without providing (or offering) refreshments to others attending. Such actions display a lack of humanity and regard for others, whilst transmitting a subliminal message of their perceived higher status in relation to others present. This may appear insignificant to some professionals, and it might be their only opportunity to take refreshments, but this approach establishes the tone of the meeting at the outset (and not necessarily a favourable one!) The effect is that other professionals and parents tend to perceive a divide between participants even before the meeting formally starts.

Messages and De-briefing

Following meetings, parents are likely to have their own private debriefing sessions, re-playing events in their minds, considering whether they successfully achieved their objectives, weighing up words spoken to them and dealing with the emotions attached to such words which may have caused despair, anger, frustration and occasionally relief and positive feelings. If parents have been accompanied to the meeting by a friend, family member, voluntary sector representative or their local Parent Partnership Service (which might also be in the voluntary sector), they are likely to have a further opportunity for debriefing, either immediately after the event or within a few days. Having an opportunity to discuss the meeting is invaluable as there may have been too much information for the parent to absorb all at once and it's possible that parental perceptions may be different from what actually occurred, or they may have placed undue emphasis on specific aspects of the meeting, which is not necessarily helpful. It is invaluable to check with another person any action points that have been agreed, statements made by participants and the context in which they were meant. This presents an opportunity to check one's own reality with that of another person who was present, someone who is impartial, without any vested interest in the outcome from the proceedings; to check whether concerns were taken seriously and whether the response received was fair and appropriate in the circumstances. It is of particular help when a *'supporter'* is experienced in the field of education as this permits specific advice on statutory requirements and procedures. Parents will require a debriefing session, whether the meeting achieved its purpose or not. Even when matters appear to be resolved, representatives, who have provided support, should still present an opportunity for parents to have closure on the previously contentious issue. On such occasions, a brief conversation after the meeting may suffice, enabling the last vestiges of turmoil to be settled, whilst ensuring parents are made aware of the option of returning for further support should they need it.

Professionals are also likely to *'debrief'* internally, going over the sequence of meetings in their minds, with consideration of their personal conduct and their success at achieving meeting objectives. In addition, they should debrief, either with colleagues who were present, or with their line managers, in order to gain a realistic perspective to events and how to take things forward, if necessary. Debriefings help settle any turmoil that might follow from a meeting, helping to re-establish some inner equilibrium so the effects are not long lasting, thereby avoiding any subsequent impact upon peace of mind and professional practice.

Communication and Motivation

It has already been acknowledged that parents and professionals approach communication with each other from different perspectives, with different goals to satisfy. Professionals, in particular, may endeavour to present a particular kind of image to parents. When they were interviewed as part of my research, they were questioned about how they had conducted themselves in recent meetings with parents. The responses were open-ended in that any amount of detail could have been provided, but the majority stated *'professionally'* in addition to claiming other characteristics such as empathy, being open and honest. The fact that so many used the word *'professionally'* appeared to indicate they felt it necessary to wear a *'mask of professionalism'*, putting on a façade when meeting with parents, which has the effect of creating distance between them, rather than revealing any aspect of their characters and personality. One would, naturally, expect anyone in employment to act *'professionally'* in their role, it being a *'taken for granted assumption'* that should need no further comment. This seemed to suggest that some educational professionals perceive the need to act in a particular manner with parents, rather than relating to them as one human being to another. There may be times when it is advantageous for them to act in this way, such as when dealing with matters of school discipline, but further questioning revealed this had only applied to one headteacher and one parent. It could be suggested that some teachers, therefore, are reluctant to form any type of *'relationship'* with parents, no matter how transitory that may be, which does not translate well into working in partnership with them, which is discussed further in Chapter 7.

An element of my research *(Attwood, 2007: 66)* involved asking professionals what they thought parents focused on most during meetings with them, choosing from the following three options:

a) The general message.
b) Specific words and phrases.
c) The manner in which information is conveyed.

The following statements indicate some professional responses.

"I think it's definitely the manner, it's your body language, it's how you are with people when they come in, whether you invite them to sit down or whether it's very informal, but definitely your body language and how you are and how you speak to them, is what they pick up the most."
Headteacher
(ibid D4: 14)

"I think the manner in which you talk to parents will be particularly important because you need to create an atmosphere where they feel comfortable talking to you, but also where you are professional and you have thought about what you are going to say. I also think they would focus on the overall message that you are stating. It is difficult to generalise as it depends upon which parent you are talking to."
Class teacher
(ibid D15: 80)

"The manner in which things are communicated can be a problem, especially when some teachers have stepped outside the school's expectations as to how a particular child should be dealt with, or they have phoned the parents' home and given a message in a particular way which is unhelpful and that can be a barrier to moving forward."
Headteacher
(ibid D8: 38-39)

"I think it's like going to the doctors, they only focus on the bits they are worried about hearing, so they'll listen for some terminology, but they will look at your body language to see if you are relaxed about giving that sort of information. As long as you give a positive persona to them, then they can see it in a positive light."
SENCO
(ibid D6: 25)

"I think they often remember phrases – I'm usually very careful about what I say because phrases can be hostages to fortune, and you need to speak with the clarity of a solicitor or a barrister in terms of not leaving things open to misinterpretation."
Headteacher
(ibid D7:31)

"I had one meeting with someone who picked up on a specific word – when we said, 'when we decide' and we generally meant everybody who was around the table, but they took it to be 'we' as in the school."
Head of Year
(ibid D5: 20)

"I think it all depends upon the tenor of the meeting and what is being conveyed to parents. I think if it is a slightly difficult situation – perhaps when you are talking to parents about unwanted behaviours that have been seen in a pupil, they do actually pick up on specific words and phrases."
Teaching Assistant
(ibid D10: 51)

"I think probably specific words and phrases. I think when humans are worried about something they tend to listen out for things they are expecting, which are probably the 'bad news' bits and will not take on board, as readily,

the 'good news' which can often come within. So I think it's human nature that people pick out words and phrases rather than general messages."
Headteacher
(ibid D11: 57)

Taking into account all professional responses, overall, they believed the primary focus for parents, in order, was:

1) The manner in which information is given (78%), followed by:
2) Specific words and phrases.
3) The general message.

Parents were asked what is most significant to them when meeting with educational professionals, and their responses, in order of importance, were:

1) The message is most important.
2) The use of specific words and phrases (almost as important as Number 1).
3) The manner in which information is conveyed.

This result overturned a commonly held view that body language is the most important aspect in communication. Obviously, there will be occasions when this is true, but within professional contexts such as parent and professional relationships, the emphasis is somewhat different. Some professionals may focus too much on their manner, rather than the content of the message, which is what parents are most concerned with; this also includes the use of language, not only from the perspective of terminology (which parents may not understand), but in how children are referred to in discussions which, at times, is derogatory, in nature. Professional responses may be understood from the perspective of them being intent on presenting a particular *'front'*, which is likely to be connected to earlier responses of *'professionalism'*. This suggests that professionals wish to be seen *'in a certain light'*, which may vary according to the reason for meeting with parents in the first place *(Attwood 2007: 87)*.

Non-verbal communication is complex and, broadly, includes consideration of the physical environment in which people meet, their emotions, the reasons for meeting and whether meetings are formal or informal. People will relate differently according to how well they know each other, as well as the basis of their relationship, for example, whether it is based on friendship or of a business nature *(Ekman and*

Friesen 1969 cited in Hargie 2006: 83). Added to this are variables such as culture, age and gender *(ibid 80-83, 92-93)* and it is, therefore, not possible to be definitive about the extent to which NVC influences communication as there are so many factors to consider.

Parents interviewed for my research *(Attwood 2007)* stated their primary focus was to listen to the message and subsumed within this was attention to specific words and phrases; this also applied to those parents supported on an everyday basis when they had meetings with professionals relating to concerns about educational provision, when they were anxious to hear whether their children had made any progress and what strategies were being implemented to help them. An educational psychologist summarised this position:

"It's surprising what parents take on board and what they don't take on board and sometimes many years later, a parent will say that some professional said X, and why it's stuck with them is anyone's guess, and people take from the message what they want to take from it.."
(Attwood 2007 Appendix E1: 7)

With respect to disciplinary matters, parents focused on *'what would happen next'*, especially if their children had been excluded from school or there was a risk of exclusion. Inherent within both types of communication, parents listened intently to the language used to describe their children and/or their difficulties, especially noting when derogatory terms were used, as illustrated by the following quote.

"I have seen parents, in the past, wincing when some professionals have talked about their children in a derogatory kind of way. It's patronising really."
Educational psychologist
(ibid E1: 9)

When asked about the professional's manner, parents had little recall, as their focus had been on what was being said. Another possible explanation for parental perceptions could be due to the heightened anxiety they experienced during meetings, meaning that they could only focus on those aspects considered to be most important - those parts of communication that satisfied their own goals and purposes for attending the meeting, with the rest of the experience fading into the background. There are possible reasons for such perceptions, which will be briefly explained in the next section.

How the Past influences the Present

The messages we hear and take away with us will be affected, to some extent, by influences from our past. As human beings, we are products of our histories, whether good or bad, they will shape how we think, feel, perceive and act upon situations in the present. From experiences, we will form opinions about events and people, including categories of people such as teachers, parents, shop assistants and so on, generalising them into a *'particular type'*. This will affect our attitudes towards specific types of events and people and the expectations we have of similar events and people in the future. For example, *Sonnenschien (1984 cited in Hornby 1995:4)* asserted that parents of children with Special Educational Needs and disabilities are often stereotyped, being viewed as vulnerable and anxious, which then enables professionals (if they so choose) to disregard parental concerns in the belief that the root cause is their anxiety. This perspective validates issues being brushed aside resulting in no action being taken to address prevailing matters affecting some children.

Notwithstanding, it is acknowledged that parents of children *can* experience enduring grief, which might be precipitated upon contact with professionals when they must (yet again), discuss their children's difficulties or they are highlighted in some other way, such as the *'good news'* scenario, already referred to *(Bruce and Shultz 2002: 10, Attwood 2007)*. Even if parents do experience enduring grief, they will vary in the extent to which they can function in everyday life, with some *'embracing'* their circumstances, determined to make the best of their situation and live their lives as normally as possible, whilst at the opposite end of the spectrum are those parents who are wholly defeated by their circumstances. It must be remembered that having children with Special Educational Needs may comprise only one element of the difficulties they experience in their lives. So whilst the professional assumption of parental anxiety states may have some validity (but not always), such stereotyping is unhelpful and creates a barrier to the professional being able to help the parent objectively, such as when concerns are dismissed. Not only that, but professionals themselves are sometimes the *cause* of parental anxiety – they may become defensive when they perceive the parent as being critical whilst parents sense judgemental attitudes and know when their concerns are being dismissed. Such reactions simply serve to heighten their emotions, especially when they *know* their children need additional support which is being denied them because professionals are not being constructive in their approach.

Furthermore, whilst training professionals, it became apparent that they sometimes fail to realise that mental health concerns are not just the province of parents, but that they might also experience such difficulties, and that this does not reduce the significance of *their* concerns. Illuminating this possibility has sometimes been a shock to professionals who often distance themselves from the type of experiences shared by parents. Too often, professionals acting in their professional capacity, separate themselves from their other roles in life such as that of parent, and fail to make any connection, even if they are also parents of children with Special Educational Needs. From this level *'playing field'*, we are *all* likely to carry *'baggage'* into meetings and this will affect how we conduct ourselves, our perceptions of events and what we remember.

Psychological Explanations

There are many psychological theories that explain how and why we perceive things the way we do, and how people who attend the same meeting, may leave with a totally different impression about what took place. A simplistic outline of some theoretical perspectives may contribute to some awareness of why communication may fail to achieve its desired purpose, or have an unexpected outcome. Each theoretical model is followed by an example that demonstrates *'theory in action'*.

Personal Construct Theory: *Kelly's (1963)* theory is based on the principle that individuals make sense of their world as a result of their past experiences. From such experiences they form *constructs* (a set of ideas) about the world, sorting out their likes and dislikes, grouping them into categories of *similarity* and *contrast*. Throughout life, *constructs* are constantly being replaced, modified or created. Experiences and the *constructs* arising from them influence how individuals anticipate future events and how they respond to the world *(Kelly 1963: 13,51)*.

Theory in Action: A parent anticipated a pre-arranged meeting with their child's headteacher was going to be difficult. When they met, the headteacher was convivial, considerate and attempted to work in partnership. However, the parent's perception of events was that the headteacher had been authoritarian, dismissive of their concerns and failed to take their views into consideration. The parent's perspective may have been influenced by childhood experiences of being disciplined at school, resulting in a dislike of authority and a belief that those in authority will discount their concerns. Memories of their past experiences might therefore have influenced the parent's anticipation of the meeting and how they perceived events as they unfolded, thereby distorting what really took place. The parent's construction of events, on this occasion, reinforced their pre-existing dislike of authority and their expectancy regarding the outcome. The headteacher may have perceived the meeting went well, although acknowledged the parent had been reserved, without knowing the reason for this.

Gestalt Theory: This theory, developed by *Korb et al (1989)* is predominantly based on figure/ground relationships. *'Gestalt'* is known as *'the figure'* which represents those aspects of an event which *'stand out'* whilst the *'ground'* relates to the environment or context in which an event takes place. On any occasion, individuals will remember some aspects more than others, whether they are words spoken, colours, room layout, people present or other detail associated with the situation. At the same time, some aspects *'fall away'* and will either be forgotten or only vaguely remembered. Unresolved issues from the past influence what individuals focus on in the present and this can have the effect of distorting their perception of events *(Korb et al 1989: 1-5)*.

Theory in Action: A meeting with a teacher is going well, until certain words *'jump out'* at the parent, who views them as derogatory. The historical significance is that similar words were spoken to the parent during their childhood and the hurt remains. Complimentary statements made by the teacher both before and after this event fade into the background and are not remembered whilst the derogatory statement remains the focus and is remembered for a long time. This is because the earlier hurt had not been resolved which had the effect of heightening the parent's awareness to any personal slights in the present.

Rational Emotive Theory: Whilst *Ellis' (1962)* acknowledged that individuals have the capacity to be both irrational and rational, he claimed there is a predisposition towards irrational thinking. This means that when individuals receive both compliments and criticism, they will be more inclined to remember and accept as *'truth'* any words which are negative. Once internalised, words then impact upon an individual's thinking, actions and attitudes *(Ellis 1962 cited in Patterson 1986: 5-8)*.

This theory particularly emphasises the power that words can have on individuals, especially if they already have a predisposition towards irrationality. Vulnerable adults and children, who often lack confidence and self-esteem, are more likely to remember derogatory phrases, not only because of their *'stinging'* effect upon hearing such words, but because they are quite likely to accept them as truly representative of themselves.

Theory in Action: A boy at school whilst being bullied is called *'stupid'* by his peers. Instead of dismissing the insult, the child takes it to heart and believes it to be true. He considers himself stupid and starts to act in a manner that supports this view and his school performance suffers. Due to being bullied, the boy starts to feel unworthy as a person, resulting in poor self-esteem and the belief he is no longer a valued person.

Cognitive Theory: *Beck's (1976)* theory is based on the premise that what people think and say about themselves affects their psychological well-being. Individuals have a lack of objectivity and are *'locked in'* to their own rule system in how they respond to situations. This means that events are interpreted in relation to themselves without acknowledgement of other factors being relevant. At the same time, they will tend to respond consistently to situations whilst their thinking can be polarised – from one extreme to the other *(Beck 1976 cited in Patterson 1986: 32,36)*.

Theory in Action: Parent (A) wants to meet her friend, Parent (B) for coffee. Parent (B) declines because of another appointment. Instead of accepting this as a valid reason, Parent (A) takes it as a personal slight, believing she has been rejected and her friend is avoiding her. To explain this *'rejection'*, Parent (A) turns her thoughts inwards and considers all her faults, believing that it is because of them that Parent (B) refused to meet with her. In her mind, Parent (A) exaggerates her faults and thinks that everyone will be repelled by them; this makes her anxious about meeting people and she consequently stops socialising.

Behaviour Theory: The underlying principle of *Wolpe's (1958)* behaviour theory is that human behaviour is either innate (within the individual) or learned through social learning experiences which are acquired through the family or wider community. From such experiences, individuals develop fears as a result of classical conditioning being employed (possibly through reward and punishment techniques) or from believing misinformation about themselves. This can result in individuals over-reacting to situations which are perceived as threatening *(Wolpe 1958 cited in Patterson 1986: 110).*

Theory in Action: A boy wants his father to attend school to watch the play he is acting in. Although his father wants to attend this event, he is overwrought with anxiety about being on school premises. The father's memories of school life are littered with forms of discipline and permanent exclusion. As a consequence, schools are associated with punishment and he responds with fear. To please his son, the father manages to attend the play, but has a panic attack that results in him having to leave early.

End Note: These theories are much more detailed and comprehensive than the outline provided here, as my purpose has been to illustrate some core elements which can underpin communication and relationship breakdown. There are, of course, many other psychological theories that explain how communication and events can be distorted in our minds because of experiences from the past that affect how we respond and think about situations in the present. These examples should provide a flavour of the many facets involved in communication between parents and professionals, as well as other relationships in our lives.

Chapter Summary

Whilst the majority of individuals have the ability to communicate effectively in everyday situations, there are formal types of communication that take place within an occupational context for which professionals would benefit from counselling and communication skills training in how to communicate effectively with their clients – whether they are patients, parents or children. Interpersonal communication extends beyond the spoken word and the nuances of non-verbal communication, but the meanings derived from such communication should be arrived at through consideration of social, cultural, and relationship factors *(Hargie 2006: 8),* consideration of motivators for specific communication as well as any psychological influences which may detrimentally affect perceptions of events and, thereby, impact upon relationships. Professionals should have particular regard for how they break *'bad news'*, being mindful to avoid derogatory language, when explaining children's difficulties. A suitable social environment should be selected in which private matters may be discussed at a pace that parents can understand, permitting them the opportunity to ask questions for further information. Finally, listening is a fundamental requirement of all communication, with it being demonstrated through Active Listening Skills and subsequent professional follow-up, when parents truly *'know'* they have been heard. Chapter 7 will explore views on partnership and how partnerships between parents and professionals may collapse because of poor communication, with repercussions for parents and their children.

Chapter 7
The Impact of Parent and Professional Relationships

Introduction

The Warnock Report (1978) continued to develop the theme of *'partnership'* that had originally been launched in the *Plowden Report (1963)*. Warnock acknowledged the significance of parental knowledge and the pressures associated with parenting children with additional needs, noting such responsibilities could hinder parental engagement with their children's schools. *Warnock (1978)* further recorded that parents often felt *'guilt, shame, frustration and disappointment'* about their circumstances which could act as additional barriers to interacting with others. To counteract this, it was recommended that professionals should encourage parental involvement, dispense *'practical advice'* and listen to their concerns *(Warnock 1978: 154)*.

This report was published during an historical period when teacher accountability was less onerous than the standards expected of the profession today, at a time when this idealistic perspective may have been achievable, when the general assumption was that those entering the profession *really loved* children and always strived to achieve the best for them. But time has moved on and educational professionals are now subjected to a myriad of demands placed upon their time, with government curricular demands to be adhered to whilst endeavouring to achieve exacting professional standards. As a consequence, it might be assumed that teachers must love children and working with parents to contemplate entering such a demanding profession. For the majority of professionals, such assumptions are accurate and evidenced in their daily commitment to fulfil all aspects of their role to an exemplary standard. I have personally known and worked alongside many who possessed a *true heart* for helping children and their parents, some of whom contributed to my own research, in an endeavour to improve relationships between parents and professionals. However, it is unrealistic to assume this applies to everyone in the profession and there will, inevitably be educationalists whose career choice has been determined by reasons other than having a strong desire to work with children and parents. This is not to infer there is anything wrong with this approach, as probably all career choices are influenced by practical considerations and lifestyle choices, but the point being made is that for some professional roles it is helpful if people have a *true heart* for those with whom they must work. The reality is that some teachers appear unenthusiastic about aspects of their role, especially in relation to working with parents, despite the requirement to convey an ethos of *'partnership'* and their approach can sometimes be the source of parental despair and children's heartache. On the other hand, there are parents who enthusiastically attempt to work in *'partnership'* (whether or not their children's teachers are responsive) as well as those who are unable or unwilling to engage for a myriad of reasons.

Many parents of children with Special Educational Needs and disabilities have *more* contact with their children's school than the average parent, with their concerns often being associated with their children's education and the provision being made for them. This chapter will take the reader through some causes and effects of relationship breakdown; when parents and teachers fail to see eye-to-eye with each viewing situations from different perspectives, sometimes with professionals rejecting or disbelieving what parents claim. As a starting point, the concept of *'partnership'* will be discussed, in terms of political intentions, parents' and professional perspectives, and how from such notions, relationships may ultimately break down.

Partnership as a Concept

The historical overview in Chapter 5, demonstrated that over the last fifty years or so, there has been a significant movement towards involving parents in their children's education, with this gaining momentum following *The Warnock Report (1978)* when *'partnership'* was adopted to describe different types of relationship in educational contexts. From my experience of working with parents and multi-agency professionals, the concept of *'partnership'* often promises more than it actually delivers. As a result of political rhetoric and media attention, parental expectations are sometimes elevated above that which the majority of parents may realistically expect on a day-to-day basis, especially when concepts such as *'partnership'*, *'power'* and *'equality'* are promoted in government papers relating to education *(Warnock 1978; DfES 2005)*.

The Department of Health has adopted a *'partnership'* approach since *The Community Care Act 1990* which became further embedded with respect to children under the *National Service Framework for Children,*

Young People and Maternity Services (2004), with professionals being expected to have regard to information provided by parents, as their children's advocates. The notion of partnership, albeit an unequal one, is probably easier to understand in relation to health services where parents generally have specific, fairly restricted roles in relation to their children - acting as advocates, being informed about diagnoses and treatment programmes, and more often than not, being reliant upon medical professionals making decisions in the best interests of their children.

With respect to educational matters, parents continue to advocate for their children and educational professionals are expected to work in partnership with them, with the primary function of parents being that of co-educators. *Hornby (1995)* and *Vincent (1996)* detailed several types of role often undertaken by parents, where the range of functions include *'helpers'* who listen to children read in class, being co-educators to their own children, helping with projects and other homework activities, or by influencing school strategy through the roles of Parent Governor or School Council member. Whilst these activities may be described as *'partnership'* the extent to which parents can make decisions and exert any influence will depend upon the particular roles undertaken (*Hornby 1995: 24; Vincent 1996: 44*).

'Partnership' means different things to different people and for parents it often leads to the expectation that they will have the same rights and privileges that someone would have in a business partnership, in particular, encompassing mutual respect, the sharing of power and exchange of knowledge with parties who are unified with respect to decisions being taken and moving forward *(Armstrong 1995: 16; Roffey 2002: 15)*. Both parents and professionals will have their own ideas regarding the parameters of partnership and may be disappointed when such relationships or systems of working together fail to live up to their expectations. Unless parents hold formal positions such as that of Parent Governor or School Council member, which usually have guidelines for undertaking such roles, *'partnership'* frequently remains a *'woolly'*, undefined concept between those involved in such working relationships *(Pinkus 2005: 185)* with the effect that such arrangements often engender hope and raise expectations that for many, remain unfulfilled and lead to disappointment.

Vincent (1996) and *Attwood (2007)* have identified that, within educational contexts, *'partnership'* may be expressed through use of other words, which more specifically represent the role of participants in relation to each other *(Vincent 1996: 3; Attwood 2007 Appendix G2: 15)* such as:

- **Collaboration** – working together as a team.
- **Participation** – this term often applies to groups of parents, such as Parent Forums, which are strategically engaged with local authorities in shaping service provision.
- **Cooperation** – parents complying with school requests, ranging from car parking arrangements around the school to supporting the school in disciplinary measures.
- **Community** – represents a reciprocal relationship with the school being the heart of the local community, serving the population whilst the community is allied to the school and supports its activities.

Of these terms, *'partnership'*, *'participation'* and *'cooperation'* tend to be favoured with respect to many aspects of school organisation and discipline *(ibid G2: 15)*. *'Partnership'* and other terms that represent the same type of activity are emotive – often encouraging involvement through the stimulation of *'warm and fuzzy feelings'* that generate hope and anticipation for participants although for some individuals, such notions generate negative and uncomfortable responses. *Edelman (1964)* asserted that terms such as *'partnership'* are *'condensation symbols'* which conjure ideas regarding relationships and systems of working which only become apparent through subsequent interactions between parents and professionals *(Edelman 1964 cited in Vincent 1996: 3)*. Whilst government legislation and policy defines specific circumstances under which parents and professionals should engage with each other, promoting potential benefits to children's well-being and educational achievement, there are some individuals who perceive *'partnership'* in a negative light and are therefore, reluctant to embrace this system of working together.

Formal relationships that involve *'partnership'* are more likely to have *'ground rules'* that detail the expectations and remit of each party; in particular, when there is parental participation in strategic groups (that influence the design and delivery of services), a remit will define operating principles (otherwise known as *'terms of reference'*) to ensure that roles and boundaries are not over-stepped in an effort to maintain clear communication channels and to ensure that partnership is productive, whilst avoiding dissent between members. Relationships involving *'partnership'* do not remain static and boundaries may shift once members have established rapport, learnt to trust each other and have become familiarised with members' skill sets and knowledge base. This sometimes results in a degree of flexibility with respect to the range of activities undertaken and, with regards to parents, *may* enable their influence to become stronger but it's not a guaranteed outcome.

Politicians frequently make *'power statements'* that gloss over the detail of reforms and include specific *'buzz words'* that attract the public's attention. These words are remembered and may subsequently be taken either out of context or generalised to take on meanings over and above that which were originally intended. As a result, it's not unknown for parents to believe they hold positions of influence, with equal rights regarding *all* decisions being made, which then results in much frustration, bewilderment and anger when they cannot bring about the changes they hoped for. What sometimes isn't evident, from initial publicity, is that few parents hold positions of influence and that decision-making powers are primarily reserved for those who participate in strategic aspects of educational provision, excepting for some tokenistic concessions for parents such as when they contribute to new educational or behavioural targets for their children to work towards.

Raising unrealistic parental expectations can, in fact, become a hindrance to successful partnership working between parents, teachers and local authority professionals. For example, following publicity associated with the Labour Government's schools' *White paper, Higher Standards, Better Schools for All* (2005), I was contacted by parents who believed they could influence aspects of educational provision (such as marking and discipline methods). Upon being informed that such matters were the province of educational professionals, they advised that publicity had raised their expectations regarding the extent to which they could *'lead'* with respect to their children's education.

The reality is that when educational professionals *'work in partnership'* with parents, they will listen to parents' concerns (or should do), which may have a degree of influence in classroom strategies, but when they disagree with parents, school and local authority professionals, have ultimate power to make decisions, resulting in parents virtually having no influence, as illustrated by the following statements:

"If it were appropriate for parents' views to have equal status, the demonstration would be through the minutes of the meetings and the action that then happens. However, the kind of meetings in which the parents' views would have equal status, in terms of actual influence, I'm trying to imagine what kind of meeting that would be, because a lot of the time, I don't think schools should be pretending to offer power to parents that they cannot have..."
Headteacher
(Attwood 2007 Appendix D7: 36)

"... the voice can be heard but it doesn't mean that you have to give into it each time. You have to take on board experience, what is best for the child and for other people as well, so they have a right to a voice, but they don't have a right to make a decision – a decision that affects not only themselves but other people.

... it is up to the parent to make that decision for the child in their own experience of what they think is right. They should have a say if they don't agree with something, but it won't necessarily mean that it's going to happen."
Headteacher
(ibid D18: 101)

"We tend to just record action points now to keep things manageable. If a parent suggested an action point, we would make sure that it was recorded. It tends to be the educationalists that drive forward action points, and parents will perhaps have one or two ideas about that, but given that they have fewer, it seems more important, I would argue, that the ones they have are recorded and acted upon."
Deputy Headteacher
(ibid D16: 91)

For many parents of children with Special Educational Needs, when professionals disagree with their viewpoint, the best they can hope for is that their opinions will be recorded, as a sign of respect to them. But for parents, the purpose of 'partnership' is to effect change, either at strategic level or one-to-one in relation to their own children, to improve provision for them, based on what they, as parents, know they need. Fundamentally, 'partnership' on an every day level is dependent upon educational professionals embracing the opportunity to work with parents and to emphasise this point, one school advised that when parents failed to attend multi-agency meetings, they were cancelled and re-arranged for another time, as the following statement illustrates:

"We have had times when we cancelled a meeting and not run it at all because a parent was not there – so I think that demonstrates our view of how important it is that parents are there."
SENCO
(ibid D9: 48)

As already stated, if professionals relinquish some of their power, this will permit more opportunities for parents to be influential; another important factor is that professionals should have the humility to recognise they have limited knowledge of the children in their care; only seeing them for a restricted period, five days a week, under relatively controlled circumstances and, therefore, cannot possibly know the child *'inside-out'* in the way that parents do. As a consequence, it is vital to know how children present in other situations, especially when there are concerns regarding their behaviour or learning. One headteacher described this approach as *'humanity'*, as illustrated by the following statement:

"Humanity, showing that you are a human being and not too distant from the parents, openness and a willingness to take on board what is being said by parents, to take on board their concerns and to show that you are responsive to those concerns. I think there is a danger with teaching professionals that they can be a little bit defensive, if criticisms are made or implied and they can rather dig in and close their minds to a lot of what is being said, rather than seeing it as an opportunity for development and better ways of doing things."
(ibid D13: 71)

Many educational professionals have an awareness of the positive benefits associated with developing and maintaining relationships with parents, as indicated by the following statements:

"I think it is vitally important. I think that we can only hope to achieve what we want to achieve in this school in partnership with parents. Education is about a three-way partnership between pupil, parents and school. I believe that children's attitudes to their learning are fundamentally influenced by their parents and by parental validation of what goes on in the school, and I do feel that a healthy school is one which feels like a community of all stakeholders

involved in it. So I feel quite passionately that there has to be a partnership between school and parents."
Headteacher
(ibid D13: 69)

"Well, if you don't work in partnership with parents, then really you have no basis for anything to work on. You have to have that partnership, you have to have that daily contact and I think we do. We work really hard to establish a relationship with parents, and I think that's paramount."
Teaching Assistant
(ibid D3: 11)

"... and if any one of those relationships is breaking down, and not working, then the work within the school impacts on that child and the children are not getting the most out of the experience they could be getting, so we need to be listening to the children. And the children need to be having that relationship with their parents and we need to be having that relationship with their parents as well, so it's very, very important. If you don't have it, everything falls to bits."
Headteacher
(ibid D7: 33)

"For the benefit of the children, at the end of the day, if they see that you are working together, their progress and their happiness is so much more evident."
Teacher
(ibid D4: 15)

"It's absolutely crucial to work in partnership with parents. I always say to parents if schools and parents are singing from the same hymn sheet, then we can make progress with children. So building bridges with parents and being open to them is very important."
Headteacher
(ibid D8: 40)

It's evident that some teachers clearly recognise the benefits gained from investing time in working with parents and have daily witnessed how children thrived as a result. As a consequence of supporting parents, Parent Partnership Services, acquire knowledge of their local schools and can often determine which schools (in their own local area) work ineffectually with parents due to their representation in case work. This is not to say, that 'better' schools are never in conflict with parents, but it does suggest they are more successful in being able to address their differences and achieve resolution to matters of concern. As one headteacher, committed to working in partnership stated:

> *"I think my overwhelming experience of dealing with parents since being Headteacher is that I have found it positive and enjoyable, and I think that it's well worth investing in time and energy and everything that goes with it to bring parents into school – to make them feel they are valued and their views are valued and that we don't have a monopoly on wisdom in the school, but we have certain professional expertise which we want to use to benefit them and their children. I think it is very important that they feel that we don't stand apart from them in our aspirations for their children, but actually their aspirations for their children and ours probably coincide a huge extent..."*
> (ibid D13: 73)

There are, however, some professionals who profess to *'work in partnership'*, but when presented with situations that could demonstrate such commitment, they instead reveal their *true* position in relation to working with parents. For example, at meetings they can demonstrate their disinterest and disengagement from events by staring out of windows and through other aspects of body language whilst others can be abrupt when parents seek help and support from them. From my experience, when parents are supported at meetings by *'professional supporters'* the dynamics between the parties usually changes, with previously unresponsive professionals becoming more friendly and constructive, whereas parents sometimes become more assertive. However, some professionals remain averse to modifying their approach, irrespective of the circumstances.

Educational professionals further hinder *'partnership'* when they address parents as if they are pupils *(Crozier 2005: 53)*, shout at them or use derogatory forms of expression, usually about their children. Such tactics represent the imbalance of power between parents and educational professionals, despite the rhetoric of *'partnership'* and the requirement to work together to help children achieve their best at school. It could be surmised that in other social contexts, such behaviour might be challenged, but some parents are weary, troubled and lack the confidence to challenge educational professionals. Furthermore, parents have reported their fears of reprisal being directed at their children, if they challenged professionals, all of which contribute to maintaining parents in a subservient position, which eliminates any possibility of meaningful *'partnership'*. The following quotation illustrates:

"Most parents would not say anything overtly because of the imbalance of power in the relationship. Professionals need to realise most parents are experts on their children. It is an emotional time for parents discussing their child – it is not the best time to raise issues."
Parent
(Attwood 2007 Appendix G6: 41)

Other strategies that create distance include professionals conveying *'bad news'* to parents, over the telephone, without presenting opportunities for face-to-face meetings to discuss matters more fully, raise questions and take on board the information they are receiving. Although quite rare, some teachers simply refuse to meet with parents, under any circumstances, although this approach is more usually reserved for headteachers and others in senior management roles than for class teachers, who would find this exceedingly difficult to implement. In recognition of the broad approach to *'partnership'* a local authority educational professional stated:

"It's very much about people's attitudes. It's about whether people want to work in partnership with parents. It's about valuing the contribution of parents and if you don't value that, then it won't happen."
(ibid E3: 23)

"I'm sure that sometimes it can be quite tokenistic. For example, for report evenings, the letter goes out with schools not necessarily being actively engaged in the process of working in partnership with parents. Working in partnership is listening, informing and engaging – with parents having a say and then acting on what the parents want."
(ibid E3: 24)

When headteachers refuse to meet with parents, it's not necessarily due to pre-existing animosity between them, but simply because their position means *'they can'*. This, of course, denies parents additional support in having existing concerns dealt with; at the same time, it suggests that *'power games'* are being employed, as illustrated by the following statement:

"Concerns are regularly raised that teachers won't talk to them (parents) and don't provide information when they should, for example, with Individual

Education Plans and Annual Reviews. Many parents have stated they have no way of negotiating targets or of being involved in reviewing progress. They are approached in the playground to sign IEP's without chance to read and discuss the contents. Annual Reviews are often arranged well in advance and notice is given to professionals so they can attend. However, a significant number then do not tell parents until a few days before and refuse to rearrange as the professionals are busy people!"

Parent Partnership Service representative
(ibid G9: 57)

As a result of legislation and national policy, schools often have policies that refer to their commitment to *'work in partnership'* with parents; their websites and newsletters may also promote this ethos but from my own professional experience, this does not guarantee *'partnership in action'* by all school staff. In schools where headteachers are resistant to *'partnership'*, their staff may covertly adopt *'a partnership approach'* as illustrated by the following parent's statement:

"By and large, they are very willing to try and meet our needs, but it's not always the case. I feel quite strongly at the moment that the headteacher isn't in partnership with us, but I feel that the staff are. I think that sometimes the teachers go out on a limb to actually help him do things that aren't necessarily in the rules, according to the headteacher. In fact, I know that happens."

(ibid C1: 4)

On the other hand, there are headteachers who fully embrace working with parents but have teachers on their team who don't work to the same standards and who appear to resent this *'unnecessary'* aspect of their role. There will inevitably be occasions when parents experience inconsistency, due to the variances of human nature, irrespective of the *'whole school ethos'*. Research and anecdotal experience acknowledge that whilst parents may select their children's school on the basis of perceived ethos, until their children actually attend the chosen school, they will not know to what extent they work in partnership and whether it actually meets their expectations *(Woods et al 1998: 2001 cited in Crozier 2005: 119)*. Even when schools have been recommended by friends and family, parental experiences will be unique to them and will, in part, be influenced by how much contact they have with the school, for what reason and, of course, the particular dynamics between individual parents and teachers.

Partnership and Relationship

'Partnership' involves effort from both sides; it entails the establishment of relationships from which parents and professionals will work together. Ideally, there should be a period during which the parties may *'get to know each other'*; some schools organise home visits, both as a means of getting to know the family and in preparing children for moving from one school setting to another. Social events, such as skittles evenings or barn dances, provide an informal opportunity for parents and teachers to relate to each other on a basic human level, as illustrated by the following statement:

> *"We have lots of events and activities which we encourage parents to get involved in. So there are a lot of activities – not just the learning and academic things, but social and sporting events as well, where parents are encouraged to participate and be involved. I think there is a very good partnership with parents ..."*
> SENCO
> *(Attwood 2007 Appendix D9: 47)*

However, not all schools present such opportunities and not all parents feel comfortable attending school social events anyway. There will inevitably be some disparity between parents and professionals regarding the extent to which they acknowledge each other as human beings with both varying in their need and desire for *'relationship'* and this will impact upon the extent to which any social niceties are included in their communication with each other. Contact with each other may be viewed as a *'functional necessity'* in order to extract information or cooperation, rather than being as *'relationship'*, but that is exactly what it is – *'relationship'*, no matter how transitory it may be, and without this element underpinning interactions, communication may be less successful. The establishment of rapport is vital to forming relationships; often within a professional/parent context this may be entwined in discussions around children's educational provision, where the parties explore common ground and differences. Social elements may take place following instrumental discussion, rather than at the beginning, if they take place at all.

The majority of schools will present an ethos of partnership through the schools' organisation, with educational professionals creating an environment which is conducive to forming relationships with parents and, thereby, working in partnership with them. Through their actions they will demonstrate a willingness to engage with parents, as shown by the methods adopted by primary schools to demonstrate their *'availability'* to parents. As an element of my own research, educational professionals were questioned about which characteristics contributed to successfully working in partnership, with the most significant characteristics being:

- Warmth and approachability
- Availability and flexibility in being able to meet with parents.
- Empathy and understanding.
- Listening.
- Honesty and trustworthiness.
- Being supportive of parent and child.
- Being open.
- Good and clear communication between home and school.
- Professional competence and being able to take action.

Many of these characteristics comply with *Rogers' (1967: 36-57)* principles (explained in Chapter 6) which underpin the skills necessary for *'helping'* relationships, further corroborated by *Egan (1990); Nelson-Jones (1997) and Davis et al (2002)*. Training in these skills contributes to professional development, although 78% of school professionals reported that educational professionals *'learnt on the job' (Attwood 2007 Appendix G2: 19)*.

Parental Approach

Chapter 6 has already acknowledged that parents sometimes lack the necessary skills and diplomacy to communicate effectively with professionals, sometimes unleashing years of pent up frustration and anger, especially when they perceive their concerns have been disregarded by professionals. This occasionally results in headteachers requesting mediation between themselves and parents, especially when they have previously been on the receiving end of volatile and abusive communication.

Headteachers have a number of strategies at their disposal when they are unable to *'build bridges'* with parents and work effectively together. For instance, they may deflect conflict by delegating responsibility to another member of staff to meet with parents, as illustrated by the following example:

"Where parents continue to be oppositional to anything I might say, and I'm not making progress, or indeed if another colleague is not making progress, my view tends to be that the parents are better off working with someone else with whom they can make progress ... I distance myself, while keeping myself well informed."
Headteacher
(ibid D8: 39)

As last resort tactics, when teachers perceive they are at risk of harm, they may formally advise parents they can no longer enter school premises, and in extreme cases might have a police presence to ensure that *'banned'* parents comply with instructions not to enter school grounds. It is unhelpful, for all concerned, when matters escalate this far and sometimes the only way forward is for parents and headteachers to meet, with a mediator present (or someone acting in that role). Otherwise, whilst parties remain at *'stalemate'*, there is no hope of resolution and concerns about children remain unresolved. A potential way of achieving resolution is to use an impartial service, such as the local Parent Partnership Service, where representatives can sometimes act as an intermediary, presenting an opportunity for parties to meet and air their grievances, with the possibility of reaching some agreement between them. A solution will need to be sought by each party and the outcome cannot be guaranteed. If these strategies fail to work, mediation can at least provide an opportunity to clear the air and bring about closure to an unpleasant situation.

Benefits of Partnership

For a number of years, government has consistently promoted the positive benefits of parent and professional relationships with respect to children's outcomes *(Plowden 1967; Warnock 1978; Desforges and Abouchaar 2003; DfES 2007; DfES 2008)* with home-school agreements *(DfE 2013)* being further evidence of the need to work together. Whilst investigating other aspects of parent and professional relationships, fifty percent of teachers, in the research sample, identified specific areas in which partnership between parents and professionals benefited children's outcomes *(Attwood, 2007:76, 88)* which included:

- Improvements in discipline and behaviour.
- A reduced number of detentions and exclusions by specific children.

- Improvements in school attendance.
- Improved educational outcomes in SATs, tables and reading (primary school).
- Improvements in examination preparation and, ultimately, examination results (secondary school).
- Improvement in attitudes, relationships with peers and friendships, developing all-round skills.

Other professionals noted that not all evidence is quantifiable, but can easily be observed, as the following quotations illustrate:

"It's easier to measure things like the extent to which young people are getting into trouble and then you bring about some intervention, like a meeting with a parent and then you can see what difference it makes."
Deputy headteacher
(ibid D16: 89)

"The most obvious one would be with 'difficult' children and the parents will often be involved for a short time and the improvement is seen and then it drops back."
Headteacher
(ibid D11: 59)

"… we are not able to quantify – it's just an internal thing that you can see the change in the parent's views and the children's attitudes …"
SENCO
(ibid D6: 28)

A number of activities come under the umbrella of *'partnership';* many of which have been in operation over a considerable number of years, where each party invests different amounts of time, according to the type of activity engaged in *(Hornby 1995; Vincent 1996)*. In my own research, professionals identified the following activities as representing *'partnership' (Attwood 2007: 76):*

- Attendance at curriculum evenings (secondary schools).
- Parent support groups, facilitated by a school's member of staff.
- Voluntary activities within school (primary schools).
- Parents' evenings (primary schools).
- Parents being given advice on which resources to use to help their children.
- Helping children with homework.

- Attendance at parenting classes.
- Raising funds so that schools could purchase vital resources.
- Newsletters.
- Parents attendance at Academic Review Days (secondary schools).
- Consultation with parents, either through annual questionnaires or through formal capacities such as Parent Governors and School Councils.

These results corroborate the earlier findings of *Hornby (1995)* and *Vincent (1996)* thereby illustrating the range of partnership activities has changed little over time. Benefits of partnership are particularly evident when parents cooperate with professionals with respect to behaviour modification strategies, where children might be saved from permanent exclusion if programmes are diligently applied and implemented early enough *(Attwood 2007: 76)*.

The following professional quotation illustrates this point:

"We have prevented many, many permanent exclusions and what would have been longer fixed-term exclusions, and we have helped children to settle in school and become happier at school and progress both behaviourally and academically as well.

We are hoping that the strategies we use have long-term benefits because we are physically teaching social skills to children that are going to enable them to maintain their mainstream school placements and that they will carry those skills into industry or out into the community as well..."

(ibid E4: 30)

'Partnership' is established by the 'quality' of the interaction between parents and professionals and is not about the quantity of engagement that takes place although with primary schools traditionally having an 'army' of volunteers that support a range of school activities, it can sometimes appear that 'quantity' is what is important. Research by *Desforges and Abouchaar (2003)* examined the range of activities that parents undertake such as road safety training, cookery and supporting teachers on school trips at primary school compared with the more formalised mechanisms for parental involvement at secondary school and deduced that some in-school parental engagement activities are not significant with respect to contributing to children's eventual outcomes, nor is the quantity of engagement necessarily significant *(Desforges and*

Abouchaar 2003: 30,49). Secondary schools secure parental engagement through more formal mechanisms such as workshops for parents (to help them become co-educators), Academic Review days or in association with Special Educational Needs procedures such as Individual Education Plans or Annual Reviews (which also apply to primary school aged children). Whilst contact with secondary school professionals is generally less than for primary schools, effective partnership may be achieved through the development of reciprocal supportive relationships. Parents of children with SEN will, inevitably, have additional contact with their children's schools, which should place all such contacts within the *'ethos of partnership'*.

Under Coalition Government reforms, policy and procedures are placing emphasis on parental *'choice'* and *'control'* (DfE 2011), with little overt reference to *'partnership'* although new initiatives may only successfully be achieved through a *'partnership approach'*. Perhaps this is due to the assumption that *'working in partnership'* has now become embedded in professional practice and there is no further requirement to overtly state this.

Partnership in Action

Some partnership activities have already been alluded to, but it's worth explaining some additional approaches adopted by professionals which demonstrate *'partnership'* with parents, as follows:

Primary Schools: During primary school years, parental relationships with their children's teachers tend to be less formal and easier to establish. Class teachers often make themselves readily available by welcoming parents and children in the morning, either at the school gate or the entrance to the school building; equally, teaching staff may see the children off the school premises at the end of the school day. This position of obvious availability makes it easier for parents to *'grab a quick word'* about any concerns they may have and, of course, parents have an opportunity to meet on the school premises, either by pre-arrangement or by taking their conversations inside, to retain privacy. This approach was one of the original recommendations contained in the *Plowden Report (1967)* which was designed to break down barriers between professionals and parents. Whilst teacher accessibility is often key to establishing *'partnership'*, this approach can be perceived as threatening to some parents, who shy away from such contact, preferring to remain *'invisible'* to professionals in authority so this approach isn't necessarily successful for *all* parents *(Attwood 2007 Appendix G6: 44)*.

Secondary Schools: Contact with professionals is usually by pre-arrangement, unless headteachers hold open *'surgeries'* where parents may simply turn up within allocated time periods. Surgeries will be advertised through the schools' websites or newsletters, so all parents should be aware if their children's school operates such a system. Other opportunities tend to be at Academic Reviews or when educational professionals facilitate workshops, as *'experts'* on specific aspects of the curriculum to help parents support their children. Through *'transplanting'* educational knowledge to parents, teachers encourage parents to become co-educators in their children's education *(Hornby 1995: 19)*.

Special Educational Needs: For parents of children with Special Educational Needs and disabilities, the scenario is quite different. Some parents may contact teachers daily, either to discuss concerns, check on progress, inform teachers of any events at home which could impact upon their children's day at school, or to report upon behavioural situations when both are working together to change patterns of behaviour, and the list goes on. In addition, home-school diaries are often used to facilitate communication between parents and professionals.

Multi-Agency Meetings: A primary way of demonstrating *'partnership'* is through parental attendance at multi-agency meetings. Currently, this should include Annual Reviews, Common Assessment Framework (CAF) and transition meetings in relation to post-school provision when the child may be in attendance for, at least, part of the meeting. The exact format of the multi-agency Single Assessment Process is still awaited, but early indications are that, where possible, children should have multiple appointments on the same day (if they are under the care of several specialists) or that some assessments may take place at the same time *(DfE 2013)*.

Parental attendance at multi-agency meetings presents an opportunity for them to ask questions and present their own views on what works for their children, advising professionals of their difficulties and reactions under specific circumstances and stating what help they consider is most important. These meetings are highly stressful for parents, irrespective of whether they are employed in a professional capacity in their own right or whether they are unemployed – sitting with several professionals (sometimes as many as a dozen), who have a view on their child (and probably of them) is somewhat intimidating and threatening for many parents. Unless they are familiar with such encounters through their own working lives, and have the confidence and assertiveness necessary to state their case, parents may visibly shrink in such surroundings and be unable to *'fight their child's corner'*. Professionals should not underestimate the effect that such meetings can have on parents and should strive to reduce their stress.

Parent and Teacher Expectations

For much of the time, relationships between parents and professionals will be calm and convivial and fairly easy to maintain. Parents will have the expectation that teachers and support staff will listen and respond to their concerns, whilst supporting their children and helping them to make progress. Educational professionals will usually find relationships with parents relatively easy when they are cooperative, share the school's values *(Plowden 1967)* and from my experience in supporting parents, are generally uncritical of teachers and school practices, they don't *'swamp'* teachers with a myriad of problems and do not present as highly emotional. So far, so good; basically, as long as each party has their objectives satisfied, relationships may *'jog along nicely'*. Obviously, there are exceptions where some parents have little or no contact with their children's schools (due to their own reasons, family circumstances, or cultural expectations around the role of education) although the point being made here revolves around parents who *do* have contact with educational professionals.

When politicians speak and write about national policy that involves parents and professionals working together, it could be assumed that such *'partnerships'* are desirable by all stakeholders and are easy to establish and maintain. Through promotion of *'partnership'* as being the optimum method by which children's outcomes can be improved, the underlying assumption is that teachers and parents will naturally gravitate towards each other, intent on having a professional relationship for the common good. However for many, the reality is somewhat different; whilst being relationships of mutual exchange, the parties often have different goals and objectives, they view situations from different perspectives (if shared at all) as well as having specific motivational needs to satisfy that impact upon the maintenance of such relationships *(Attwood 2007)*. How the parties conduct themselves will inevitably, have some bearing on the extent to which children's outcomes will be enhanced.

The Disintegration of Relationships

This is delicate territory; as with any human relationships, there may be a tendency to become defensive when aspects of character, professionalism, ability and lifestyle come under scrutiny or criticism. As already mentioned, educational professionals tend to encourage families to adopt the norms of the school, whilst families, obviously, prefer to live their lives as they choose. When home routines impact upon children's ability to learn, headteachers may consider it appropriate to broach this delicate area, through open, honest communication and use of negotiation skills, as the following example illustrates:

"I think there is a certain conflict between the lifestyles of a lot of families and expectations the school have of children coming in. Something that sounds pretty trivial and mundane is bedtimes – when children are going to bed (late) and how tired they are when they come to school and what they see on the television. We daily get anecdotal evidence of children referring to things they have seen on television, which without being too stuffy about it, you might deem to be unsuitable, and their exposure works counter to the ethos and culture that we are trying to engender here. We have to be brave and have those debates with parents ..."
Headteacher
(ibid D13: 73)

When children fail to make educational progress, parents may regard *'poor teaching'* as the cause *(Croll and Moses 1987 cited in Armstrong 1995: 53)* and approach the issue from this standpoint, which may result in educational professionals becoming defensive rather than solution focused. When parents take educational concerns to their children's teachers, the situation will either be diffused, due to teachers taking action to resolve the problem(s) or nothing changes. When the problem remains constant, parents believe that teachers are *'not listening'* to them. From anecdotal experience, as well as research, it became apparent there were three primary professional behaviours that have the potential to initiate a *'conflict response'* in parents *(Attwood 2007)*. These responses will be outlined, with a more detailed explanation following.

1) Professionals who don't listen nor acknowledge parental concerns as being valid.
2) Professionals committing to undertake specific actions and then not following these through.
3) Professionals communicating insensitively, using disparaging or derogatory terminology to parents and/or their children.

These will now be explained more fully.

Number 1: The significance of listening has already been referred to in Chapter 6, where it not only comprises the *'act of listening'* with associated behaviours that demonstrate the speaker is being heard and understood, but that lack of subsequent action to remedy problems also denotes lack of listening. Listening and follow-up actions appear to *'prove'* to parents they are respected, their views are valid and that they are considered as *'partners'* in their children's education.

Number 2: When professionals have committed to undertake specific actions, parents may initially feel relieved and elated that their concerns are being taken seriously, with the anticipation that existing problems will soon be resolved. They leave meetings with the confidence that *'something will be done'*, but this initial elation is sometimes soon replaced with distress, frustration and anger, when no remedial action subsequently takes place. This scenario connects with Number 1 (above).

Number 3: This type of situation is different as few parents will overtly express their displeasure at hearing derisory comments. Some might seek emotional support from friends, whilst others may contact an advocacy service that may offer both emotional and practical support, by being in attendance at further meetings. Professional support of this type can empower parents and give them the confidence to challenge communication that makes them feel uncomfortable. Unless parents feel that they and their children are respected, they will tend to minimise contact with educational professionals.

A simplistic hypothetical example outlines common sequences that occur when parents attempt to persuade professionals to take action to support their children (Numbers 1 and 2 above). The scenario has been set against a parent's request for additional support, which despite professional assurances is never forthcoming. The trigger for relationship disintegration might be any number of different situations involving professionals, taking place over short or long time periods, depending upon the frequency of meetings and parental endurance. However, the bottom line is that parents reach a point at which they must make a decision about how to move forward, as illustrated below.

Parent: explains to class teacher that their child is experiencing difficulties with a particular aspect of learning.

Teacher: acknowledges the concern and advises they will use some additional resources to help overcome the difficulties.

Parent: checks with their child whether additional support has been implemented. Over a reasonable period of time, it becomes apparent that no additional support is being provided and the parent returns to speak to the class teacher.

Teacher: provides reasons for inaction and promises strategies will be implemented immediately.

Parent: questions their child again to ascertain whether any additional support is being provided. When strategies have still not been implemented they return to speak to the class teacher.

Basic Cycle: depending upon the patience and tolerance level of the parent, they may repeatedly visit the class teacher, in the hope of getting something done.

Escalation: parent eventually escalates the situation by taking concerns to senior staff (either headteacher at primary school or Head of Year/House, at secondary school). Senior staff listen to parent's concerns and agree to meet on a future date with the class teacher present, with a view to resolving the issue.

Group School Meeting: parent attends another meeting with senior staff and class teacher present. Strategies are agreed for resolving the difficulties.

Elevated Cycle: despite verbal support from senior staff, no action is taken to resolve matters and further meetings take place. Parent continues to speak informally to class teacher as well as attend pre-arranged meetings with senior staff present, over weeks or months.

Parent: eventually realises that their child's teacher has no intention of addressing their concerns, despite apparent support from senior staff, leaving them with the following options:

A. Change their child's school in the hope of getting better support elsewhere.
B. Become like a *'dog with a bone'*, determined to *'make them do something'*.
C. Give up and *'go away'*.

Change school (A): Some parents may choose to move their children to a new school, although others may not have this option due to family circumstances such as transport considerations, health and disability issues, work commitments or lack of a suitable alternative. This is aside from the fact that parents and their children should not be forced to change schools because of a breakdown in parent and professional relationships.

'Dog with a bone' (B): A few parents will become more persistent, in the hope of *'making'* teachers fulfil their commitments, as it becomes a matter of trust and integrity, adding to the fact that their children are being denied the additional support they need. From anecdotal experience, all that appears to happen is that parents become increasingly frustrated and angry, whilst school teachers maintain their position of inaction or may undertake a tokenistic gesture, as appeasement. How parents respond will obviously depend upon their personalities, but could range from passive aggression to more overt displays of annoyance. Parents may speak to the class teacher and/or senior staff so frequently that teachers begin to dread further contact. Relationships disintegrate and educational professionals attempt to avoid further contact with such parents wherever possible. One parent who experienced this type of scenario observed:

"I always feel like they're going to say, 'oh no, it's Mrs F again, oh no! What does she want now?' And you can see it in their eyes. 'What's it now?"
(Attwood 2007 C6: 38)

Professional integrity and trustworthiness can become all consuming. It's about professionals following through actions they have committed to, as well as demonstrating that parents have been listened to and that their concerns have been taken seriously.

Parents have sometimes sought support following repeated discussions with class teachers and/or headteachers about difficulties being experienced by their children, often associated with *'hidden'* disabilities, in particular, about how their children's behaviour at home had been influenced by events at school. A common occurrence was that their children *'kicked off'* at the end of the school day, when they were met by their parent(s), if they attended primary school, or when they returned home if older children at secondary school. When such parents have reported their concerns to their children's teachers, having been able to connect emotional and behavioural reactions to upsetting events that had occurred at school, it was not uncommon for teachers to disbelieve them when children had shown no outward signs of distress at the time of specific events occurring, as illustrated by the following statements:

"At the moment, the biggest one is school, and that he is perfect. The question mark seems to be whether he has the problem, because they don't see it and that we, as parents, don't know what we are doing. That is what we have been told."
(ibid C4: 25)

Such responses fail to acknowledge children's ability to *'hold it together'* at school, which is a common feature of children with *'hidden'* disabilities and therefore, should have been recognised by their teachers. Instead, they tended to respond with disbelief, or attribute such behaviours as being due to parenting styles or other factors emanating from the home environment. The same parent further elaborated as follows:

"When you say he is fine at school, they accept that and he has been congratulated no end on that, but then at home because of everything he has stockpiled from school, he explodes. We were told we obviously needed help to control him at home. They won't see that what they do has a knock-on effect and we had one incident at school where his shoe came off and a 'nice' child kicked it out of school boundaries into the mud. Somebody had to go and retrieve it and the teacher said to me that they were so pleased with him because he didn't react at all, but stayed calm. They got his shoe and cleaned it up – no worries. That night he took a fist to me and his sister, and when I went back into school to tell the teacher what had happened, she said to me, 'you need help with him.' You cannot win."
(ibid C10: 77-78)

When concerns are not acknowledged, parents do not receive the support and advice they need, nor are strategies implemented in school, to help address situations, even when *'triggers'* from the school environment have been identified and reported upon. Parents will persist for a period of time in an effort to influence educational professionals, hoping that they will recognise what is *'going on'* and that relevant support will be provided. At the same time, parents will experience a range of emotions – frustration, anger, despair and emotional upset about their predicament. Following meetings at their children's school, parents are likely to verbalise their feelings about the events that have taken place, either in the home environment or outside – who was there and what they said. Even when emotions are held inside, children will be aware of the turmoil experienced by their parents, following their contact with school professionals. Children may have a sense of guilt, knowing that their parents have been meeting with educational professionals because of them, and will observe their parents' attitudes towards the school and specific teachers, especially if they start avoiding contact with the school altogether, as illustrated by the following parent's statement.

"The school is the main problem. I think our son picks up on the grief between home and school, and we have to weigh it up and say, 'why are we going through this for him?' It just causes aggravation between us and it's every single day. To not communicate with the school makes it easier because there is no aggravation.

I don't think he sees school in a positive light because it causes grief, but then he's usually on a downer about school anyway, so it just impacts upon that."

(ibid C4: 26)

From supporting parents who have reported their experiences and through my own research, it has been possible to ascertain a particular sequence of events which can lead to parental disengagement. The extent to which this type of reaction occurs in children will be mediated to some extent by the type of learning difficulty or disability as well as the age of the child. Relationship breakdown will not always lead to this scenario being experienced as, inevitably, personal characteristics and temperament can affect the outcome; furthermore, if parents are aware they are on the cusp of this cycle, they can then take action to repair any emotional damage. I have termed this process the *'spiral of disaffection'* which is illustrated by the following chart:

Promises and Pitfalls of Special Education

Spiral of Disaffection

Parents' concerns receive negative or unhelpful responses.

↓

Parents become defensive.

↓

Parents persist to prove their concerns are justified.

↓

When efforts have been repeatedly unsuccessful, parents reject the school and avoid further contact.

↓

How do parents' reactions affect their children?

↓

Children become aware of the grief and tension their parents experience because of the reactions of teachers.

↓

Children feed off negative feelings about school.

↓

The school is no longer viewed in a positive light.

↓

An *'anti-school'* attitude is added to pre-existing difficulties.

↓

Negative attitudes affect children's application to learning and ultimate learning outcomes.

↓

Children unlikely to achieve potential. Disaffection impacts upon behaviour which further compounds difficulties associated with Special Educational Needs and disabilities.

From experience in training educational professionals, it appears there is little recognition of the harm that may result from poor parent and professional relationships. Parent and teacher hostilities may have significant repercussions for family life and children's achievements and the trauma experienced by families may endure for considerable time. Ultimately, there will need to be difficult decisions regarding children's education – such as whether to *'sit it out'* or change schools, neither of which are necessarily preferred solutions to the dilemma. Sometimes, headteachers pre-empt any parental response, by permanently excluding children from school, due to an escalation of undesirable behaviour or simply *'one time too many'* occurrences of poor behaviour. I hope that by including this aspect of parent and professional relationships that it will prevent some unwanted outcomes for families; that parents will be empowered when meeting with professionals whilst being aware that, with the best will in the world, there are some things they cannot change. Additionally, parents may become more attuned to their children's reactions, resulting from their own conflict with the school, and can therefore, mediate any affects this may have on their attitudes towards education. Now for the final scenario.

'Give Up and Go Away' (C): Sometimes there comes a time when even the most strong-willed and tenacious parent has to conclude they are unable to achieve their objectives and there is little point in expending further time and energy trying to do so. By then so much time may have elapsed that their children may be on the brink of entering a new phase of their education where they will have different teachers. When weighing up the effects of prolonged stress both on themselves, as parents, and the repercussions for their children, parents may decide to *'bide their time'* until events take their natural course and they no longer have to deal with unresponsive individuals. This is not an easy decision to arrive at as it means that their children do not receive appropriate support, but to retain sanity and well-being, it might be the right decision for some families.

The Effects of Derogatory Language

Derogatory terms and *'put downs'* cause considerable grief for parents and their children. Usage by professionals implicitly conveys their belief that they have *'superior'* status in relation to parents and this entitles them to form judgements and reinforce the secondary status of the other party. Whilst supporting parents, they sometimes recalled callous and hurtful comments that had been spoken by educational professionals. Invariably, such comments were delivered to children with challenging behaviour so they were viewed as *'problems'* and more often than not would be on the school's disciplinary stages – a pathway, that can lead to permanent exclusion. In addition, they would usually have a diagnosis of a *'hidden'* disability which was sometimes accompanied by speech, language and communication difficulties thereby affecting their ability to understand, follow instructions and to respond appropriately to questions. Teachers were not necessarily consistent, and would acknowledge *'hidden'* disabilities on some occasions whilst refusing to accept their existence, in relation to particular children, on other occasions.

Derogatory language and forms of expression are sometimes spoken to children who are already struggling with their disabilities and might be unable to modify their behaviour without appropriate support and medical intervention. Such children will, most likely, have a pre-existing sense of failure due to previous comparison between them and their peers, and as a consequence will be wrestling with low self-esteem which can be exacerbated through inappropriate forms of communication *(Beck 1976; Ellis 1962 cited in Patterson 1986; Purkey 1970: 17)*. Such comments can become a *'self-fulfilling prophecy'* with behaviour and attitudes conforming to what had been spoken.

An individual's self-concept is influenced by how other people have treated them, especially during their formative years. In simplistic terms, individuals may have high self-esteem, as demonstrated by their confidence and self-assurance, due to having received encouragement and praise about their abilities and/or personalities, whilst others may have low self-esteem, due to having received excessive criticism, discipline or rejection; added to this is the impact of any comparisons they make between themselves and their peers *(Purkey 1970: 2)*. Teachers can be viewed as *'significant others'* and be highly regarded by pupils, so that any statements they make are then accepted as *'truth'*, ultimately affecting children's achievements and how they perceive themselves and their capabilities *(Deutsch 1963 cited in Purkey 1970: 40)*. Educational professionals frequently attribute any difficulties that children experience as being due to events and influences from the home environment *(Roffey 2002: 9)*, without acknowledging their own influence on children's development and well-being, which may be of a positive or negative nature *(Crozier 2005: 51)*. Disparaging words spoken to children can cause irreparable harm to their self-concept *(Purkey 1970:14)* with repercussions for educational achievement as well as mental health.

Even parents, when meeting with professionals, may be affected by hearing derogatory terms used about their children. Such terms are absolutely *'stinging'* for parents and may result in parents' own loss of confidence, due to how professionals regard their children. Ultimately, parents may become reluctant to meet with the same professionals again as illustrated by the following statement:

"What is spoken can add to the grief that is already being experienced. I can still remember specific events. Professionals have a lot of power in what they say about your child. They need to be responsible about how they give information."
   (Attwood 2007 Appendix G6: 40-41)

Accidental Faux Pas

Having now alluded to harsh words that may be deliberately spoken, it is time to consider the effects of insensitive words which may be carelessly spoken or written down. Being spoken about as a *'deficit'*, within the context of the Medical Model of disability, can be harmful to children where reference is made to everything they can't do or where their behaviour does not conform to what are considered normal standards. Multi-agency meetings are frequently the source of such comments, where a number of professionals of different disciplines, meet with the parent(s) sometimes with their children in attendance, for at least part of the time. Meetings can be intimidating, irrespective of parental background and professional experience, and parents may be reluctant to speak out against the negative tone of such meetings, as the following statements demonstrate:

"I have seen parents wincing when some professionals talk about kids in a derogatory kind of way without meaning to; it's a patronising way really."
Educational Psychologist
   (ibid E1: 9)

"I have been to quite a few meetings that were derogatory from the point of view that the whole tone of the conversation is about what the child cannot do, the child cannot do this, this, this and this, without talking about what the child can do. I think some professionals can be very pessimistic about future outcomes. I think professionals need to be realistic but I think they can be so

negative (sometimes) that the parents at the end of the meeting probably feel there is no hope at all for their child."
Local Authority Educational Professional
(ibid E2: 17)

"I might be in a meeting with a teacher or another professional and they might be saying something about their child. I have been in meetings where a parent has taken offence about what the teacher has said and has got quite angry and shouted."
Educational Psychologist
(ibid E2: 15)

Professionals meeting with parents and their children should have regard to the circumstances of the meeting and be mindful that they have the power to influence events outside the *'consulting arena'*. Sensitivity is an essential characteristic when meeting with parents and their children and professionals should develop an awareness of how their words and actions may either display partnership and encourage families, or instead cause emotional turmoil to the extent that pre-existing difficulties are exacerbated as the following quotations illustrate:

"He always gets very nervous about meetings in advance. He doesn't like going to them at all. He always believes it's a criticism of him and we have had to work very hard at that."
Parent
(ibid C1: 7)

"A lot of negative stuff was said in front of him, and he was feeling bad enough about himself as it was, about everything and about not fitting in. So, I think that was all very detrimental actually…"
Parent
(ibid C2: 15)

Although this chapter is primarily about interpersonal relationships, it's also worth noting the damaging effects of written communication, as illustrated by a parent who received paediatric correspondence about her son.

"Doctors and other professionals were not always very sensitive. I remember once that I received a letter from a doctor and it spoke in detail about our son's facial features – he looks like me actually, but they spoke quite

brutally about his facial features, and I remember feeling quite angry and thinking that nobody else would comment and certainly not in writing about how another child would look, and I remember feeling, 'how dare they talk about my son like that'."
   Parent
   (ibid C8: 52)

Parents of children with Special Educational Needs may feel *'under attack'* from all directions and experience many indignities because of their children's difficulties. Chapter 8 through *'structured'* case studies, will further demonstrate the *'battles'* that parents experience in having their *'voices heard'* and their children's difficulties recognised and addressed.

Chapter Summary

The reality of *'working in partnership'* is that personalities tend to predominate and individuals do not always see eye-to-eye, egos as well as lack of confidence will affect people's reactions; one party may attempt to dominate the other (either deliberately or unintentionally), whilst the other may easily take offence or become defensive in response to what they hear. Teachers and parents may be territorial, believing the other party has *'crossed a line'* into areas that are not of their concern. Each party will defend their position whilst a lack of empathy may prevent them from understanding each other's perspective. This chapter has attempted to present a realistic picture on how parent and professional relationships can deteriorate to breaking point, with an explanation of some of the primary reasons that contribute to relationship breakdown.

We are dealing with the idiosyncrasies of human nature, with individuals having innumerable characteristics, behaviours and personal agendas that can impact upon how they conduct relationships with others; not forgetting, of course, that individuals are additionally influenced by events from their past which can influence current perspectives in any situation (see Chapter 6). Having *'partnership'* imbued into policy does not guarantee a lack of conflict. Sharing the same (overall) goal does not necessarily mean that parties will agree on how to achieve it. Even goals may be contentious – with parties working together to improve children's educational outcomes, but each having different expectations with respect to what *'improvement'* looks like; they have different ideas about standards to be achieved (or what is possible to achieve) and it may apply to different aspects of the curriculum. There will always be opportunities for parents and professionals to operate in parallel rather than in *'partnership'*.

This chapter will, hopefully, have addressed some of the pitfalls of parents and professionals *'working in partnership'*, but inevitably, there will be many other situations and examples which have not been addressed. It is hoped that parents who have already experienced some upsetting events, will become empowered in their engagement with professionals, whilst those just embarking on this journey, will have a realistic perspective of what they might face and will be prepared with their armour on! It is hoped that professionals reading this will have acquired greater insight into the parental perspective, which can beneficially impact upon their professional practice in a way that will enable their relationships with parents and children to flourish.

Finally, along the journey, parents will meet many exceptional professionals, those who genuinely respect and value working with families, always willing to *'go the extra mile'* because they desire to give their best (within limited resources), but starting the journey with supportive professionals does not necessarily mean that it will continue; conversely, a number of negative and stressful experiences can be followed by meeting someone extraordinary, whose skills, wisdom and commitment are just what parents need at that time.

Chapter 8
Parents' and Children's Experiences

Introduction

Case studies included in this chapter will help illustrate some of the stress and turmoil that is experienced by parents in their quest to obtain accurate diagnoses and appropriate educational provision for their children whilst managing many (sometimes daily) interactions with professionals that can add to pre-existing tensions in daily living. From experience in supporting parents, substantiated by my own research, factors that exacerbate stress, when parents interact with professionals, are insensitive communication, judgemental attitudes and professional prevarication. It's not uncommon for parents of children with Special Educational Needs to find themselves in a *'battle'* with professionals – an experience which has been acknowledged in both the *Lamb Inquiry (DCSF 2009)* and the Coalition Government's *Green Paper, Support and aspiration: A new approach to special educational needs and disability (DfE 2011)*. Too frequently parents find themselves having to *'fight their corner'* with respect to school provision and the need to *'prove'* their children's difficulties at every turn. From my experience, schools are often reluctant to implement *reasonable adjustments* or access additional resources for children with *'hidden'* disabilities without a paediatric diagnosis, corroborating earlier research by *Pinkus (2005: 186-187)*. Even with an unequivocal diagnosis, there is a requirement to *'prove'* to what extent children's learning difficulties or disabilities impair their ability to access the curriculum, with such proof being necessary to escalate educational or medical intervention. *'Proving the case'* is likely to become even more critical when children only receive additional support if they meet stringent eligibility criteria. With signs indicating that thresholds are being raised before children become eligible to receive individualised Additional SEN support or obtain Education, Health and Care Plans, there is a risk of only the most significant and obvious needs being addressed.

Scarcity of resources could result in increased parental tenacity in their quest to obtain additional support for their children. Parents might perceive professionals as uncaring and lacking in compassion, when they have no option but to apply strict eligibility criteria in relation to making additional resources available. Unfortunately, under the current economic climate, despite having sensitivity and empathy towards others' situations, professionals may have little room to manoeuvre when they respond to individual requests and needs. Whilst possessing *'a true heart'* for helping others, many professionals experience constraints in how they must respond to requests, sometimes resulting in tough (possibly reluctant) decisions being made that involve saying *'no'* to parents and young people.

'Professionals', as human beings, encompass the full spectrum of characteristics and behaviours and are as fallible as anyone else. One major difference is that for people who hold professional roles, the expectations from those that use their services are often higher than they would be for people not holding such positions. As a consequence, parents may have high regard for the professionals that support them and their families but experience significant disappointment and anguish when such expectations are not lived up to, however caused.

Confidentiality and Research Ethics

Case study information was obtained through one-to-one interviews which were recorded and subsequently transcribed verbatim. Parents responded to open-ended questions by providing as much information as they considered appropriate. All information was obtained in accordance with research ethics, applicable at that time[3] and in compliance with the eight Principles of the *Data Protection Act (1998)*. This meant that all data was obtained for research purposes and that no other information in my possession, through my professional role, was used or referred to. Parents consented (in writing) to their stories subsequently being published, in any format. To safeguard anonymity, pseudonyms have been used for parents and children (where appropriate) whilst professionals are only alluded to in respect of their professional role. Case studies are historical but are representative of the struggles still experienced by families. The *'stories'* are typical of those reported to Parent Partnership Service representatives around the country and are not specific to any local area.

Diagnoses

School provision is frequently dependent upon having a medical diagnosis, and not only that, but the correct diagnosis. As some of these

---

[3] British Educational Research Association (2004) and Bath Spa University (2002)

case studies will reveal, the diagnosis may change over time, as children grow and develop, or the presenting picture may be so complex, that it takes a number of health and educational professionals considerable time, to ascertain the true nature of the difficulties being experienced by the child.

Format of Case Studies

Each case study starts with an introduction which provides some background information in order to contextualise the situation. Side headings have been used to help distinguish particular events or parental concerns. Statements have been edited, where necessary, to improve clarity of expression and to retain anonymity. End notes inform readers of the position of parents and their children when research was completed.

Case Study 1: Mrs B

This case study illustrates some of the difficulties experienced in obtaining a diagnosis for a child with an *'invisible'* disability, both in terms of timeliness and accuracy with respect to having all aspects of the disability (or multiple disabilities) recognised, recorded and provided for. Mrs B was initially unable to persuade educational professionals to acknowledge her concerns and take appropriate action; not only with regards to an application for Statutory Assessment but with on-going support as well. This study illustrates the *'blame culture'* that is endemic within the educational arena, when parents are blamed for their children's undesirable behavioural characteristics. Furthermore, the study highlights that once a Statement of Special Educational Needs has been issued, there is no guarantee that educational provision will be consistent between settings and that needs are always addressed, in compliance with the Statement. Failure to deliver services may be attributed to insufficient funding which limits the extent to which specialist services, such as speech and language therapy, may be purchased whilst at other times, for example, lack of provision could be due to not recognising the severity of children's difficulties or being unwilling to implement the right amount and type of support.

This case study highlights the dilemma of where to send a bright child or young person with a significant disability. Local authorities are often, understandably, reluctant to send bright children to a special school, even when it's the most appropriate environment for supporting their disability or current emotional state. Parents, on the other hand, may prioritise their child's emotional well-being, when deciding upon the suitability of a school – often preferring an environment perceived to be calm, secure and having the professional expertise to address manifestations of their child's disability. In contrast, educational professionals tend to assess school appropriateness based on cognitive (ie intellectual) ability. So even when a Statement of Special Educational Needs exists, and technically, parents may *'choose'* their child's school, they must sometimes *'prove'* why their child should attend a special school (usually by way of medical evidence), although with admission procedures evolving for Academies and Free Schools, this might present a different landscape in the future. Mrs B had moved around different parts of the country so not all experiences were in the same area.

Nursery School: *"When Barry went to nursery school they didn't know what to do with him; there were complaints from the staff that he had been pushing the other children and the other parents would look at me a bit darkly, although nothing was said to me directly. So there were situations when I would feel uncomfortable, even though things were never said directly to my face. You kind of live with it and feel that it is around you all the time because you can't join in the same way, you can't sit around with parents when you have a child that's kind of running around like a lunatic. And we did have to stop going to playgroups and stuff like that because he would just go mad, pushing other children over and wouldn't listen to anything I said. I'd go to the park and he'd take all his clothes off and run around and throw himself in the pond. Some parents would go, 'How do you cope?' I was just very careful where we went. Nobody suggested to me that I should take him to see a doctor and get him assessed; it just seemed like he was really out of control and I just felt that I was inadequate at dealing with that. It was only when I had my second child that I actually realised I wasn't a bad parent; that it had nothing to do with my parenting actually. It transpired he had much more complicated problems."*

First Primary School: *"When Barry was four he went to the local infants' school and I said to them that I thought he had some problems and they put him on an Individual Education Plan (IEP) and basically nothing (more) was done. I subsequently found out that the Special Educational Needs Co-ordinator (SENCO) had told the headteacher he needed a Statement but she completely ignored it. He really struggled at infants and I used to dread going to pick him up because I knew there would always have been a problem* during the day. The staff would be negative about the things Barry had done and the way they dealt with him was to sit him at his own little desk and he would spend time drawing. It solved the problem for them, but didn't help him integrate. It was probably the worst thing they could have done, but it was my lack of knowledge and experience. But now I know that if things are in place for him, he will adhere to behaviour and get himself together, but I didn't know enough in those days. I think he just got really far behind with all the basic learning so we thought he had learning difficulties."

Second Primary School: *"It felt like a struggle for years until we moved to another area and he went to a new primary school. Within the first weeks, they said he needed a Statement (of Special Educational Needs) and they rushed it through to get it sorted out quickly. He was assessed by an educational psychologist and he got a Statement within six months. That was a turning point really and they were very good at providing the right support for him so those were calm years. So, between the ages of 7-11 years old, I felt he was in the right caring environment of a small school, with very supportive staff. There was a bit more coming through for me in the way of information, but I can't say it was through many professionals.*

We addressed his diet, went to see the doctor and attended the Child and Family Therapy Unit, where they made some suggestions. But you know, I would really have liked a diagnosis. I would have liked things to have been much clearer from the outset and then I would have felt more empowered to have gone to professionals and say, 'you know, this is what we need for our child'."

First Secondary School: *"And then we had the maelstrom of secondary school which was a nightmare for probably the best part of eighteen months. Barry was allocated someone to look after him but she broke her arm and when he went in they had nobody there to support him. I phoned the school and asked 'what's going on?' and they told me that he didn't have a support assistant, so this child who'd had a support assistant for four years, went into secondary education without any support. So, in a way, the writing was on the wall, right from the start. They turned round and said to me, 'we think he's got very complex special needs; we don't think we can deal with him' so it just spiralled downwards. It was the most disastrous thing; he felt he had failed; that he was worthless and useless and cut his arm – we had terrible things to deal with – that was in the first term.*

I contacted the Education Authority and Barry was re-assessed. It was all going horribly wrong. He'd been excluded (from school) and then got excluded again for a week. It was a whole catalogue (of events) because the initial support wasn't there. Everything went downhill very quickly. He'd get the bus to school, but that didn't work out as he would get into arguments on the bus, so I ended up having to drive him to school every day – the whole thing was such a mess, and it got worse.

It's been like living in a time bomb really, but we coped because I have loads of stamina and I have always been very healthy - I'm constitutionally strong. Meetings at school were just awful. I used to come out really disappointed and wanted to cry and felt that people were really pointing the finger at me - that I wasn't an adequate parent. I felt I was being spoken down to, that nobody was listening to me, that nobody had any respect and that people were patronising ... this whole thing about complex Special Needs was quite a shock to me. I had meetings constantly about my son - they just thought he was some sort of delinquent and so he was treated like he was just trouble and I kept saying to them that 'he had been fine for four years at primary school, he had the right level of support and he is having all these problems because the support isn't in place for him'. But still nobody was actually listening to what I was saying."

Second Secondary School: *"Then we transferred him to another school and it got even worse. They said they would be able to support him but when he got there, after about a week, they said, 'we can't support him actually, we haven't got the kind of support staff in place that can support him.' So we were completely stuck.*

I wasn't getting anywhere basically and he was constantly being excluded from secondary school. It has certainly been complicated trying to get his problems acknowledged - I was just banging my head against a brick wall – it was very frustrating. Then I got a private diagnosis and I actually felt that people were taking me seriously and they had to sit up and take notice."

Special School: *"Barry went to special school where there are two members of staff supporting three children. So I feel that everything pretty much fell down on the support issue and that's when it all spiralled downwards for us actually. It has been a whole different thing with him going to special school and they have tried to support him. He is pretty bright and they knew he wasn't in the right place, but there was nowhere else for him to go. So the whole thing has turned around really. Most people have been great, and we've had all different assessments of him and everybody has been very good about* *giving me information and I feel that when I go to meetings, my voice is being heard. I now feel fine because I do feel that I have got a lot of back-up and now I'm much more informed.*

Barry's Reactions to Meetings: *"He would feel terrible. He would just be crying, he would be really upset and not understand why things were going so wrong for him and those were very difficult times actually. A lot of negative stuff was said in front of him and he was feeling bad enough as it was - about everything and about not fitting in. So I think that was all very detrimental actually, but it's not like that anymore so a lot of that is in the past really."*

Exhaustion: *"It has been very exhausting. It's been very hard having a child with problems because I found that I had no experience (of the system) and didn't know where to start. He had problems in getting a clear diagnosis when he was young and it has been a learning curve really, so the whole thing has been quite a big thing in our life because my other child is fine, so he has had quite an easy, normal kind of childhood. But with Barry, it has been fairly complicated from the time that we realised he had problems – probably from when he was a toddler and it became more apparent. And it is all the stuff that goes with it – you feel like you are not being a good parent; you can't understand why this child is the way that he is.*

I was very much on my own, and there was nobody backing me up and I was at a loss as to where to start with this child who was very hyperactive – who wouldn't sit down for a meal. He wouldn't sit down and eat properly at the table until he was probably about 7 years old, so I basically fed him on the run for years; I literally put food in his mouth as he was running around. Then when we moved and he went to the infant school they didn't know what to do with him either.

It has been very hard having a child that doesn't fit in, having a child that finds it really hard to make friends because you, as a parent, want everything to be okay for your child and you want to give them the best support, the most loving environment, but if they are just kicking against everything all the time, where do you go? When he was younger, he could be physically quite aggressive and he didn't seem to have any boundaries. I used to take him to places so he could be outdoors and completely wear himself out but we had to be really careful where we went. Small environments were not good at all – we used to go to soft play places and then he just got into trouble because he couldn't cope in an environment with lots of noise and activity; he used to spin out of control so we were very restricted with regards to where we could go.

I knew he was hyperactive and found out as much information as I could around any kind of hyperactive condition that would give me more information really. He already had an organic and whole food diet and I made sure that he had no additives or anything like that – no chemicals. So I eradicated anything that might set him off and make him more hyper.

He didn't understand danger at all, so there were always potentials for danger out there. When he was little especially, you had to have eyes in the back of your head, even walking down the street was hazardous because he would just run off. We have lost him so many times in crowds, when I thought I'd never see him again. To have all these kind of scares because he never had any understanding of danger or anything. I would try to explain to him afterwards what he had done, but he just couldn't take it onboard – he had no comprehension of that. I used to have nightmares and constantly wake up in the middle of the night, with this image of him being run over. You are just living with stress a lot of the time when you are living with a child like that because they are very, very impulsive – but far less so now he is older."

Family Life: *"My husband wasn't around very much (because of his job), but when he was around he just couldn't cope, I think he found it really hard. He tried to discipline Barry when he was little, but because it didn't work, he got very frustrated. I knew that he was really good if he went outside; if he climbed trees and did lots of active stuff then that would be really beneficial to him, so I would try and make sure that we incorporated that into the day. I had a different relationship with our son. I could see his potential – like how artistic he is, even from being tiny. I tried to look at the positives but my husband found that quite hard; he found the whole thing of having a child with Special Educational Needs very tough and he didn't come home filled with joy. He got quite depressed about it.*

When I separated from my husband, our youngest son wanted us to stay together, but Barry just seemed to accept it. I think that in many ways, he is quite accepting of a lot of things because of his condition – he seems to be able to take lots of things in his stride. Children with Asperger's seem able to cope because they have an internal world and it is like they are really driven by their obsessiveness so a lot of other emotional stuff doesn't quite touch them in the same way."

The Diagnosis – Part 1: *(Barry was about 7 when)* *"the hospital said it was definitely ADHD (Attention Deficit Hyperactive Disorder), so all the strategies were around his hyperactivity rather than his obsessive stuff – we* didn't know there were other problems as well. About eighteen months ago, we had a private educational psychologist's assessment as we needed a proper diagnosis." (Barry was about 12-13 years old).

The Diagnosis – Part 2: "*When we got the final diagnosis, I was just relieved really, because lots of people had said to me 'he is only ADHD, he doesn't have Asperger's', but I kind of knew enough about Asperger's to know that he had quite a lot of Asperger type stuff going on, and some people had said to me that he was quite destructive and there was a lot of (other) behavioural stuff. Because I live with him, I had an instinct that some of the stuff he was doing, he wasn't that aware of, he really couldn't help himself – he was very impulsive and also obsessive and I was proved right because once a diagnosis came through it was much more combined – it was Asperger/ADHD/other related literal learning problems and things like that; and not understanding language. It was a relief to finally know that all the stuff I had been privately thinking actually came through in the diagnosis, so I felt that I had been right all along.*"

Mrs B's Additional Comments: "*There were little pockets of time when I felt that professionals were pretty informative and helpful, but we still had the problem when he left. They thought he would be fine at secondary school but, of course, he wasn't. Nobody pre-empted the fact that he would have problems at secondary school and how complicated those problems might be. So I've had very mixed experiences with professionals.*

It's absolutely crucial to get an early diagnosis sorted out; it's crucial to have really good liaison between primary and secondary school. A lot of children (with Asperger's Syndrome) need full-time support when they have that transition period, but it is really underestimated how traumatic it is for children who have been used to that small calm and nurturing environment. Now I think it is so great that he is much calmer because the memory of all those years running after him and trying to think of places to go where he would be safe was quite a strain.

Looking to the future, I hope that Barry will do his GCSE's successfully, and with the right type of support, he will go onto 'A' levels and then into Further Education. As to whether he could look after himself, I really don't know; he will probably have to keep on having support. It's really good for him to focus on his obsessions because when they are not carried through, he gets very frustrated, but if he can see a solution to the obsession, then he is much happier.

I'm hoping he will be successful with his creativity because he is very talented, I think, but he will need the right sort of support to go through sixth form and he will have to be at a school where they are very understanding about his quirky ways. He is very chaotic at the moment and very untidy and that is something we will have to address as he gets older; he just has no concept of putting anything away.

At 14 years old, Barry is now becoming more independent and school are trying to find the balance by giving him independence but making sure that he is actually supervised. In his own eyes, he is more normal now and thinks that he can cope with many more situations compared with when he was younger; he is much happier at school, so he doesn't feel that he needs this extra support, but if it wasn't there, things could go downhill really quickly, and I am really aware of that.

It needs to be acknowledged that you know your own child, you live with them day-in, day-out and suddenly you have no voice, no say. Parents should be given the opportunity to be involved in the whole process and not feel sidelined and not made to feel that they haven't got anything to contribute. I was busting a gut to go to the schools and get involved and tried to get the right support in place, but nobody wanted to know. When your child needs a certain level of support and that is not being provided and everything is going downhill and you have to deal with the repercussions of that at home, it's just horrible and everybody is stressed and it need not be like that. You can have support, but it's not necessarily the right kind of support because the support Barry was given at his first secondary school was not the right support and that made things much worse. If you haven't got the right kind of support in place it can really exacerbate situations."

End Note: When Mrs B separated from her husband, she brought both sons up alone although they spent weekends and holidays with their father. The study indicates that around the time of adolescence some difficulties fall away although these are replaced by new challenges, which involve longer-term planning for post education and into adulthood. Mrs B felt more positive about the future, with respect to Barry's potential achievements and felt she would soon be able to return to work.

(Attwood 2007 Appendices C2: 9-15, C9:61-69)

Case Study 2: Mrs G

This case study illustrates the trauma which can be experienced by a parent when they hear, for the first time, that their child has a severe disability with distress being further compounded by the manner and circumstances in which the diagnosis was conveyed. Mrs G's story illuminates some of the struggles experienced over a fifteen year period in having her daughter's needs addressed.

Initial Concerns: *"... at the three month check, the GP noticed the spacing between her eyes and referred her to an opthalmologist who diagnosed a pseudo-squint. I was asked if our daughter could attend a paediatric doctor's examination, which I agreed to. There was no indication there could be something seriously wrong."*

The Diagnosis: *"The consultant viewed all the cases before returning with the trainee doctors. In a room full of people, I was given the diagnosis, advised that she might be deaf and informed that the baby I was expecting might also be deaf. My world fell apart. I fell apart – literally."*

Professional Sensitivity: *"There were no facilities. I was dumped in somebody's office at the hospital, literally bawling my eyes out."*

Audiology Tests: *"She was immediately referred to an audiologist who confirmed that she was profoundly deaf."*

Professional Support: *"They were all into practical things such as hearing aids and what-have-you. Professionals need to realise that they are talking about a child – not a case study, not a number - it's somebody's whole life. I still get uptight because people don't acknowledge that she is a person and that she is my daughter. They should try putting themselves on the other side of the table, just for once, and think, 'how would I cope if somebody was telling me that about my child'.*

There is no time to talk. The issue that makes her a Special Educational Needs child is that she is profoundly deaf, but I wanted to know more and it took a very long time and mostly my time to find out about the condition and what it meant. I remember us mentioning cochlear implants soon after her diagnosis, but that was too early and it all had to come later. She has since had a cochlear implant, and that was something else we had to fight for, but you just do, don't you? You get used to it. I suppose, they did their job well in terms of dealing with the diagnosis, but they don't take into account the other needs."

The Statement: *"It's very hard at the beginning. At the first Statement meeting, there was my husband and I and it felt like about twelve others. Our daughter was about 4 and it was about where she was going to go to school – that was very daunting. They are better now because a lot of the same people come every year, but they still get me in a stew, and I'm a professional person – I'm used to coping in meetings with other professional people. Somebody with less confidence would just not stand a chance.*

We argue constantly (with professionals). We had a meeting a couple of weeks ago about our daughter's lack of speech therapy. I don't care that the PCT (Primary Care Trust) are saying the post can't be funded, it's in our daughter's Statement, and somebody should be doing something. Then they pass you round – you go from the school to the local authority to the Speech and Language Therapy service and back again, you know, and I'm going, 'stop it!' Somebody take responsibility for this problem!"

Professional Pessimism: *"We fight tooth and nail, and I am sure that everybody must get absolutely sick of us, but we have people telling us constantly, 'you know your child best' and then when we want something different, they always think that they are right. In the early years, they said, 'everything was going to be difficult and a struggle and all the rest of it' and we kept arguing that she was an intelligent child. Just because she is deaf, she couldn't demonstrate in the traditional testing way, and it has taken us an awful long time. Now most of them agree that she is a bright little girl."*

Additional Comments: *"You do get the feeling that they have got in their minds what suits them best and if you don't go along with it, then you are a pain, and you have to be prepared to be a pain to get what you want."*
(ibid C7: 44-51).

End Note: When Mrs G's second child was born, audiology tests confirmed his hearing was normal. At the time of being interviewed, her daughter was doing well at school.

Case Study 3: Mrs E

Mr and Mrs E suspected there was something wrong early on; they had two older children and were aware that, developmentally, their third daughter was distinctly different to her siblings. This case study demonstrates how parents' concerns may be dismissed over a considerable period of time, which in this case spanned two years until

Mr and Mrs E took the initiative in commissioning a private assessment. On this occasion, the parents became *'lead partners'* in relation to their daughter's educational provision. As well as obtaining a diagnosis for their daughter, they provided teaching staff with reading materials on dyspraxia so they could implement the most appropriate strategies for their daughter, whilst potentially benefitting other children.

Raising Concerns: *"We had our suspicions (there was something wrong) when she went to playgroup. They asked us whether they could involve an outside agency to see her, but actually that never happened. When she was in reception class at primary school, we voiced our concerns at the first Parents' Evening – it was sound work, concentration and other things. From an academic point of view things weren't really clicking into place, so we did discuss our concerns with the school at that point. We kept speaking to the school and nothing was done. Eventually we got to Year 1 – nothing was done. We seemed to be going backwards and forth. The school was saying she was just making slow progress, but there was progress, and perhaps naively, we feel now, we went along with that until she went into Year 2. I telephoned the local authority and voiced our concerns and said we wanted an assessment of some sort because we really weren't happy with the way things were progressing at school. And that is how we ended up getting an Individual Education Plan in place.*

The educational psychologist went into school, when we asked for it to be done, and identified quite a few things that needed working on. This was followed by a meeting with the school SENCO (Special Educational Needs Co-ordinator) - we went through the Individual Education Plans for a little while, but were still concerned."

Outside Agencies: *"We then involved other outside agencies and help from a Special Needs Teacher who does work with our daughter at home; she confirmed our suspicions so we asked our GP for a referral to a neurologist. We feel we could have had more information. Our daughter was showing signs of developmental co-ordination disorder and I think we could have been guided a few months earlier, even if it was said, 'look she is exhibiting signs of DCD, dyspraxia or whatever and you could go to your GP and ask for a referral to take this further', but we weren't given that advice. We were very much in the dark and there were no pointers for us and we had to do research on the internet. Then the Special Needs teacher said to us, 'have you thought about* dyspraxia, because she seems to be exhibiting a lot of the characteristics of it?' Nobody else had suggested this to us and you just think, 'we wasted two years and I don't think she really learnt anything new and we could have had a lot of these things in place by now'. Instead we have got to the situation now where we are trying for a Statement and she is due to go to junior school soon – time isn't on our side now. We feel very let down."

Diagnosis: *"We only saw the neurologist last week, and he has basically confirmed our suspicions. We had a private report done ourselves where the occupational therapist tested everything and she confirmed dyspraxia too. We had to do all of that off our own back. I do feel that the school are trying to implement things now to help us, but we feel that we are all the time saying, 'can you do this, can you do that?' especially now we need as much evidence as possible (for Statutory Assessment). But we do feel let down by the system. We feel it has failed her. I know that a lot of children with dyspraxia don't get picked up until later on, but on the other hand because she has so many characteristics, we wonder how it slipped through the net. Now the school advise us that 'she doesn't sit still and doesn't concentrate and you think, 'well surely alarm bells should have been ringing a long time ago'."*

Professional Approach: *"The occupational therapist is very positive with lots of advice and is very good. She is actually going to go into school for us to give the teachers and assistants a talk on things that they can do with our daughter to help her through the day. But we have had to initiate everything ourselves."*

Working in partnership: *"Since we have had the diagnosis and have given the school the report, we have had quite a few long chats and they are trying to put things in place that we have asked them to do. Some of it is simple strategies that we use at home with her, that we have asked them to try, which at the end of the day, will make their job easier if they know how to get the most out of her. I wouldn't have said that was the case in the first two years and I'm not sure that it would have been the case if we hadn't been as forthcoming as we have been. We have provided them with all information about the condition and have loaned them books, etc. I think the school thinks we are not going to give up on this so they might as well do as we ask; there are quite a few things we have initiated that I don't think they necessarily would have. I think they know we will push to get our daughter all the help she really needs, whereas we did feel fobbed off at first. Now they have sent two teachers on a study morning about the condition and things like that, so it is positive.*

We haven't had any contact with physiotherapists and other people like that – it's all been quite quick with just the educational psychologist, the occupational therapist, neurologist and the school. The school haven't actually come forward and asked us to try and arrange something; I think it's because we have been very proactive and that is why they are doing things."

Keeping school informed: *"We have always been very open with them; we have told them she has extra lessons at home and what she is doing, we told them when we asked for a referral and when we had spoken to the local authority – we haven't hidden anything. There has never been any going behind their backs and not keeping them informed because we have given them a copy of the occupational therapy report and have been very open and I think that is the only way for them to support us and for us to support them really."*

End Note: Parents and teachers were continuing to work well.
 (ibid C5: 28-33)

Case Study 4: Mrs H

Mrs H was married, with two sons, one of whom was born with a number of disabilities and health concerns which resulted in regular medical appointments. Over the years, the family had lived in different parts of the country.

Initial Concerns: *"When our son was about two years old, he had speech and language difficulties and wasn't able to form words. He was ill as a baby – he had holes in his heart and he got pneumonia and was in hospital for about three months and then he was discharged. I called the health visitor who made a referral to the speech and language therapist."*

The Diagnosis Part 1: *"That was quite a long story because to begin with they thought he had speech and language problems but then they thought he had some physical differences and perhaps even cerebral palsy. Professionals were not always very sensitive to what they said. I remember the first time when they said they thought there was some long-term difficulties or Special Needs; I was quite devastated and phoned friends to come round. I feel quite emotional now (just remembering it) because it is a big thing – it's a huge thing when you are told that your child has got differences and difficulties that are going to be on-going. Of course, we love him dearly, but it just means that your course of life is different. It was an emotional time."*

The Journey of Diagnosis: *"At one stage, he was under nine different consultants for different parts of his body, and it was a relief when he was 10 years old, to be assigned a paediatrician who would actually oversee all of it and pull it together. From the age of 3 to 10, we were passed from pillar to post – somebody to look at his head, somebody to look at his legs, somebody to look at different parts of his body and we were spending an awful lot of time going to different professionals, who all considered different parts of his body separately."*

The Diagnosis Part 2: *"The diagnosis was quite complicated in that it wasn't just one diagnosis; it was almost the start of a journey and that nobody really knew what the issues were, and in fact, our son wasn't diagnosed with Asperger's until he was 11 years old, following my request for a Statutory Assessment. There have been different diagnoses along the way and different thoughts because the professionals themselves hadn't been clear about the diagnosis."*

Attributing Blame: *"Doctors looked to me to have caused the problem. I remember once we went to somebody and they accused me of talking to him too much whilst somebody else claimed it was because I tried to explain things to him before they happen. I can see now, that actually, I knew he was much happier and calmer when we did explain things before they happened, and, if in fact, he's had Asperger's for many years, that actually would explain that, but it was more of a gut feeling. I remember thinking 'they are all looking for a reason and they are actually looking to me to have created the reason', and I felt blamed for the situation."*

Different Professional Approaches: *"We have a wonderful paediatrician, who although he can't do any more for our son, is always on call and he gives real dignity to myself, my family and our son; he really listens. The speech and language therapist is also wonderful. Some professionals have been great, particularly when they have been really interested in our son and been really nice to him – that's made an awful lot of difference, but there have been times when they have simply 'been professional' and looking at him as a case, rather than an individual. We have been in lots of hospitals and all types of provision, and I think the best ones have been when people have been quite humorous and funny and human. The worst ones have been when people may be good at their academic side and their professional role, but they are almost like dealing with a case or piece of paper, rather than a human being. Schools' staff have been defensive from the outset."*

Professional Time: *"Professionals are clearly under a lot of pressure and stress, which I am well aware of, but actually they don't always show you that for actually this twenty minutes, or whatever, this is actually who I am dealing with and this is the most important thing at this time. I think however busy they are at the time of the appointment, they should make that individual be the most important person at that time, then obviously go onto the next person and do the same for them. There should be real respect and looking for good things. I think the problem with a diagnosis is that people are always looking at the things they cannot do and the things they find difficult and that actually is quite disconcerting and depressing. I know why they do it, but I do think they should start with what the child can do and make them feel that they are really important at that time."*

Professional Sensitivity: *"We went to a Speech and Language Assessment Unit and the speech therapist was playing with our son. He had been given some not very good toys – really not very nice toys to play with; they were not very attractive and they included a fence and some animals and he made a crown out of the fence. The speech therapist advised the doctor that he hadn't done anything imaginative with any of the resources, and I thought that was quite imaginative – it might be imaginative in an unusual or bizarre sort of way, but it was certainly imaginative. And I remember they made comments to each other about it. I know that I have been left feeling very small and very powerless as people discuss my son.*

I remember going to a hospital appointment and we had to go and wait a huge amount of time for a scan and I had a lump in the pit of my stomach and was wondering what we were going to find. The waiting room was horrible and we had to wait a long time and nobody kept us informed about how long we would have to wait. And then they took my son in as a piece of anatomy that they were looking at. Those health professionals did not really take into account what a huge thing this was for a parent – he was a little boy and didn't really understand. But they were doing the scan and they were talking about it and discussing it between themselves, but it was a huge thing. The findings could have been really very significant and I don't think they had taken on board how significant that was (for a parent) and I remember that."

Addressing Negativity: *"I do think he knows when people have been nice to him and he goes out with his head held high, whereas if people have talked about him, he feels that he has missed out on something and does not like people talking about him in his presence. We emphasise things that are* *good and things that aren't we just say, 'well that wasn't very nice' and try to link a hospital, medical or learning appointment with something like going for a coffee ..."*

Additional Comments: *"Whatever a professional's personal or time pressures are, that all the people they are seeing are individuals and they do matter and it's really important that they go out feeling as good about themselves as they can."*

End Note: Many of the events recalled here had taken place years earlier. Such was their impact that whilst recalling her *'story'*, Mrs H re-lived emotions that she had thought were long buried. At the time of interview, the family were experiencing a period of calm.
(ibid C8: 52-57)

Case Study 5: Mrs W

This is separate (unpublished) research reviewing the effectiveness of transition arrangements since the Labour Government required local authorities to produce Transition Protocols, under the Aiming High for Disabled Children Transition Programme *(DCSF 2008)*. The study illustrates that transition planning can be time consuming and sometimes repetitive. It further demonstrates the need for professionals to convey children's lack of progress to parents, thereby preventing unexpected challenges at the critical time of transition planning. Research ethics have been applied and details are published with consent. To establish context, information regarding earlier years has been provided.

Early difficulties: *"Zac never settled at playgroup and this continued throughout the infant stage of education. When he was 8 years old, a referral was made to the educational psychologist and a specialist language teacher. These were quickly followed by appointments with a paediatrician and speech and language therapist."*

Diagnosis and Support: *"There was a diagnosis of autistic spectrum disorder, dyslexia, dyspraxia and severe speech and language difficulties, accompanied by a low IQ. A Statement of Special Educational Needs was obtained in Year 5, just before he started secondary school. When Zac arrived there, a support worker would meet him before school and talk through* *changes. He always tried to please others - he would do his best and was generally quiet and withdrawn."*

Post-Sixteen Transition: *"During Year 9, Zac met with a Connexions officer who discussed possibilities for his future and completed a form that detailed his needs. Options included local colleges, a special school and a special college. All places were visited and were initially a possibility. As the Special school had pupils with physical disabilities, it was thought this environment would cause Zac to freeze and want to bolt so this was mentioned as a possible problem. Professionals attributed this concern to 'bad parenting' whilst advising it was 'politically incorrect' to hold such views. A local college eventually offered Zac full-time provision whilst a college outside the area, could offer him a two year placement which would enable him to stay over.*

Further Diagnosis: *"Zac started to vomit on the way to school and was referred back to the paediatrician and educational psychologist, who also made a referral to the Child and Adolescent Mental Health Service (CAMHS). Further tests revealed he had severe communication difficulties and was bordering on school phobic. The clinical psychologist provided coping strategies for acute anxiety and the educational psychologist undertook ability assessments which revealed Zac had learning difficulties and the reading age of a 6 year old. This was shocking news as secondary school teachers had always been reassuring, saying he was doing well within his capabilities, and there had been 'lovely' comments made about him at Annual Reviews. It was now becoming apparent he had limited literacy and numeracy abilities and was unable to participate in every day social interactions that most of us take for granted. As Zac became more anxious and withdrawn he found escapism through computer games and television programmes. Further enquiries indicated there had been no specialist provision for Zac and he had made little progress at school.*

Arrangements took over a year and involved numerous meetings, telephone calls and e-mails, as well as further visits to educational settings before Zac was finally granted an out of area placement.

End Note: Zac had settled into his new setting and was making progress *(Attwood 2012)*.

Chapter Summary

Case studies demonstrate the need for parental tenacity and determination in having their children's needs recognised and addressed.

They raise questions about how long is an acceptable time period to wait before serious intervention occurs and then whether such interventions are even appropriate. It's evident that for most parents, *'partnership',* on an everyday level, is unequal in nature, where their voices are but a whisper against the powerful voice of professionals. Nevertheless, it's hoped that parents will be encouraged – that no matter how dire the situation for a period of time, with much struggle along the way, children's circumstances can be improved upon and they can learn to manage their disabilities (at least to an extent). Family life may acquire a degree of calmness and predictability, if not entirely the normality hoped for.

Chapter 9
SEN Reform – Will it deliver?

Introduction

In 2011, the Coalition Government published a *Green Paper, Support and aspiration: A new approach to special educational needs and disability* in which it outlined the intention to overhaul educational provision for children with Special Educational Needs and disabilities with a view to enhancing the educational and life chances of such pupils. The intention is that reform will remove the adversarial nature of the system for parents and that by making specialist training available for both experienced teachers and students in training that all educational professionals will have the necessary expertise in managing and teaching children with a range of Special Educational Needs. Parents are being granted more *'control'* with respect to aspects of provision, the strategic role of local authorities is being strengthened whilst the voluntary and community sectors are becoming more integral to the delivery of services *(DfE 2011)*. Prior to publication of the *Green Paper,* there had been a period of consultation with parents of children with Special Educational Needs and professionals with responsibility for delivering services to families; this presented an opportunity to evaluate the proposals and to advise on areas of contention within the existing system whilst noting aspects which were more successful. The *Green Paper* prompted a range of responses from the media, local authorities and charitable organisations with some of the changes being welcomed, whilst others have caused consternation. Since then, a number of local authorities, referred to as *'pathfinders'* have been trialling some of the new systems, with the intention of disseminating *'best practice'* before full implementation of the reforms from 2014. *Draft Provisions (2012),* setting out the legal framework, were consulted upon, and subsequently formed the Special Educational Needs section of the *Children and Families Bill (2013),* which is expected to receive Royal Assent in Spring 2014. This means the legal framework for SEN reform has largely been settled and we are only awaiting professional guidance on implementation in the revised SEN Code of Practice. In my opinion, there are some new proposals which are likely to bring about positive benefits, some virtually replicate systems already in place, except for some re-packaging, whilst other elements raise concerns about whether some vulnerable children will receive the support they need. This chapter comprises my commentary on SEN reform - it evaluates contradictory elements and illuminates both benefits and disadvantages associated with new systems of working and entitlements. My views have been influenced by several factors which broadly include experience gained from managing a statutory service and providing direct support to parents of children with Special Educational Needs, employment on the pilot stage of the Single Assessment Process for Older People and, of course, experience gained from teaching in schools, colleges and universities. I have particular concerns that elements of this reform have wider implications for society and these too, will be addressed in this chapter. Whilst some changes to SEN provision have been explained in earlier chapters, the following review will examine some of the wider elements, including health and social care aspects. The *Green Paper (DfE 2011)* published specific aims and objectives, including the measures necessary to achieve them; these will be alluded to only insofar as necessary to contextualise my commentaries.

Early Identification and Assessment

Target: To improve the early identification of children's needs and put into place appropriate provision as early as possible. The aim is to help every child have the opportunity to achieve their potential, with as many as possible, continuing into further education, training and employment *(DfE 2011: 28)*.

Achieved by: Further development of the Early Support programme for children with Special Educational Needs and disabilities. It's intended that a further 4,000 health visitors will be in post by 2015 and they will be trained to identify children with Special Educational Needs with some being located in Children's Centres to increase their accessibility to parents. Health visitors will continue with their long-standing functions such as home visiting, co-ordinating the involvement of other professionals, completing developmental assessments for two year olds and working within multi-agency teams to provide support to families *(DfE 2011: 30)*.

Commentary

Early identification and intervention *is always valuable. As a starting point, when families are being supported and helped, it alleviates some of their* stress and provides them with a 'contact' for seeking further information. When children have their difficulties identified early it should automatically result in educational support being provided to help them manage their condition. Furthermore, early interventions have the potential to alleviate frustration in children which can ultimately manifest in behavioural difficulties.

Children's Centres: Whilst the previous Labour Government's programme both increased the number of Children's Centres, their accessibility and appeal to a wider range of service user, the Coalition Government, has reverted to the original objectives of Sure Start Children's Centres by strengthening the 'deficit' model that is both targeted and preventative in its approach (DfE 2011; DfE 2012; Gaunt 2013).

Through delivery of Parenting Programmes, parents can be educated on parenting techniques which benefit their children both at school and home. Pre-school provision for two year olds has been introduced to help parents undertake (limited) training or employment, as a means of reducing the number of households on benefits. However, whilst the principle is sound, eligibility is being restricted to children in care, families on very low incomes, receiving benefits or those with children with Special Educational Needs and Disabilities (DfE July 2012). This narrow criteria excludes families with a 'barely sufficient' income from benefitting from free pre-school provision, and yet the difference between such families and those who are eligible may be minimal; certainly insufficient to regard them as not requiring help to improve their circumstances. It also prohibits more affluent families from accessing free early years provision when attendance at such settings could be of considerable benefit to children who may be living with a parent with mental illness or some other health concern; it could deprive children of having a period of normality and an opportunity to socialise with their peers. Whilst recognising the need for eligibility criteria, this targeting has been based on stereotypical assumptions of wealth and need thereby precluding other families which could benefit from free early years provision if some flexibility was permitted. It has not been publicised whether special concessions might be granted, in certain circumstances, such as applications being supported by general practitioner or health visitor recommendation.

Types of Assessment

Target: Reduce bureaucracy and timescales for statutory assessment and increase multi-agency working between agencies in relation to Special Educational Needs provision *(DfE 2011: 37,40,58).*

Achieved by: Improvements to multi-agency assessment.

School-based Additional SEN Support *(DfE 2013)* will be of a single level, replacing School Action and School Action Plus (and the Early Years equivalents). Statutory Assessment will become known as an Educational Health and Care Needs assessment and the process through which this will be achieved is the Single Assessment Process. Education, Health and Care Plans (EHC Plans) will replace Statements of Special Educational Needs and will span 0-25 age range. Informal assessments will be undertaken for those children and young people with less significant difficulties *(DfE 2011:29-30)*.

Commentary

Multi-Agency Assessments

Multi-agency assessments for children became a feature of professional practice upon introduction of the Common Assessment Framework (CAF) which formed part of the Every Child Matters: Change for Children Agenda (2004) under the previous Labour Government. So the principle of multi-agency assessments is merely being maintained as opposed to being a new operational feature. The Common Assessment Framework has broad similarities to that of the Single Assessment Process (SAP) which will be implemented under the new system although whether CAF will be incorporated into the Single Assessment Process or remain a separate assessment system is currently unknown. The Common Assessment Process is instigated when children are identified as having unmet needs; they may already be receiving support from a number of services but their needs may be so complex or wide-ranging that some difficulties are not being addressed; this is when CAF comes into its own as a means of organising provision that 'fills the gaps'. Upon completion of individual professional assessments, a multi-agency meeting is arranged, to which the parents are invited and may contribute to Action Plans being agreed. A key requirement of the Common Assessment Framework is that a Lead Professional must be appointed from among the multi-disciplinary team which supports the child. The professional who undertakes this role then has responsibility for co-ordinating future meetings and for ensuring that action points agreed are actually fulfilled within agreed timescales. The Single Assessment Process will also require a Lead Professional, with the same type of responsibilities so there will either be two similar systems operating in parallel or one will be subsumed into the other. One benefit to parents, children and young people is the reduction of the statutory time frame in which formal assessments must be undertaken, reducing the period to twenty weeks. However, even when governments stipulate time periods, some local authorities are better than others in being able to fulfil their statutory obligations and some, for a variety of reasons, may be unable to achieve the target for each applicable family in their area.

Single Assessment Process: *As its name implies, this assessment process is meant to eradicate the need for multiple assessments, reducing the number of times that 'history' is explained by parents before each professional can determine the next course of action. The Government indicated its preference for professionals to meet face-to-face in order to agree action plans and types of support, instead of being reliant upon written reports and correspondence between agencies (DfE 2011: 37). This approach, if taken literally, is beset with its own logistical difficulties around the practicalities of organising meetings when all professionals actively supporting a child can be present at the same time. It is somewhat idealistic to expect all multi-agency professionals to attend every multi-agency meeting; unless there is a significant increase in the number of paediatricians, speech and language therapists, educational psychologists, other health professionals as well as social workers, the likelihood of eliminating the submission of assessment reports on at least some occasions, seems somewhat unrealistic. Being familiar with the process for Annual Reviews, it's a rare occurrence for all professionals working with a child to attend such events. Realistically, there is a greater likelihood of multi-agency professionals being able to attend assessment meetings when a reasonable time period has been 'blocked out' for a number of assessments on a back-to-back basis, thereby maximising effective use of resources. However, the production line format is likely to prevent any prevarication and indecision and could heighten the stress experienced by parents and professionals who could feel pressurised in such time limited environments.*

One Assessment? *The Green Paper (DfE 2011: 37) alluded to the possibility of health, education and social care assessments being undertaken together. Whilst this would be an economical use of resources, this approach fails to consider the emotional impact upon parents and their children. Imagine this scenario - a room with as many as thirteen professionals in attendance with parent(s) and child. Each professional would take their turn to assess the child's difficulties, symptoms and history, relevant to their area of expertise. Such meetings would be extremely time-consuming, as well as being absolutely daunting for children and their parents. Children would be 'objectified' whilst* each professional focused on different aspects of their difficulties. Assessments undertaken this way would 'de-humanise' children and it's unreasonable to expect vulnerable children to cope without any untoward effects from such experiences. Whilst this might be an acceptable approach for some families, for others, the ensuing effects from such processes, undertaken in the 'the best interests of the child', could actually cause significant emotional harm. As the Children and Families Bill (2013: 19) intends to protect children's emotional well-being, families should be able to choose whether they attend 'single' multi-agency assessments if this operational format becomes policy. My own research highlighted the detrimental effects upon children following their attendance at multi-agency meetings, after they had listened to their limitations and difficulties being discussed. The stress and significant impact on self-worth resulted in some children either self-harming or developing a range of anxiety responses. Parents then had to engage in 'damage limitation' by putting a 'positive spin' on what had been said and in building up their children's self-confidence (Attwood 2007: 81 Appendices C1: 7, C2: 15, C8: 57). Fundamentally, it doesn't matter how caring and well-intentioned professionals are, from my perspective, placing children in a multiple assessment scenario could be construed as being similar to a rat being observed in a laboratory. This type of situation is not necessarily a safe option. It's, therefore, hoped that children's attendance at multi-agency meetings isn't developed beyond (part-time attendance) at Annual Reviews.

Time and Trust: It takes time for cultural change to become embedded in professional practice and some professionals will initially be reluctant to base their own professional decisions on the 'history' noted by professionals in another role. Therefore, it will not totally eradicate the need for parents to repeat medical, educational or social history. For effective implementation, it's absolutely vital that each geographical area is fully networked to the national database and that relevant professionals from each agency, can access information. There could be potential difficulties for families who have opted out of having their medical notes uploaded onto the system as this could necessitate recourse to more traditional ways of working.

Information sharing within and between agencies requires formal protocols that address how information is shared and the criteria for doing so, including which professionals are entitled to have access. When information has been collected and recorded, parents and children will benefit if this can then contribute to applications for other services and benefits such as Short Breaks and Disability Living Allowance, which the Government is exploring.

Education, Health and Care Plans

Target: To provide education, health and social care support to children and young people aged 0-25 years *(DfE 2011: 28).*

Achieved by: Multi-agency working between agencies. Education, Health and Care Plans will incorporate goals for education, health, employment and independent living *(DfE 2011: 28).*

Commentary

This holistic approach to supporting children and young people, whilst commendable, is not entirely new policy. Labour Government policy was also holistic with respect to the 'Five Outcomes' for service delivery to help children thrive as part of the 'Every Child Matters: Change for Children' Agenda (2004). The 'outcomes' addressed maintenance of children's health, their safety, enjoyment of life, achievement, their contribution to society and achieving economic well-being (DfES 2004: 9). Therefore, aspects of reform cannot fail to appear as re-packaging of aspects of Labour policy. Theoretically, Education, Health and Care Plans, with their provision extending beyond compulsory education and into early adulthood should alleviate the possibility of young people 'falling through the net' with respect to accessing adult health and social care services. The new system will emphasise the need for thorough planning and more co-ordinated working between children's and adult services. It's worth noting that the Labour Government's Aiming High for Disabled Children Transition Programme (DCSF 2008) required local authorities to produce Transition Protocols, with a view to ensuring multi-agency working achieved optimum results for young people. However, the Coalition Government's Comprehensive Spending Reviews (2010 and 2013) have had a considerable impact upon local authority budgets resulting in fewer staff to deliver front line services. With such commitments being written into Education, Health and Care Plans, the difficulty lies in having sufficient human resources available to implement transition planning effectively.

A further consideration with respect to the new Education, Health and Care Plans is the involvement of parents. Whilst children are of compulsory school age, parents are entitled to participate in any planning associated with their children, but when they reach the legal age of adulthood, parents can be excluded from any decisions relating to young people. Therein lies a difficulty – some young people are expected to make their own decisions regarding their care when, in fact, they have the mental age of a child. This situation produces a significant conundrum, as young people do not always have the mental capacity to decide upon what is best for them, but services historically, at least, disregard the 'voice' of parents once their children become adults (or the age to receive adult services). Parents speak of their powerlessness, when young people have rejected services that could have helped them or presented a different reality to the actual circumstances due to their inappropriate responses to professional questions. It is, therefore, hoped that Government Regulations will address this dilemma and permit parents to act as advocates for the life-time of Education, Health and Care Plans and that their 'voices' will be heard with respect to such provision. For some parents, the solution may be achieved through becoming Power of Attorney for their adult children (where mental capacity justifies such action) which can then ensure they will not only be consulted about their young person's needs, but their voices will have a measure of influence.

Professional Development

Target: For all teachers to be able to identify and meet the needs of children and young people with Special Educational Needs *(DfE 2011: 59)*.

Achieved by: Continuing Professional Development, new scholarship schemes and improvements to teacher training *(DfE 2011: 60)*.

Commentary

Professional development and additional qualifications are considered as being significant to children's learning experiences and educational outcomes (DfE 2011: 19). However, whilst there is evidence that teacher expertise is significant to improving children's outcomes, this is only one aspect within a range of factors which should be considered. Teachers need to have sufficient opportunity for observation, which in an average class size of 30 children with differing demands, may be easier said than done. If observations only take place in 'snatched' moments, it might take considerable time before there is sufficient information upon which to act. In addition to this, there is the possibility of professionals adopting a 'wait and see approach' whilst a scenario develops, which then evokes the question about what time period is acceptable before any action is taken. Professional attitudes and behaviour will influence professional practice (DfE 2011: 65) with their perceptions affecting the speed at which concerns are acted upon. Professional qualifications and training are important but the characteristics of individuals and their approach to situations are often over-riding factors.

Giving Parents Control

Target: To give parents more *'choice'* and *'control'* regarding their children's Special Educational Needs provision *(DfE 2011: 45, 47)*.

Achieved by: Local offers which detail services available for children with SEN, increased transparency of SEN funding and the option of personal budgets *(DfE 2011: 49)*.

Commentary

The Green Paper (DfE 2011: 41-42) perpetuated the notion of parental control through the option of having personal budgets for their children's Special Educational Needs and in relation to choice of school. Such statements can create unrealistic expectations regarding the extent to which parents may influence decisions and exert parental power. Historically, parents have been categorised as 'equal partners' with school professionals (Warnock 1978: 150) only to have this subsequently re-aligned as a collaborative relationship. The concept of 'consumerism' has evolved since its original inception under the 1988 Education Reform Act (Vincent 1996: 31), with patients now having the freedom to select where they access certain health services and parents now having the right to establish Free Schools which are funded by central government. As the Labour Government previously stated that parents would be able to establish their own schools (DfES 2005), the current Free Schools programme illustrates how initiatives, which are initially launched by one government, are often carried forward by successive governments, albeit with re-modelling of the concepts to comply with their own ideology. We will now examine what these 'new' initiatives really mean for parents.

Do all parents have Control? *In principle, all parents of children with Special Educational Needs can exert 'control, but the reality is that not all parents either want to or can take up this option. Only a minority of parents are in a position to undertake the long-term and sustained commitment necessary to establish Free Schools. Even when parents are dissatisfied with their provision, many will be unable to pursue such initiatives because they lack the time, skills and energy rather than being due to any lack of motivation or interest on their part.*

Will Local Offers make a difference? Parental 'choice' can be exercised through publication of Local Offers for parents; it's a requirement that local authorities collaborate with local education providers (schools and colleges) and the NHS to indicate which education, health and social care services are 'expected' to be available in the local area as well as providing information about provision outside the area for children who attend out-of-county placements (DfE 2013).

'Expected' provision is not the same as that which is categorically available; presumably it is only 'expected' because, under the current economic climate, there is no guarantee of services being available long-term or who will be providing them. For parents to be certain about provision, they will inevitably have to pursue their own enquiries to ascertain (as far as possible) whether any imminent changes are being planned. However, it's welcomed that local authorities will consult with parents and young people to enable them to influence decisions regarding the delivery of existing services and the planning of future provision. This will ensure resources are targeted to more effectively meet local needs (DfE 2013).

Local Offers are fundamentally an extension of the information already provided by Family Information Services (FIS). Parents are already advised about local services and support through advertisements in the local press and on service websites, directories, information packs and publicity materials are distributed via health visitors, general practitioner surgeries, voluntary organisations and Children's Centres. Sometimes FIS representatives attend school Parents' Evenings and Parent Partnership Service events, both to publicise their services and to offer support to parents. In this technological age, Local Offers will inevitably be accessible through the internet, but there will need to be alternative arrangements for parents who cannot access the internet otherwise this could exclude those parents who most likely need support. Whilst attendance at promotional events is a heavy use of human resource, and is not necessarily time and cost effective from a business perspective, this is still an effective way of establishing contact with parents who otherwise might not know how to access information or they may have a particular reluctance to contact local authorities – perhaps viewing them as bureaucratic bodies to be avoided! Already, some local authorities are publishing their Local Offers through Family Information Services and it might therefore, be assumed that such responsibility will be maintained in the future. Local Offers will not provide information that is usually obtained directly from schools. Parents who wish to view Special Educational Needs and Behaviour Policies (which are *particularly relevant for parents of children with behavioural difficulties) will still need to access these directly from school websites, providing that schools have transparently placed such documents in the public domain, otherwise, parents are entitled to request paper copies from school offices. As the Local Offer is being produced under an ethos of transparency, it might positively encourage all schools to make their policy documentation accessible to parents, especially when having regard to the parental role of 'consumer'.*

Local authorities, as 'parent champions' (DfE 2010) are being tasked with ensuring parental information is accessible from a single source, but ensuring such information is always accurate and up-to-date may prove an onerous task. The Coalition Government's rationale for producing Local Offers is to help parents make informed decisions about their children and young people's education, so that having made 'right choices', they believe there is less likelihood of subsequent dissatisfaction with the elected provision (DfE 2011: 45). Unfortunately, this perspective fails to acknowledge the whole picture. Not all parents are successful in obtaining their preferred choice of school; some parents are unsuccessful in obtaining any of their stated preferences which means that some will be sending their children to specific schools under sufferance. Written policies, whilst stipulating how specific situations are likely to be handled, provide no guarantee about how situations will be dealt with. Educational professionals sometimes refer to their policies as 'evidence' of professional practice, even when the experience of parents and their children has been 'outside' that of the policies to which they have been referred.

The human factor always affects any situation. Subjective judgements are made about the need to take certain actions, professional inexperience may not recognise the need to take action, 'short-cuts' may be taken resulting in some policy 'stages' not being implemented, individuals may be apathetic or simply unwilling to undertake protocols in accordance with school, local or national policies. Some of the primary reasons that parents contact Parent Partnership Services are because 'promises' are not fulfilled, provision is not implemented and children fail to make progress. Publication of additional information is only a starting point for parents; it cannot guarantee what will take place in educational settings. Reform will not necessarily eradicate parental dissatisfaction with their local authority or the service provided by their children's schools.

Personal Budgets

Target: Increase parental control over support provided for their children *(DfE 2011: 47)*.

Achieved by: Personal budgets for children with Education, Health and Care Plans *(DfE 2011: 47)*.

Commentary

Personal budgets have been promoted as an optional arrangement for parents. It is one of the systems through which the Green Paper stated that parents and young people could have 'greater control' (DfE 2011: 47, DfE 2012:) although the Children and Families Bill (2013:) only referred to parents 'being involved' (DfE 2013: 34). There is a significant difference to being in 'control' to that of being 'involved', with the latter position implying that parents will collaborate with professionals to agree how the budget is used whilst the former implies parents will have a lead role, although this may depend upon their particular budgeting arrangements. Key Workers will assist parents and young people (with their own budgets) in planning services (DfE 2011: 49) so decisions regarding expenditure are unlikely to be taken in isolation. Local authorities and health services are expected to jointly commission services whenever possible; for example, health services such as speech and language therapy are sometimes purchased by local authorities on 'block' contracts, where a number of hours are purchased to service several children, with a specific number of sessions allocated per child. Such arrangements could restrict the amount of influence that parents may exert. For some, 'control' may be illusionary rather than literal although they might still 'feel' empowered (DfE 2011: 47) as participants in the process.

With parental 'involvement' comes additional responsibility which requires wisdom in prioritising their children's needs, based on their difficulties. Service costs must be transparent to enable parents to calculate the cost of services over each academic year or for whatever time period specific support is required. There is a significant risk of parents being disappointed when allocated budgets only address their children's needs at an adequate level as opposed to a higher standard.

Some parents and young people will opt for personal budgets to be paid through the Direct Payments system, which means that money, for specific services, is paid directly into a special account for this purpose. The Coalition Government's Spending Review (2010) significantly impacted upon the ability of local government and health services in being able to meet their statutory obligations, resulting in eligibility criteria for some services, such as Short Breaks becoming more stringent. Specialist support services previously provided by local authorities are now mostly commissioned from the private sector, which may prove costly, resulting in budgets being insufficient to purchase the same quantity of services as previously. In the current economic climate it is unrealistic to expect all needs to be met; there will inevitably be difficult decisions regarding what is most important for children and what can be provided within the funds available. Parents will need to make tough decisions regarding which aspects of their children's difficulties must be addressed first. Part 3 of the Children and Families Bill (2013: 35) indicates that local authorities will have complied with their statutory obligations upon transfer of funds under the Direct Payments system. From this position, it can be construed that parents will have responsibility for providing relevant services to meet their children's needs. Whilst many parents are likely to welcome the prospect of commissioning services for their children, there is the potential for a 'blame scenario' to develop if children subsequently fail to make progress; parents could be accused of making poor decisions, when the cause could be due to insufficient funding to deliver necessary services.

Looking Ahead: *The Indicative Draft: The (0-25) SEN Code of Practice (2013) indicates there will be three types of personal budget. This includes the Direct Payments system, 'notional budgets' and 'third party' arrangements (DfE 2013). Obviously, specific details will be advised in the new Code of Practice, upon publication.*

Choice of School

Target: To give parents a real choice of school *(DfE 2011: 51).*

Achieved by: Having a wide range of high quality provision *(DfE 2011: 51).*

Commentary

The Green Paper (DfE 2011) developed the Coalition Government's earlier commitment, published in the White Paper, The Importance of Teaching (2010) to give parents a 'real choice' of school by increasing the range of schools available. In keeping with this commitment, Free Schools have opened and significant numbers of maintained schools have converted to Academy status. When parents express their 'preferences' for which schools they wish their children to attend, Academies and Free Schools are among the options from which they may choose. In a new ruling by Government, children without Statements or Education, Health and Care Plans will be eligible for admission to specialist Free Schools, provided their difficulties match the specialism offered by such schools, thereby creating even greater choice for parents. I will now attempt to clarify the notion of parental 'choice' in relation to which schools their children attend. Whilst local authorities have a duty to provide sufficient school places for all children living in their area, this does not necessarily mean that there are sufficient places available at every school chosen by parents when applying for school places. Some schools are exceptionally popular and may be over-subscribed meaning that some parents will be unsuccessful in gaining a place for their child. The School Admissions Code (2012: 7) states that parents have the 'right to express a preference' and, therefore, any reference to 'choice' should really be understood as being 'preference'.

Mediation

Target: Reduce stress for parents and make better use of public funds *(DfE 2011: 54)*.

Achieved by: Advice from an independent mediation service before Appeals can be lodged *(DfE 2011: 54)*.

Commentary

Mediation: The Children and Families Bill, Part 3 (DfE 2013: 36), in its quest to reduce applications to the First-tier Tribunal (SEND), has introduced the requirement that parents and young people who wish to submit an Appeal regarding aspects of Education, Health and Care Plans (excepting school places), must obtain a certificate from a mediation adviser; this confirms that applicants have received information and advice about mediation and whether they have refused to participate in the process. Instead of reducing bureaucracy, this process has added another tier, and by so doing, has reduced parental 'choice' and 'control' due to the mandatory requirement to receive advice from a mediation adviser, when they might prefer not to. This process will act as a deterrent to parents and young people pursuing costly Appeals which could otherwise be resolved at local level, but there is a risk that through mediation, some cases may be 'resolved' through compromise which results in less than satisfactory solutions. This process only applies to children's educational provision and there is no requirement to receive advice from a mediation adviser with respect to disability discrimination claims.

Learning and Achieving

Target: Reduce over-identification of children with Special Educational Needs *(DfE 2011: 58)*.

Achieved by: Replacing School Action and School Action Plus with a single school-based category of SEN *(DfE 2011: 58)*.

Commentary

Through the Schools Funding Reform Arrangements for 2013-14, delegated funding is being increased to enable schools to adequately resource Special Educational Needs provision and contribute towards the budgets for children with Education, Health and Care Plans. Unless schools provide their own in-house specialist services, there is a need to commission such support from outside providers.

Whilst the legal definition of Special Educational Needs remains fundamentally the same, there will be strict criteria and protocols to be addressed before such definition applies. This suggests the 'threshold' for SEN is being raised – being only for children whose needs cannot be supported by school resources alone (DfE 2011: 58). It could, therefore, be deduced that elevated criteria will apply to Education, Health and Care Plans as well. This has potential implications for children who already have a Statement of Special Educational Needs, who may not meet the new criteria, especially if their needs were only borderline when the Statement was issued. Parents will obviously be aware if their children only just met the eligibility criteria. Children currently experiencing difficulties at School Action may no longer be viewed as having Special Educational Needs and, therefore, may not qualify for individual support, unless their difficulties escalate and they meet the new criteria.

In view of these 'shifting sands', it could be deduced that only children and young people with the most complex needs will qualify for Education, Health and Care Plans. When local authorities have refused to undertake formal assessment or issue EHC Plans, parents should be mindful that Appeals to the First-tier Tribunal (SEND) will be considered in relation to the new criteria being adopted under reform, which will obviously reflect upon the success of any Appeals.

It has been the practice for some time that health services such as speech and language therapy are often delivered by educational professionals such as teaching assistants and this is likely to continue; obviously specialist programmes are overseen by therapists who have responsibility for ensuring appropriate training and delivery of the programme. The use of lower skilled professionals and, therefore cheaper resources might be the only way that schools can attempt to provide for children's needs through their own budgets and unless experienced staff deliver such programmes, children's progress may be affected.

Chapter Summary

SEN reform has been approached from a perspective that grants parents *'choice'* and *'control'*, with parental choice being enhanced through the availability of additional school performance data upon which parents can make informed decisions. However, the extent to which *'choice'* and *'control'* may be exercised is inequitable, being subject to socio-economic and psychological influences as well as the particular roles undertaken within the educational arena.

Government strategies are designed to raise professional standards from initial teacher training through to Continuing Professional Development that include professional qualifications and networking between schools with teachers being incentivised by the possibility of achieving further qualifications and leadership positions. Additional skills and knowledge are usually accompanied by increased responsibility and teachers will be expected to more accurately (and easily) identify a range of Special Educational Needs and disabilities and manage them appropriately in the classroom.

Access to educational psychologists is becoming increasingly rarefied, with many now operating in a consultative capacity. Schools might be reluctant to purchase such services unless there is clear evidence of need. In the past, it was common for educational psychologists to assess children experiencing a range of difficulties, even before the question of Statutory Assessment arose, as well as undertaking assessments as part of the process. With stretched resources, there is a risk of over-burdening teachers by expecting them to undertake some of the lower-order functions, previously undertaken by educational psychologists. If such practice ever occurs, it could be detrimental to both teacher morale *and* children's outcomes.

This SEN reform is well-intentioned - designed to improve children's outcomes and well-being, motivate and up-skill professional staff, improve upon multi-agency working, including the voluntary and community sectors, whilst satisfying parental need to be involved in decisions that affect their children.

There remains one concern for readers to consider; that is children's eligibility for Education, Health and Care Plans (and Statements) and for receiving school-based Additional SEN support. Legally, the definitions of SEN and disability remain fundamentally the same but the qualifying criteria are being re-framed. Under the new regime, teachers must evidence the strategies and resources that have been implemented, demonstrating they have explored all options before children are eligible for Additional SEN support whereas under the current system, such stringent criteria usually applies in respect of an application for Statutory Assessment. Obviously, there will be similar mechanisms in place in respect of applications for Education, Health and Care Plans. This is likely to result in fewer children receiving statutory provision *and* school-based support; the number of children formally identified with SEN and disabilities will inevitably decrease, thereby achieving one of the goals of reform.

There are children who currently receive support, which under reform are likely to become *'normalised'* and denied individual support to help address their needs. Instead, they will be required to operate from a position of *'false consciousness' (Low 2006: 108)* as if they had no difficulties at all. Their only hope of a measure of support will be through whole-class strategies which cannot address the idiosyncratic presentation of *all* learning difficulties and disabilities.

The new approach adopted by educationalists will likely impact upon other professional roles. For example, if schools no longer accept that certain (probably low level) behavioural characteristics can be attributed to disabilities, there will be little benefit in children having a paediatric diagnosis if this will not qualify them for Additional SEN support. Parents may then discover it's harder to *'prove'* their children's difficulties; this is further compounded when presenting difficulties appear less severe than they actually are until investigated more thoroughly. Schools invariably require written paediatric evidence of disabilities, and without such evidence, they are unlikely to implement *reasonable adjustments*. As adults, if children have been failed by the education system, there may be difficulties in obtaining employment and in proving they have genuine difficulties that require support. This is an issue that requires further consideration.

Chapter 10

Academies and School Discipline

Introduction

This chapter will provide an outline of the position of Academies before highlighting some of the practices with respect to school disciplinary procedures and Independent Review Panels in relation to permanent exclusions.

Raising Standards

The Labour Government introduced City Academies in the year 2000, adopting the view that by raising educational standards, inner city poverty could be relieved. Despite these intentions, few Academies actually existed until the General Election in 2010, which resulted in a Coalition Government being formed. The new Government prioritised education, viewing this as being a route to individual opportunity whilst, at the same time, addressing many social ills. As a consequence, the Academy programme, which had its origins under the Labour Government, has been rapidly rolling out, in the quest to achieve educational excellence.

The Department for Education has established the operating principles of Academies and determined which schools can become Academies. The core principles are that maintained schools which have been rated by Ofsted as *'outstanding'* as well as those described as *'failing'* are permitted to convert to Academy status. School improvement is then achieved through *'partnership'* or *'federation'* arrangements between successful and less successful schools where headteachers of high performing schools help raise the standards of their less successful partners by contributing their experience, formulae for success, and helping to drive forward improvements with respect to school organisation, teaching and pupils' learning and educational achievements. The current position is that selective schools, usually known as Grammar schools, may also become Academies, but must remain selective and equally non-selective schools cannot become selective after converting to Academy status. Furthermore, the Coalition Government encourages Academies to have sponsorship from universities, charities, businesses, religious and other organisations which then influence specific areas of study, with schools becoming *'centres of excellence'* in subject specialisms such as the Arts, Languages, Sciences or Technology *(DfE 2013)*

School Funding Reform: Arrangements for 2013-14 are introducing greater transparency in how maintained schools and Academies are being funded, with Academies being brought more in line with other mainstream schools. This is partly being achieved by an increase in delegated budgets to all schools and new formulae for calculating school funding which places greater emphasis on pupil characteristics as opposed to consideration of school organisation and premises *(DfE 2012: 3)*.

Accountability and Operation

Under the *Academies Act 2010,* the Secretary of State can enter into an Academy Agreement with any person or body such as businesses, other organisations or modern day philanthropists. Conversion to Academy status is granted for a minimum of seven years, although the time period can actually become indefinite. The majority of pupils who attend Academies will be those who reside within the area in which the Academy is situated.

Academies operate in compliance with their Funding Agreements which are agreed between them and the Secretary of State. There is some variance between Funding Agreements, depending upon the time period in which educational settings converted to Academy status although under the *Academies Act 2010* any person or organisation entering into an Academy Agreement must:

a) *"Establish and maintain an independent school in England".*
b) *"Make Special Educational Needs provision for pupils with SEN".*

Academies must, therefore, address the needs of all their pupils, including the brightest children as well as those who struggle. Under the *Children and Families Bill (2013: 21),* Academy proprietors are expected to co-operate with their local authority with regards to fulfilling their obligations in respect of children with Special Educational Needs and disabilities and in keeping education and care provision under review.

Academy Freedoms

As independent schools, Academies operate outside of local authority control and have autonomy and freedom with respect to school organisation. For example, proprietors can determine staff pay and conditions, term dates, duration of the school day and are permitted to employ unqualified teaching staff for specialist subjects, in line with other schools in the independent sector. Furthermore, they also purchase their own specialist support services and negotiate their own contracts *(DfE 2012)*.

School Admissions

The *School's Admission Code (2012)* explains the mandatory requirements of all maintained schools, Academies, Free Schools, University Technical Colleges and Studio Schools with respect to admissions arrangements for children moving through the schools system. Academy Funding Agreements state they must comply with the Code, although there could be circumstances when the Secretary of State may vary this requirement *(DfE 2012: 3)*. Before children enter the educational system or move into a new phase of education, each local authority will distribute Admissions guidance to parents informing them of the procedures for applying for school places and how to state their school preferences. The guidance contains information on each type of school within the local authority area and informs parents of the responsible bodies for determining admissions criteria in the event of more applications being received for schools than they can actually accommodate. For example, local authorities are the Admissions Authorities for maintained schools whilst governing bodies are responsible for Voluntary Aided Schools, whereas Academy Trusts are responsible for Academies *(DfE 2012: 5)*. Academies must, therefore, specify how they allocate school places and determine their admissions arrangements in the event of there being more applicants than places available. Parents of children with additional needs, but without Statements or Education, Health and Care Plans must apply for school places in competition with other parents.

Families who move into a new area during the academic year or decide to change their children's school will be subject to *Fair Access Protocols* which are designed to ensure children are quickly placed into school settings. Whilst parents can state their particular preferences, the *Admissions Code (2012: 26)* advises there is no requirement for Admissions Authorities to satisfy parental requests for particular schools. Local authority Admissions teams can advise parents about specific procedures.

'Named' Schools and Statutory Provision

Admissions procedures for children with Statements or Education, Health and Care Plans involve direct liaison between local authorities and the *preferred* schools, chosen by parents. Before finalising a Statement or Education Health and Care Plan, the local authority should consult with parents regarding which school they would prefer their child to attend; the local authority acting in an advisory capacity, will present their views regarding the suitability of specific schools, taking into consideration factors such as age of the child, their ability and whether the school is appropriate for meeting their Special Educational Needs, having regard to the *"efficient education of others and efficient use of resources" (DfE 2013: 30)*. The *Children and Families Bill (2013)* has indicated this established protocol will continue under reform. Most parents will be successful in having their request granted and their local authority will then proceed with admission arrangements and in having the school named in the Statement (or Education, Health and Care Plan).

Whilst Academies are classified as *'independent'* schools, their Funding Agreements contain equivalent SEN obligations to that of maintained schools. Academies are, therefore, expected to have reciprocal relationships with their local authorities in relation to the execution and delivery of Special Educational Needs provision *(DfE 2013)*. Both the *Children and Families Bill (2013)* and the *School Admissions Code (2012)* are written with the intention of bringing Academies into alignment with other schools in relation to the admission and provision of children with Special Educational Needs and disabilities, as it's intended that such guidance and legislation should over-ride any anomalies contained in Academy Agreements.

Schools might sometimes refuse to admit children with Statements (or EHC Plans) on the premise that such admission would be *'incompatible with the efficient education of other children'* or that they are unable to meet their needs. The *Equalities Act 2010* specifically addresses inequalities and in removing barriers to full participation in society. As a result, parents and young people may have the option (depending upon their circumstances) of appealing to the First-tier Tribunal (SEND) on the basis of Disability Discrimination, in an endeavour to have decisions overturned, although obviously this process takes time. If an Academy has been named on a child's Statement (or EHC Plan), when they have previously refused admission, they can Appeal against such actions to the Secretary of State, who will then make the final decision.

School Discipline

Behaviour Policies: Schools sometimes place these policies on their websites or parents may obtain copies, upon request. Behaviour policies will usually indicate the procedures that are implemented following minor misdemeanours and the sanctions used when behaviour progresses to more serious incidents. A staged system is usually adopted from which parents may ascertain whether their children are at low risk of exclusion or at serious risk of being permanently excluded although it is not necessary for children to go through all the stages before being permanently excluded; the disciplinary stage will be determined by the seriousness of the incident(s). Obviously, parents will have an idea of the risk of permanent exclusion if their children have already received a number of fixed-term exclusions and will likely have been advised of this by headteachers.

School Exclusions: Some children are more susceptible to being permanently excluded or receiving fixed-term exclusions than others. For instance, the *Department for Education Statistical First Release for permanent and fixed period exclusions 2010/11* indicated that children with Statements of Special Educational Needs were at least nine times more likely than those without Statements to find themselves permanently excluded and six times more likely to receive fixed-term exclusions. However, children with Special Educational Needs but without Statements, were eleven times more likely to be permanently excluded due to disruptive behaviour. The next most significant category was children in receipt of Free School Meals followed by minority ethnic children. Categories often overlap, but overall, boys are more likely than girls to be permanently excluded *(DfE 2012)*.

Exclusions guidance is produced for educational professionals that outlines the circumstances under which pupils may be permanently excluded or receive fixed-term exclusions and details the procedures that should be implemented in the event of exclusions. Schools have the right to permanently exclude pupils following one serious breach of the school's Behaviour Policy although permanent exclusions often result from a history of incidents, until *'the final straw'* is reached. When instigating exclusion procedures, schools *"must have regard"* to the guidance and implement its principles unless there are valid reasons for not doing so *(DfE 2012: 2)*. Factors that headteachers must consider when making the decision to permanently exclude are whether:

> *"allowing the pupil to remain in school would seriously harm the education or welfare of the pupil or others in the school"*
> *(DfE 2012: 6).*

Exclusions Guidance serves to both protect pupils whilst empowering headteachers to implement punishment in proportion to the misdemeanour. In accordance with the *United Nations Convention for the Rights of Children, Article 12,* children's voices should be heard and with respect to school exclusions (whether fixed-term or permanent), they should be permitted the opportunity to *'state their case'* during each stage of the disciplinary procedure; furthermore, under Article 3, schools are expected to consider the interests of children when making decisions which affect them. Whilst single incidents cannot necessarily be anticipated or prevented, lower level *'nuisance behaviour'* should be addressed before it escalates and results in fixed term exclusions, which can ultimately lead to permanent exclusion. Since September 2012, schools are required to more effectively manage disruptive behaviour, with the expectation that multi-agency assessments will help establish the root causes of poor behaviour and thereby avoid some permanent exclusions *(DfE 2012: 4).* In my experience, most schools will access whatever services and support are available to help children whilst others adopt the position that pupils *'are on the road to permanent exclusion'* and consider it a waste of professional and financial resources to invest in accessing costly support services. Sometimes relationships between pupils and staff deteriorate to such an extent that educationalists metaphorically *'stand back and wait'* whilst pupils *'speed along a collision course to permanent exclusion',* without either implementing strategies or support to avoid this outcome.

Some schools take the initiative and implement *'exclusions'* of an illegal kind - not following government guidance or even their own Behaviour Policies, but ensure that children are absent from school. From my experience in supporting parents of children with Special Educational Needs, the most common strategies included *'lunch time exclusions'* and *'extended study leave'*. Such strategies demonstrate a lack of regard for the well-being and education of children whose behaviour is often the result of *'hidden'* disabilities. With some of these occurrences being highlighted in the Children's Commissioner's Inquiry, *'Always somebody else's problem' (Office of the Children's Commissioner, 2013)* and with their recommendations for new accountability procedures, it is hoped that such practices will be eradicated in the future.

Independent Review Panels: Full guidance on procedures relating to fixed-term and permanent exclusions is contained in the *Department for Education's Exclusions Guidance (2012)*. The purpose of this section is to highlight changes with respect to Independent Panels, formerly known as *'Appeal'* Panels, but as part of reform, are now known as *'Review'* Panels. Previously, parents were able to request reconsideration of permanent exclusion by an Independent Appeal Panel, with the possibility of having decisions overturned but this is no longer possible. Parents can now request the attendance of an SEN Expert at Independent Review Panels, with such persons acting impartially with respect to providing information about specific Special Educational Needs, irrespective of whether such difficulties have been recognised by the school *(DfE, 2012: 23)*. Independent *Review* Panels, having heard the background to the exclusion, can take one of three possible actions, outlined in Exclusions Guidance, as follows:

- They can agree with the original decision (uphold the decision).
- They can recommend that the School's Governing Body reconsider their decision.
- Governing Bodies can be *directed* to reconsider their decision when there have been flaws in the procedures undertaken.
  (DfE 2012: 24).

For maintained schools, local authorities have previously had responsibility for organising Independent Appeal Panels, and this is likely to continue for Independent Review Panels. Academies, on the other hand, are responsible for organising their own Panels, which must operate impartially.

Parental Support: If parents find themselves in the position of having to attend school disciplinary procedures, with respect to either fixed-term or permanent exclusions, they are entitled to have someone support them. If this person has professional expertise, such as a Parent Partnership Service representative, or is a member of a recognised support group (for specific disabilities), they may also assist in presenting the case; there are a number of organisations which can advise and support parents in this type of situation.

Chapter 11

Where do we go from here?

In writing this book, I have strived to provide a realistic picture on SEN provision by including current practice and informing readers of some of the new processes that are already in the public domain – in the hope of allaying concerns for the future. I have provided my own perspective on SEN reform, based on my knowledge of how the system tends to work in practice, whilst briefly raising concerns about elements of future provision. I hope that by doing this, parents will become more knowledgeable of how the system works, whilst being aware of possible pitfalls, should they start to develop.

We cannot ignore the financial implications of any reforms, no matter what sector they apply to – there will inevitably be a finite amount of money with which to implement the system, especially during the current economic climate. No system is ideal, despite best intentions, but the Government, in my opinion, is introducing changes which should increase parental empowerment, for those that seek this, thereby demonstrating that parents have been listened to with respect to their concerns and desires. However, during times of economic drought, resources must be rationed, with strict eligibility criteria being applied to gain access to extra provision and services. This will inevitably mean that parents cannot expect their children to receive everything they need, but if they do, this is likely to be a phased process and not all delivered at once and, most likely, being influenced in how funding is allocated each year for such provision.

Over many years, there has been much written about the concept of partnership and what exactly this means for professionals and parents. This book has examined and critiqued aspects of this phenomenon. Obviously, there are formal partnership arrangements where parties should have identified expectations of each other, but for everyday relationships between parents and teachers, there is less need to get *'hung up'* on expectations of what each can obtain from the other. Fundamentally, as long as parents and professionals can communicate in an open, honest and respectful manner, this will go a long way towards helping children achieve their goals, whilst avoiding upsetting family dynamics and causing unnecessary stress to each party. Of course, from such communication, it's key that professionals listen to parents, take heed of their concerns and act upon them. This is not to say that professionals are puppets to be pulled by parental strings, but to state that more often than not, when parents raise concerns about their children, even if those concerns are instinctively driven, as opposed to having some visible proof (which professionals often seek), they tend to be right, so these should be explored, as necessary. Parental quotations and case studies have illustrated the struggles sometimes experienced by parents - they have not been included to denigrate any professional body or acts by any person, but to illustrate there is still a culture of disregarding parental concerns, forming hasty judgements and of low expectations from which apathy prevents timely intervention.

Parents and professionals do share the common goal of improving children's educational experiences and outcomes and, of course, this will always be approached from different perspectives simply because of their respective roles. Some things we must simply accept and work from the standpoint where there is a mutual exchange of knowledge, which can be used by each party to benefit children.

The most prevalent concern arising from SEN reform is the apparent raising of the *'threshold'* before children are classified as having Special Educational Needs, although the legislative framework remains fundamentally the same. This suggests that only the most overt and serious difficulties experienced by children will be eligible for additional in-class support and, of course, the same principle will apply to those seeking Education, Health and Care Plans. There is a threat that those children currently with Statements of SEN will no longer meet future criteria for statutory provision and local authorities may, in due course, withdraw such provision which will result in them receiving a lower level of support, but it's hoped that these concerns are subsequently proved unfounded. Many children, with apparently, low-level needs will have these addressed by whole class strategies, which are not effective for everyone and every type of need. This is aside from the fact that significant needs are not necessarily recognised as being at that level, as already illustrated, which leaves us with the question about what will happen to such children. With the best will in the world, conscientious teachers can only do so much, especially when they have a class of around 30 children to manage and teach. Specialist services are less readily available than in the past and unless schools are willing to commission services when difficulties are *suspected* rather than thoroughly *identified,* there will be an increased burden upon teachers to be *'all things to all people'*. As this is an unrealistic expectation, there will likely be more teachers who *'fail to deliver'* simply because of overload and lack of capacity, aside from any other factors. However genuine the reasons, parents do not want to hear excuses when their children's needs are not been addressed and this will hardly engender good relationships between them. Aside from any capacity issues, provision will largely depend upon the subjective judgement of professionals and their value systems (as it does now). This cannot be separated from the intricacies of human nature and the fallibility of individuals. Not forgetting, of course, the inter-relationship between education, health and social care; this means that if educational professionals fail to identify or recognise needs in the classroom, this can impact upon any medical diagnosis for *'hidden'* disabilities. From my experience, assessments involve parental, health and educational input and, understandably, there usually needs to be corroborative evidence of existing difficulties before a firm diagnosis is forthcoming. This will also have implications for entitlement to disability benefits.

- Will relationships between parents and professionals improve in the future? *Some will and some won't.* With an increase in parental expectation (as a result of SEN reform), parents will expect more but teachers may be unable to fulfil the extra demands being placed upon them. This has the potential for further conflict.
- Do professionals want to work with parents? *Many do because of the known benefits from such relationships but do recognise this can involve a huge investment of time.* On the other hand, there are others who perceive such relationships as an *'add on to the job'* which they would prefer not to endure.
- Will parents meet teacher expectations with regards to collaborating appropriately whilst not exceeding a level of involvement that teachers feel comfortable with? *Some will and some won't.* The SEN system is designed for parental involvement and the extent of this is largely dependent upon children's needs and how they are being addressed. Most parents will *'fight'* to ensure the best possible provision for their children with the risk of crossing an *'invisible'* line in terms of appropriate involvement. As already alluded to, partnership means different things to different people and it can be difficult to know where acceptable boundaries lie.

Underpinning the extent to which SEN reform is implemented successfully will be the value systems held by individuals. Each person has their own set of values which they incorporate into everyday existence, including their working lives, irrespective of any legislation and policies they are expected to adhere to. The manner in which these are interpreted and the extent to which they are followed to the letter, will be affected by individual value systems and the actual value they place upon such practices.

I hope this book proves useful with respect to information on SEN systems and processes, with reference to underpinning promises, whilst alerting readers to some of the pitfalls to be avoided within the SEN arena.

USEFUL CONTACTS

Information is reproduced with permission and has primarily been provided by the organisations listed.

NATIONAL AUTISTIC SOCIETY
393 City Road
London
EC1V 1NG

Autism Helpline and NAS Information Centre
The National Autistic Society's Autism Helpline offers impartial, confidential information, advice and support for people with an ASD, their families and carers. The Information Centre provides information to students, teachers and other professionals.
Autism Helpline: Tel: 0808 800 4104 operates Monday - Friday, 10.00 am - 4.00 pm.
Information Centre: Tel: 020 7903 3553.
Email using the online enquiry form at www.autism.org.uk/enquiry
Website:www.autism.org.uk/helpline
Website:www.autism.org.uk/infocentre

Education Rights Service
The National Autistic Society's Education Rights Service provides advice and advocacy on Special Educational Needs provision and entitlements to parents and carers of children who have an autism spectrum disorder.
Tel: 0808 800 4102
Email: educationrights@nas.org.uk
Website: www.autism.org.uk/educationrights

Welfare rights and Community care services
Provides advice on welfare rights and people's rights to community care.
Email: welfare.rights@nas.org.uk
Website:www.autism.org.uk/welfarerights
Email: community.care@nas.org.uk
Website:www.autism.org.uk/communitycare

Parent to Parent service
Provides an empathetic listening ear and support service for parents.
Tel: 0808 800 4106
Website:www.autism.org.uk/p2p

NAS Education Support Service and Training
The Education Support Service provides specialist support for professionals working with young people (aged 3-19) with autism in a range of educational settings. Costs are per bespoke package. The Training department offers courses on a range of educational issues, as well as accrediting external courses, many of which have an educational focus. Contact details for both services:
Tel: 0141 285 7117
Email: training@nas.org.uk
Website: www.autism.org.uk/training

NAS Conferences and events
The NAS runs nationwide conferences and events for professionals.
Tel: 0115 911 3367
Email: conference@nas.org.uk
Website: www.autism.org.uk/conferences

NAS Supporter Care
For queries about membership of the NAS, fundraising, publications and other activities the NAS is involved in.
Tel: 0808 800 1050
Email: supportercare@nas.org.uk
Website: www.autism.org.uk/supportercare

NATIONAL AUTISTIC SOCIETY
on-line services

NAS website
The website contains a wealth of information about autism and Asperger's syndrome and details the broad range of help and services offered by the NAS.
Website: www.autism.org.uk

Community

An online community for all affected by autism.
Website: www.autism.org.uk/.community

Signpost
Signpost provides personalised information for parents/carers and people with autism spectrum disorders relevant to age, diagnosis and location. It is also useful for professionals advising parents or those with an ASD. It includes information on benefits, key services and training.
Website: www.autism.org.uk/signpost

Autism Services Directory
The directory holds detailed information on education services including schools, nurseries and colleges, local authorities, parent partnerships and educational outreach services. It also provides details of training courses for teachers and other educational professionals.
Website: www.autismdirectory.org.uk

Network Autism
A free online community for anyone who works regularly with children or adults with autism. Take part in discussions and groups, read the latest research and collaborate with others in the UK and internationally.
Website:www.networkautism.org.uk

BRITISH DYSLEXIA ASSOCIATION
Unit 8
Bracknell Beeches
Old Bracknell Lane
Bracknell
RG12 7BW
Telephone: 0845 251 9003

The British Dyslexia Association provides information and advice on dyslexia and dyscalculia. Training and accreditation for teachers and membership are also available.
Helpline: 0845 251 9002
Monday to Friday 10.00 am - 4.00 pm.

Tuesday and Wednesday 5.00 - 7.00 pm.
E-mail: helpline@bdadslexia.org.uk

DOWN'S SYNDROME ASSOCIATION
Langdon Down Centre
2a Langdon Park
Teddington
Middx
TW11 9PS

The Down's Syndrome Association is the only organisation in this country focusing solely on all aspects of living successfully with Down's syndrome. Since 1970, we have grown from being a local parent support group into a national charity with over 20,000 members with a national office in Teddington, Middlesex and offices in Northern Ireland and Wales. We also work closely with over 130 local support groups throughout the UK.

The helpline can provide information about all aspects of living with Down's syndrome including specialist advisers on benefits, education and health. The training department provides training for members, professionals and carers. Other projects include Workfit, the employment initiative and our sports programme DS Active.
Telephone: 0333 12 12 300
E-mail: info@downs-syndrome.org.uk
Twitter@DSAInfo
Facebook: www.facebook.com/DownsSyndromeAssociation

DYSLEXIA ACTION
Park House
Wick Road
Egham
Surrey
TW20 0HH

Dyslexia Action is a national charity that takes action to change the lives of people with dyslexia and literacy difficulties. We want a world where barriers to learning, employment and fulfilment have been removed for people with dyslexia and other specific learning difficulties. We take action to change lives by:

- Offering help and support direct to individuals.
- Empowering others so they can help individuals affected by dyslexia.
- Influencing change to help individuals affected by dyslexia.

Telephone: 01784 222 300
Website: www.dyslexiaaction.org.uk

NATIONAL DEAF CHILDREN'S SOCIETY (NDCS)
15 Dufferin Street
London
EC1Y 8UR

The National Deaf Children's Society (NDCS) is the leading charity dedicated to creating a world without barriers for deaf children and their families.
For more information visit:
Website: www.ndcs.org.uk

Tel: 0808 800 8880 Freephone Helpline (voice and text)
E-mail: helpline@ndcs.org.uk or www.ndcs.org.uk/livechat to chat online.

NATIONAL PARENT PARTNERSHIP NETWORK (NPPN)
Council for Disabled Children
National Children's Bureau
8 Wakley Street
London
EC1V 7QE

The National Parent Partnership Network (NPPN) supports the work of Parent Partnership Services across the country. They can help parents find their local Parent Partnership Service so they can obtain information, advice and support. NPPN is part of the Council for Disabled Children (CDC) which is the voice of the disabled children's sector.
Tel: 0207 843 6058
E-mail: nppn@ncb.org.uk
Website: www.parentpartnership.org.uk

GLOSSARY

'*Additional Needs*'- is a euphemism that is frequently used instead of Special Educational Needs. The term refers to the additional or different educational provision required for children and young people.

Additional SEN Support – this is the new school-based level of support which is replacing School Action and School Action Plus. The same will apply to Early Years provision.

Annual Review – every child with a Statement of Special Educational Needs will have an Annual Review. This review examines progress against previous targets, establishes new goals and determines any changes to educational provision.

Appeal – when this word is used with a capital 'A', it usually applies to a legal process such as an Appeal to the First-tier Tribunal (SEND) or against a school allocation decision.

Behaviour Policy – every school will have a policy that details their expectations regarding pupil conduct and the sanctions used to manage inappropriate behaviour, including specific disciplinary stages.

Common Assessment Framework (CAF) this is a holistic process which is used to assess children's unmet needs. This can include any aspect of their health, developmental, behavioural or learning needs.

Comprehensive Spending Review – Government spending reviews determine the amount of money that is allocated to government departments. They currently take place every three years.

'*Constructs*'- in relation to Personal Construct Theory, it is believed that individuals construct their reality through forming ideas about situations, events and people in order to help them make sense of their world. This is a continual process throughout life.

Early Support – this programme is for families with disabled children under the age of 5. It involves a co-ordinated multi-agency approach to meeting needs.

Educational Psychologist – sometimes undertakes psychological assessments of children when they are experiencing difficulties at school.

Education Health and Care Plan (EHC Plan) – the system that will replace Statements of Special Educational Needs for recording statutory provision for children and young people with Special Educational Needs, spanning 0-25 years of age.

First-tier Tribunal – is part of the legal system where parents may Appeal with respect to their children's statutory Special Educational Needs provision.

'Green Paper'- the Coalition Government's paper on SEN reform: *Support and Aspiration: A new approach to special educational needs and disability (2011)*.

'Hidden' Disabilities – a term frequently applied to people with disabilities that are not immediately obvious in the physical sense. Such disabilities can affect thinking processes (cognitive function), emotional responses (affective) and how individuals behave.

Independent Appeal Panel (IAP) – parents could formerly lodge Appeals with an Independent Appeal Panel in the hope of having decisions regarding permanent exclusions overturned. These Panels have now been replaced by Independent Review Panels.

Independent Mediation Advisor – is a person who gives parents advice about mediation before they submit an Appeal to the First-tier Tribunal (SEND).

Independent Review Panel (IRP) – these panels have replaced Independent Appeal Panels. They can review decisions regarding permanent exclusions and can request that governing bodies review their procedures, but do not have the power to overturn decisions.

Non-Verbal Communication (NVC) – refers to how people communicate in the physical sense such as facial expression, eye contact, body language, as well as characteristics of the voice such as intonation.

Occupational Therapist – can help children and adults with physical or mental disabilities to function more independently.

Paediatrician – is a doctor who treats babies and children. Paediatricians may be hospital or community based.

Partnership – is when people or agencies work cooperatively together in order to achieve a common goal.

Parent Partnership Services – statutory services that exist to provide information, advice and support to parents of children with Special Educational Needs. They can also support parents when their children have been excluded from school, although there are regional variations in the type of support offered.

Person-centred Planning – is a model for working with individuals to help them in making decisions regarding their future.

Self-esteem – refers to how individuals value themselves and rate their abilities.

Short Breaks – local authorities have a duty to provide a range of Short Breaks for disabled children. Eligibility criteria apply.

Single Assessment Process (SAP) – an assessment process for children and young people which might lead to Education, Health and Care Plans being issued. Due to closer multi-agency working and improved information sharing, the process should reduce the amount of repetition that parents experience in explaining their children's difficulties.

Special Educational Needs (SEN) – the legal term for children and young people who require additional or different support to help overcome barriers to learning.

Special Educational Needs Code of Practice – statutory guidance for professionals that details procedures and processes in relation to Special Educational Needs provision.

Special Educational Needs Policy – each school will have a Special Educational Needs Policy which outlines their approach to addressing children's additional needs.

Special Educational Needs Co-ordinator (SENCO) – is the teacher or Early Years Practitioner with responsibility for the assessment, planning and co-ordination of educational provision for children with Special Educational Needs.

Speech and Language Therapist – can work with children and adults in connection with disorders which affect speech, language, communication and swallowing.

Statement – is the legal document that details children's difficulties and the support required to help them learn. Statements also include a named school. These will soon be replaced by Education, Health and Care Plans.

Sure Start Children's Centres – primarily focus on the needs of families which are socially and financially disadvantaged. They offer a range of universal services to support children and parents.

Transition – refers to the strategies used by professionals to ease the process of children moving from one educational setting to another. This also applies to young people leaving school and entering into further education, training or employment.

Bibliography

Armstrong, D. (1995) *Power and Partnership in Education*. London: Routledge.

Attwood, L. (2007) *An Evaluation of Communication between Educational Professionals and Parents and its impact on Families and Working in Partnership with Parents*. MA Dissertation submitted to Bath Spa University. Copy available in Library.

Bercow Review (2008) Department for Children, Schools and Families. Nottingham. Reference: DCSF-00632-2008.

Bruce, E. and Schultz, G. (2001) *Non-finite Loss and Grief: A Psychoeducational Approach*. London: Jessica Kingsley Publishers.

Bruce, E. and Schultz, G. (2002) *Non-finite loss and challenges to communication between parents and professionals*. British Journal of Special Education: Volume 29 Number 1.

Buckman, R. (1994) *How to Break Bad News: a Guide for Health-Care Professionals*. London: Pan Books.

Butler, P. (2013) *Hundreds of Sure Start centres have closed since election, says Labour*. The Guardian (28/1/2013). Available online from: www.theguardian.com/society/

Children's Commissioner's report (2013) *Always someone else's problem: report on illegal exclusions*. Available online from: www.childrenscommissioner.gov.uk

Children's Workforce Development Council (2006) *Common Core of Skills and Knowledge*. Leeds: Children's Workforce Development Council.

Coles, C. and Hancock, R. (2002) *The Inclusion Quality Mark*. Bristol: TLO Limited.

Council for Disabled Children (2004) *Come on in: The Disability Discrimination Act 1995, Part 3 Access to Goods and Services; A practical guide for Children's Services*. London: CDC.

Council for Disabled Children (2007) *Every Disabled Child Matters: Disabled Children and Child Poverty (briefing)*. London: CDC.

Crozier, G. & Reay, D. (2005) (eds) *Activating Participation: parents and teachers working towards partnership (Chapter 3)*. Staffordshire: Trentham Books Limited.

Customer Service Excellence. Information about the Standard is available from: /www.customerserviceexcellence.uk.com/aboutTheStandardCSE

Davis, H., Day, C. & Bidmead, C. (2002) *Working in Partnership with Parents: The Parent Adviser Model*. London: Harcourt Assessment.

Department for Children, Schools and Families (2009) *Inclusion Development Programme, Primary and Secondary Supporting Pupils on the Autism Spectrum*. Available online from: *www.gov.uk/publications* Reference: DCSF-00041-2009

Department for Children, Schools and Families (2009) *Lamb Inquiry: Special Educational Needs and Parental Confidence*. Nottingham: DCSF Publications.

Department for Children, Schools and Families (2006) *Parenting Support: Guidance for local authorities in England*. Nottingham: DCSF Publications.

Department for Children, Schools and Families (2007) Parent Partnership Services – *increasing parental confidence: Exemplification of minimum standards*. Nottingham: DCSF.

Department for Children, Schools and Families (2008) *The Impact of Parental Involvement on Children's Education*. Nottingham: DCSF Publications.

Department For Children, Schools and Families (2008) *Aiming High for Disabled Children Transition Programme*. Available online at: http://webarchive.nationalarchives.gov.uk/20100202100434/dcsf.gov.uk/everychildmatters/resources-and-practice/ig00322.

Department for Children, Schools and Families (2010) *The Pupil and Parent Guarantees*. Nottingham: DCSF Publications.

Department for Education (2012) *A profile of pupil exclusions in England. Research Report DFE-RR190*. Available online from: www.education.gov.uk

Promises and Pitfalls of Special Education

Department for Education (2013) *Behaviour and discipline in schools: guidance for governing bodies.* Available online from www.education.gov.uk Reference: DFE-00125-2013.

Department for Education (2013) *Children and Families Bill.* The Stationery Office Limited.

Department for Education (August 2012) *Early Education for 2 Year Olds.* Available online from: www.education.gov.uk

Department for Education (2011) *Evaluation of impact of DfE investment in initiatives designed to improve teacher workforce skills in relation to SEN and disabilities. Reseach Report DFE-RR115.* University of Warwick.

Department for Education (2012) *Exclusion from Maintained Schools, Academies and Pupil Referral Units in England: A guide for those with legal responsibilities in relation to Exclusion.* Available online from: www.education.gov.uk Reference DFE-00042-2012.

Department for Education (November 2010) *Government moves to free up children's centres.* Available online from: www.education.gov.uk

Department for Education (2013) *Home-School Agreements: Guidance for local authorities and governing bodies.* Available online from: www.education.gov.uk-home

Department for Education (2013) *Indicative Draft: The (0-25) Special Educational Needs Code of Practice.* Available online from: www.education.gov.uk

Department for Education (2012) *School Admissions Code.* Available online from: www.education.gov.uk

Department for Education (2012) *School Funding Reform: Arrangements for 2013-14.* Available online from: www.education.gov.uk

Department for Education (2011) *Special Educational Needs Information Act – An Analysis 2011.* Available online from: *www.education.gov.uk*

Department for Education (2012) *Statistical First Release: Permanent and Fixed Period Exclusions from Schools and Exclusion Appeals in England 2010/11.* London: DfE. Available online from: www.education.gov.uk/rsgateway

Department for Education (2013) *Statistical First Release: Special Educational Needs in England.* London: DfE. Available online from: www.education.gov.uk/rsgateway

Department for Education (2012) *Statutory Framework for the Early Years Foundation Stage: setting the standards for learning, development and care for children from birth to five.* Available online from: www.education.gov.uk Reference: DFE-00023-2012.

Department for Education (2011) *Support and aspiration: A new approach to special educational needs and disability.* London: The Stationery Office. Available online from: www.education.gov.uk

Department for Education (2012) *Sure Start Children's Centres Core Purpose.* Available online from: www.education.gov.uk

Department for Education (2010) *The Importance of Teaching.* Available online from: www.education.gov.uk

Department for Education (2010) *The Relationship between Speech, Language and Communication Needs (SLCN) and behavioural, emotional and social difficulties (BESD).* Available online from: www.education.gov.uk Reference: DFE-RR247-BCRP6.

Department for Education (2010) *What are 'P' scales and how do I get hold of a copy?* Available online from: www.education.gov.uk/popularquestions

Department for Education (2013) *What are Academies?* Available online from: www.education.gov.uk

Department for Education and Department of Health (2011) *Supporting Families in the Foundation Years.* Available online from: www.education.gov.uk

Department for Education and Employment (1997) *Excellence for all Children Meeting Special Educational Needs.* London: DfEE.

Department for Education and Skills (2007) *Aiming High for Disabled Children: better support for families.* HM Treasury.

Department for Education and Skills (2004) *Every Child Matters: Change for Children.* Nottinghamshire: Department for Education & Skills Publications.

Department for Education and Skills (October 2005) *Higher Standards, Better Schools for All, More choice for parents and pupils.* Available online from: www.dfes.gov.uk/publictions/schoolswhitepaper

Department for Education and Skills (2006) *Parenting Support: Guidance for Local Authorities in England.* Nottinghamshire. Department for Education & Skills Publications.

Department for Education and Skills (2001) *Special Educational Needs, Code of Practice.* Nottinghamshire: Department for Education & Skills Publications.

Department for Education and Skills and Department of Health (2004) *National Service Framework for Children, Young People and Maternity Services.* London: DH Publications.

Department for Work and Pensions (2008) *Exploring disability, family formation and break-up: Reviewing the evidence.* The Institute of Applied Social Studies and the University of Birmingham.

Desforges, C. & Abouchaar, A. (2003) *The Impact of Parental Involvement, Parental Support and Family Education on Pupil Achievements and Adjustment: A Literature Review.* Queens Printer. Available from: www.dfes.gov.uk/research Reference: RR433.

Easton, C., Gee, G., Durbin, B., and Teeman, D (2011) *Early intervention, using the CAF process, and its cost effectiveness:* Findings from LARC3. Slough: NFER

Egan, G. (1990) *The Skilled Helper: A Systematic Approach to Effective Helping.* Belmont, California: Brooks/Cole Publishing Company.

Ellis, M. (2013) *Sure start stop: Coalition cuts to children's centres target Labour areas.* Mirror (14/2/2013). Available online from: www.mirrow.co.uk/news

Gaunt, C. (2013) *Children's centres move away from universal services to target poorest.* Nursery World (19/7/2013). Available online from: www.nurseryworld.co.uk/article/

Hargie, O. (2006) (3rd edition) *The Handbook of Communication Skills.* Hove: Routledge.

History of the Labour Party. Available from: www.labour.org.uk/history

Hornby, G. (1995) *Working with Parents of Children with Special Needs.* London: Cassell.

HM Treasury (2010) *Spending Review.* Available online from: www.gov.uk/publications

Jacobs, M. (1996) (9th edition) *Swift to Hear: Facilitating Skills in Listening and Responding.* London: SPCK.

Kelly, G. A. (1963) *A Theory of Personality: The Psychology of Personal Constructs.* London: W.W. Norton & Company.

Korb, M. P., Gorrell, J. and Van De Riet, V. (1989) *Gestalt Therapy: Practice and Theory.* (2nd edition) London: Allyn & Bacon.

Low (2006) *Some Ideologies of Disability.* Journal of Research in Special Educational Needs. Volume 6 Number 2.

Mead, M. and Heyman, K. (1965) *Family.* London: Collier-Macmillan Limited.

National Children's Bureau (undated) *Early Support.* Available online from: www.ncb.org.uk/early-support

National Parent Partnership Network (2010) *Parent Partnership Services – Increasing parental confidence: Exemplification of minimum standards for PPS and Local Authorities.* London: NPPN.

Nelson-Jones, R. (1997) (4th edition) *Practical Counselling and Helping Skills.* London: Cassell.

New Schools Network (2013) *Special Free Schools – accepting pupils with no statement of SEN.* Available online from: newschoolsnetwork.org

Office of the Children's Commissioner School Exclusions Inquiry (2012) *They never give up on you.* Available online from: www.childrenscommissioner.gov.uk

Patterson, C. H. (1986) *Theories of Counselling and Psychotherapy.* New York: Harper Collins.

Pinkus, S. (2003) *All talk and no action: transforming the rhetoric of parent-professional partnership into practice.* Journal of Research in Special Educational Needs. Volume 3 Number 2.

Pinkus, S. (2005) *Bridging the gap between policy and practice: adopting a strategic vision for partnership working in special education.* British Journal of Special Education Volume 32 Number 4.

Plowden Report (1967) *Children and their Primary Schools: A report of the Central Advisory Council for Education (England).* Her Majesty's Stationery Office.

Purkey, W. W. (1970) *Self Concept and School Achievement.* New Jersey: Prentice Hall.

Roffey, S. (2002) *School Behaviour and Families: Frameworks for Working Together.* London: David Fulton Publishers Limited.

Rogers, C. (2007) *Disabling a family? Emotional dilemmas experienced in becoming a parent of a child with learning disabilities.* British Journal of Special Education. Volume 34 Number 3.

Rogers, C. R. (1967) *On Becoming a Person: a therapist's view of psychotherapy.* London: Constable & Company Limited.

Rose (2009) Department for Children, Schools and Families. *Independent Review of the Primary Curriculum: Final Report.* Nottingham.

Stone, J. (2004) *Parent Partnership Services: Practice Guide.* London: Council for Disabled Children.

Terzi, L. (2010) *Justice and Equality in Education: A Capability Perspective on Disability and Special Educational Needs.* London: Continuum International Publishing Group.

Tickell, C. (2011) *The Early Years: Foundation for life, health and living: an independent report on the Early Years Foundation Stage to Her Majesty's Government.* Available online from: www.education.gov.uk

The Children's Society (2011) *4 in Every 10: Disabled children living in poverty.* Available online from: www.childrenssociety.org.uk

Training and Development Agency for Schools (2010) *About Parent Support Advisers (PSAs).* Available online from: www.webarchive.nationalarchives.gov.uk

Vincent, C. (1996) *Parents and Teachers Power and Participation.* London: Routledge Falmer.

Warnock (1978) *Special Educational Needs: Report of the Committee of Enquiry into the Education of Handicapped Children and Young People.* London: Her Majesty's Stationery Office. Available online from: www.tes.co.uk

Acts of Parliament

Academies Act (2010) (c32) London: The Stationery Office Limited.

Childcare Act 2006 (c1). London: The Stationery Office Limited.

Children Act 1989 (c41). London: The Stationery Office Limited.

Children Act 2004. (c31). London: The Stationery Office Limited.

Community Care Act 1990 (c19) London: The Stationery Office Limited.

Data Protection Act 1998 (s1). London: The Stationery Office Limited.

Disability Discrimination Act 1995. (c50) London: The Stationery Office Limited.

Disability Discrimination Act 2005. (c13) London: The Stationery Office Limited.

Draft Legislation on Reform of Provision for children and young people with Special Educational Needs (2012). London: The Stationery Office Limited.

Education Act 1981. (c60) London: The Stationery Office Limited.

Education Act 1986. (c40) London: The Stationery Office Limited.

Education Act 1993. (c35) London: The Stationery Office Limited.

Education and Inspections Act 2006 (c40). London: The Stationery Office Limited.

Equality Act 2010 (c15). London: The Stationery Office Limited.

SEN & Disability Act 2001 (c10). London: Her Majesty's Stationery Office.

Special Educational Needs Information Act 2008. London: The Stationery Office Limited.